The Minor Intimacies of Race

THE ASIAN AMERICAN EXPERIENCE

Series Editors
Eiichiro Azuma
Jigna Desai
Martin F. Manalansan IV
Lisa Sun-Hee Park
David K. Yoo

Roger Daniels, Founding Series Editor

A list of books in the series appears at the end of this book.

The Minor Intimacies of Race

Asian Publics in North America

CHRISTINE KIM

UNIVERSITY OF ILLINOIS PRESS
Urbana, Chicago, and Springfield

Publication of this book was supported by a grant
from Simon Fraser University.

© 2016 by the Board of Trustees
of the University of Illinois
All rights reserved
1 2 3 4 5 C P 5 4 3 2 1
♾ This book is printed on acid-free paper.

Library of Congress Cataloging-in-Publication Data
Names: Kim, Christine, 1973–
Title: The minor intimacies of race : Asian publics in North
   America / Christine Kim.
Description: Urbana : University of Illinois Press, 2016. | Series:
   The Asian American experience | Includes bibliographical
   references and index.
Identifiers: LCCN 2015038292
ISBN 9780252040139 (hardback : acid-free paper)
ISBN 9780252081620 (paper : acid-free paper)
ISBN 9780252098338 (e-book)
Subjects: LCSH: Asians—North America—Public opinion. |
   Public opinion—North America. | Asian Americans—Public
   opinion. | Asians—Canada—Public opinion. | Racism—
   United States. | Racism—Canada. | Intimacy (Psychology)—
   Social aspects—United States. | Intimacy (Psychology)—
   Social aspects—Canada. | United States—Race relations. |
   Canada—Race relations. | BISAC: SOCIAL SCIENCE / Ethnic
   Studies / Asian American Studies. | SOCIAL SCIENCE /
   Anthropology / Cultural. | HISTORY / Canada / General.
Classification: LCC E49.2.A75 K56 2016 | DDC 973/.0495—dc23
LC record available at http://lccn.loc.gov/2015038292

For Yusuf, Zahra, and Zidan

Contents

Acknowledgments ix

Introduction: Multiculturalism, Minor Publics, and Social Intimacy 1

1. National Incompletion: Awkward Multiculturalisms and Denaturalizing Whiteness 31

2. Transnational Triviality: Print and Digital Asian North American Publics 57

3. Diasporic Fragility and Brokenness: Korean War Legacies and Structures of Feeling 91

4. Global Loss: Metaphoric Substitution and the Logic of Human Rights 124

Conclusion: Ephemeral Publics and Roy Kiyooka's *StoneDGloves* 154

Notes 161

Works Cited 165

Index 179

Acknowledgments

I am grateful to many people for encouraging, guiding, and inspiring me over the years that it took to write this book.

While this book is not a revision of a dissertation, the thinking behind this project would not have been possible without the training that I received as a doctoral student. As a graduate student at York University, I was lucky enough to work with Dr. Barbara Godard, who taught me many things about how to read literature, art, and culture, always while remaining conscious of the underlying patterns and structures of power at work. But perhaps even more important, she encouraged the pursuit of intellectual curiosity; for that, I will always be grateful. Dr. Leslie Sanders was also an invaluable teacher and friend while I was a graduate student. She asked me questions that were deceptively simple yet difficult to answer, and these forced me to be much more precise in my thinking. I am also indebted to the mentoring and learning I received from Dr. Terry Goldie and Dr. Tom Loebel while at York. Candida Rifkind, Andrew Burke, Elena Basile, Heather Milne, Kate Eichhorn, Tess Chakkalakal, Trish Salah, and Robert Stacey were a wonderful community of friends while I was a graduate student and I am much richer for the hours of conversation I spent with each of them. Candida Rifkind and Andrew Burke also provided feedback on sections of this book and I am indebted to their careful eyes, sharp questions, and enduring friendship over the years.

The bulk of this book was written when I moved to Vancouver. There are many stimulating intellectual and artistic conversations about Asian Canada taking place here, and I am grateful to Chris Lee, Kirsten McAllister, Helen Leung, Larissa Lai, Hiromi Goto, Rita Wong, and Roy Miki for welcoming me into them. I would also like to thank Chris Lee for encouraging this project and reading countless drafts of it, always with keen insights and good humor. Thanks also to Y-Dang Troeung for her thoughtful feedback on an earlier version of chapter 4. My gratitude also goes to Cindy Mochizuki and David Khang, two Vancouver-based artists whose work I engage with in this book. They have generously shared their art and had long conversations with me about their work.

In the English department at Simon Fraser University, I have the good fortune of working with supportive and thoughtful colleagues that I like a lot. I am especially grateful to Sophie McCall, David Chariandy, Deanna Reder, Jon Smith, and Dave Coley for advice on this project, for engaging with my research and writing, and for their friendship.

Dawn Durante has been an ideal editor, offering guidance and encouragement along the way. To her, I extend my sincere thanks. Amanda Wicks has also been a wonderful support at the University of Illinois Press. I am grateful to Anne Rogers for carefully copyediting this book. I also thank the two anonymous readers for their thoughtful reviews, which made this book much stronger and sharper. To the Asian American Experience series editors, Eiichiro Azuma, Martin Manalansan, Lisa Sun-Hee Park, David Yoo, and especially Jigna Desai, thank you for welcoming me into your roster. Portions of this manuscript appeared previously in the edited collection *Asian Canadian Theatre* and the journal *Interventions*, and I am grateful to the publishers for allowing me to reprint them here. An earlier version of part of chapter 1 was published as "Performing Asian Canadian Intimacy: Theatre Replacement's *Bioboxes* and Awkward Multiculturalisms" in *Asian Canadian Theatre*, edited by Nina Lee Aquino and Ric Knowles (Toronto: Playwrights Canada Press, 2011), 183–94; a section of chapter 3 was published as "Intimating Asias, Postcolonial Possibilities, and the Art of David Khang" in *Interventions: International Journal of Postcolonial Studies* 15, no. 1 (2013): 24–37. Publication of this book was supported by a publication grant from Simon Fraser University.

For all of its benefits, moving to Vancouver has also meant being separated from family. I have been exceedingly lucky and found supportive and kind friends who have helped Vancouver feel like home. I have been able to write this book in large part because they generously welcomed my family and me into their homes and lives. I am grateful for the friendship of Michelle and Mark Srdanovic, Kirstin and Paul Richter, Melissa and Nathan Thorpe, and Natalie Brenton and Mike Shepherd.

I am grateful to my parents for their unwavering love, support, and encouragement, even when my decisions have worried them at first. They have always made me feel safe in this world. To Eric, my younger brother and oldest companion, and his new wife, Lillian, thank you for your friendship over the years, even when I was at my bossiest. Faruq and Ayesha Varachia are the kindest parents-in-law and I appreciate how they have welcomed me into their family. Love and gratitude also to Yasmine, Fahmeeda, and Abdul Coovadia. To my parents and in-laws, thank you for your extended visits and nurturing my children while I wrote this book.

My biggest thanks are to my husband and children. I am grateful to Yusuf for his constant encouragement, sharp insights into cultural and racial politics, and sense of humor about the everyday. As I said on our wedding day, he has always been more than I expected. Quite literally, this book would not have been possible without my children, Zahra and Zidan. Since they came into my life, I have thought intensely about feeling and the everyday and this work lies at the heart of this book. I am grateful to them for making me feel emotions rather than just theorize them. To Yusuf, Zahra, and Zidan, I dedicate this book with all my love and gratitude.

The Minor Intimacies of Race

Introduction
Multiculturalism, Minor Publics, and Social Intimacy

On November 14, 2011, the Bank of Canada launched into circulation a new $100 bill made of polymer as part of a broader project to overhaul Canadian currency. This new currency series—like the two that preceded it in 1969–79 and 1986—was publicized as bearing increased security features that would be difficult to counterfeit, news welcomed by many Canadians. While the upgrading of banknotes is a routine occurrence, this particular one became the subject of controversy nearly a year later when several news outlets revealed that, during the design process for this new banknote, the bank's focus groups had rejected an earlier version that featured an Asian-looking female scientist on the bill. The news reports list a number of quietly, perhaps even sophisticatedly, racist reasons that the groups found this initial image unsuitable: the reinforcement of a model-minority perception of Asians excelling in the sciences, the singling out of Asians at the expense of other ethnicities, and the racialization of the banknote by pairing a bill yellow-brown in color with an image of an Asian woman (Canadian Press, "Asian-Looking Woman Scientist"). Of these, one comment stands out for the overtly racist feelings it expresses: "The person on it appears to be of Asian descent which doesn't rep(resent) [sic] Canada. It is fairly ugly" (Canadian Press, "Asian-Looking Woman Scientist"). Bowing to these criticisms, the Bank of Canada replaced the image with a female scientist of "neutral ethnicity" (Beeby, "Image of Asian-Looking"). Unsurprisingly, when news of this decision eventually leaked to the public, complaints emerged about the bank's deracialization of whiteness and rendering invisible nonwhite Canadians. In response, Mark Carney, the then governor of the Bank of Canada, quickly issued an apology "to those who were offended" (Beeby, "Canada $100 Bill").

In the wake of this breaking news, reactions to the proposed and revised bill were mixed. Many were angered by the incident and voiced their disapproval. On his *Angry Asian Man* blog, Phil Yu bluntly calls the reasoning behind the whitening of the scientist "flimsy" before concluding that the incident is "race-bending on a banknote" ("'Asian-Looking' Woman"). The Chinese Canadian National Council (CCNC) National—a national organization committed to promoting the rights of Chinese Canadians with chapters in every province—and CCNC Toronto held a press conference on August 17, 2012. They issued a joint statement about the bill's revision that denounced it as "a racist decision by the Bank of Canada" and pointed out that the bank's "term 'ethnically neutral' was inaccurate" (Chinese Canadian National Council, Toronto Chapter). Other respondents expressed their displeasure in a variety of ways: Andrew Gunadie, a young Internet personality, posted a video on YouTube that conveys, perhaps most clearly through his facial expressions, disbelief at the bank's comments; Mu-Qing Huang (a graduate student at the University of Toronto interviewed for a *Toronto Star* article) reads the bill as a sign of multiculturalism's lies and argues that "if Canada is truly multicultural and thinks that all cultural groups are equal, then any visible minority should be good enough to represent a country, including [someone with] Asian features" (Beeby, "Image of Asian-Looking"); and Sandy Ross recognizes the racist nature of this controversy by locating it within a history of "white-washing in Canadian monies." Collectively, these criticisms make the racist dimensions of this incident difficult to ignore by addressing the bill as a matter of racial injustice, in affective terms, as exposing the fallacies of multiculturalism, and as part of a longer history of racism. Nonetheless, defenders of the bank's decision did precisely this. Andrew Coyne, writing for the *National Post,* takes the controversy as an opportunity to unfairly criticize "identity politics, whose first rule is: no matter what you do it's wrong." He claims the incident has been misinterpreted and is adamant that "the underlying problem here isn't racism, or political correctness. It's blandness: a culture of banality that pervades official Canada, of which the bank notes are only a particular form." Perhaps even more indicative of a general public feeling are online comments that respond favorably to the news articles and the new bill. One poster believes that using "the dominant ethnicity ... isn't racism, but common sense," while others respond to the controversy with annoyance, perceiving the incident as political correctness searching for problems where none exist (Beeby, "Canada $100 Bill"). The trivialization of the $100 bill controversy and the complex processes and histories of racialization it gestures toward is both deeply frustrating and unsurprising given how Asian Canadian publics have consistently been excluded from the national imagination.

I open *The Minor Intimacies of Race* with this debate because it confronts us with tensions that lie at the heart of the multiculturalism project in Canada and demands that we question why the proposed inclusion of an Asian-looking woman on the $100 bill is a contentious move if Canada is a multicultural country. In many respects, the $100 bill story dovetails with the larger concerns of this book because both highlight how the politics of multicultural recognition obfuscate racialized feeling. This is exemplified by the dominant public's affective resistance to the currency transformation, which is squarely at odds with the political and legal rhetoric of the nation-state and, more precisely, with the Multiculturalism Act, which intends to "recognize and promote the understanding that multiculturalism reflects the cultural and racial diversity of Canadian society and acknowledges the freedom of all members of Canadian society to preserve, enhance and share their cultural heritage" (Government of Canada, "Canadian Multiculturalism Act"). In spotlighting this recent episode in Canadian public life, my intention is threefold: first, to emphasize how the language and logic of multiculturalism structure race and racialization for a liberal imagination in Canada; second, to note that although the rhetoric of multicultural recognition may permeate the nation, multicultural feeling does not; and third, to propose that the minimal amount of public debate about the $100 bill is indicative of a more general public inability to recognize the racialized nature of citizenship. By asking why the scrutiny over the whitening of this image of a female scientist failed to capture the interest of a wider public and to launch a more sustained exploration of race, I investigate how the cultural politics of racial representation register and circulate for a range of audiences. Why, in other words, is the debate over whether an Asian-looking scientist is an appropriate image for Canadian currency not understood to be a conversation of fundamental importance for a dominant public? Why are more publics not interested in understanding how racial logics and representations circulate within and beyond the nation-state?

Thinking Through the Public

Because there is perhaps no object more quotidian in contemporary North America than money, the deep-seated resistance to the racialization of the Canadian $100 bill is particularly conducive for analyzing the shape and stakes of everyday racial dialogues for Asian Canadian publics. In order to move beyond the limiting discourse of official multiculturalism, I resist the rhetoric of difference embedded in the language of *communities* and turn instead to *publics,* a term I explore further in this section to examine contemporary racial formations. Produced in response to particular issues or moments, publics do not require the same kinds of investments or stable structures that tend to grow communities over generations. While communities remain vital as a theoretical concept and an active force for Asian Canadian scholarship more generally, I am drawn to the public for the kind of critique of democratic citizenship it can make in the present moment.

In the $100 bill controversy, the ambiguous place of racialized bodies within the economy and attachments to whiteness as a form of unmarked and neutral universalism operate as sites of conflict. As Malaika Aleba suggests in a blog post about this debacle—one she describes as "a not-so-healthy dose of ridiculousness served with a side of racism guaranteed to leave a bad taste in your mouth"—we need to analyze the uneasy feelings of a dominant public when confronted with the image of an Asian scientist. While the anxieties produced within a dominant public might "stem from fear that Asians will, to put it in racist terms, take over," such feelings must be interrogated because they imply "that Canada has always been and should remain white, which simply isn't true and ignores our colonial history." In this regard, two aspects of the $100 bill discussions are particularly pertinent: first, the relatively brief period of public interest in the $100 bill; and second, how multiple publics—a dominant public as well as minor publics—responded to the problems of race highlighted by this new currency. To address the first point, the transitory style of these conversations speaks to the basic premise of minor publics—namely, that publics remain in existence only as long as their participants are engaged in dialogue. Because multiculturalism provides the dominant terms for understanding race in a Canadian context, conversations that contest this logic tend to occur in marginal spaces and exist as short-lived eruptions. Although moments of social engagement on the part of minor publics may leave behind traces, there is no guarantee that they will be remembered or repeated. A key distinction between minor publics and a dominant one is that, while all publics emerge by virtue of their engaged participants, there are few, if any, structures in place to sustain minor publics, and many (such as mainstream news outlets and mass media) designed to ensure the longevity of a dominant one. Minor publics, such as Asian Canadian ones, are more ephemeral than a dominant public because their conditions of possibility require that they repeatedly reconstitute themselves instead of simply continuing or redirecting ongoing conversations in order to respond to particular issues. The conflicting desires of a more stable dominant public and impermanent minor publics are visible in the contrast between the bank's efforts to quickly diffuse racialized critiques and return Canadian currency to its quotidian status and the attempts of those who wanted to pursue these examinations further. While there may have been interest on the part of Asian Canadian publics to use this incident as an entry point for more complex and nuanced conversations about racial logics and representational strategies,[1] there was little space within a dominant public to do so once the bank issued its apology.

The public is a crucial concept for this book because it provides a means of theorizing how collectives are defined, felt, and mobilized. Put simply, *The Minor Intimacies of Race* argues that feeling matters and, moreover, that feeling is core to the construction of minor publics. Thus, central to my argument throughout this book are the feelings we have about multiculturalism as well as those about racialized conditions that are displaced by multiculturalism. Philosopher Jürgen Habermas argues in *The Structural Transformation of the Public Sphere* that publics use reason to critique the exercise of political power and explore matters of interest to the greater common good in order to ensure the correct workings of democratic governments. And yet, as many scholars since have noted, the public sphere has always been defined by what it excludes—namely, the racialized, gendered, heterosexual, and classed terms of citizenship.[2] The dominant public, then, implicitly debates citizenship for a collective imagined to be normative. In light of these structural concerns, what would be the ideal place to discuss this new $100 bill in terms of the racial logics and strategies that influence how citizenship rights are exercised, diaspora is imagined, and international human rights are conceptualized and recognized? Where, in other words, could the banknote controversy be discussed as an index of the participatory style of a dominant public rather than dismissed as overblown hysteria? What kinds of shared language or common feelings are needed before a collective unpacking of racial dynamics can take place?

The other limitation of a Habermasian public sphere for the purposes of understanding racialized publics is that its rational emphasis excludes from consideration affective intelligence. By reconceptualizing the public as a forum that also includes the feelings and concerns of minor publics, it can function as a critical tool capable of yielding sharp insights into how power, citizenship, and social dynamics operate. In order to think through racialized publics as spaces that exist in relation to, but also outside of, a dominant public, I rely on Lauren Berlant's feminine publics and Michael Warner's queer counterpublics; as models of related minor publics, they demonstrate the dialogic possibilities that emerge when shared feeling exists. In *The Female Complaint,* Berlant describes intimate publics as being structured in a circular fashion: sentimental feminine culture provides the basis for a public of female consumers, and this collective identification allows for social intimacy. She explains, "What makes a public sphere intimate is an expectation that the consumers of its particular stuff *already* share a worldview and emotional knowledge that they have derived from a broadly common historical experience" (viii). These insights into the necessary preconditions of social intimacy are immensely useful for examining what happens when conversations about race replace feminine mass culture as the grounds for bonding and interaction. As an organizational strategy, race marks the limits of a dominant public at the same time that it functions as the center of minor publics, operating as a "social fact" whose implications remain contentious and unspeakable within a dominant public.

The current resistance to acknowledging that racial affect operates as a peculiar blind spot within a Canadian multicultural imaginary acts as my entry point into this investigation of the social intimacies of minor publics. Building on critical interventions that demonstrate the falseness of the public/private opposition, I consider how beliefs prevalent in the private sphere structure publics, particularly with respect to racialized discourses. Following Warner's move away from the perception of the public and private spheres as distinct entities, an assumption that obscures the power differentials that determine which bodies and what speech can be public and which and what must be private, I contemplate instead "a continuum of publicness" (25). On such a scale, the workings of power, authority, and intimacy become visible with public and private demarcating a myriad of potential positionings contingent upon content and context. The importance of politicizing cultural understandings of public appropriateness cannot be stressed enough, especially since they determine the difference between public invisibility and privacy (26). Within this revised framework, what Warner calls *counterpublics*—those "publics [that] are defined by their tension with a larger public" (56)—can be understood as formations that produce their own kinds of social intimacy.

While Warner's concept of the counterpublic enables us to theorize Asian Canadian publics generated through their opposition to a dominant Canadian public, it is less useful for analyzing Asian Canadian publics when they emerge out of a desire for social intimacy. While the counterpublic emphasizes antagonism with a dominant public, Asian Canadian publics are also produced by a desire for collective belonging and emotional recognition. Commenting on his fieldwork experiences in Greece, Thailand, and Rome, anthropologist Michael Herzfeld describes cultural intimacy as "the zone of internal knowledge whereby members of a society recognize each other through their flaws and foibles rather than through their idealized typicality as heroic representatives of the nation" (133). A sense of deeply shared identity is communicated to others through bodily gestures illegible to outsiders but familiar to other insiders; this corporeal language promotes collective intimacy through public secrecy (145). Modifying for an Asian Canadian context Herzfeld's notion of public secrecy as the basis for collective intimacy, I see something different happening within Canadian and American conversations about race. Unlike the locals that seek to preserve cultural secrets as the basis for collective identity, the unwillingness of a dominant public to be involved in extended conversations about race (such as the one about the $100 banknote) or to notice that they are being addressed is a refusal of social intimacy. The reluctance of a dominant public to critically engage with the structures, affects, and social and material consequences of race that exceed the logic of multiculturalism limits social relations and collective attachments.

In this book, I explore how minor publics struggle with social intimacy by turning to literary texts, artistic works, theatrical performances, and debates waged through print and social media. Each employs different strategies to address its particular audience, and thus presents the problem of social intimacy from a new angle. Examples such as the $100 bill controversy and the contentious responses to *Maclean's* magazine's "Too Asian?" article and Alexandra Wallace's "Asians in the Library" YouTube video (both examined in chapter 2) demonstrate the dominant public's refusals of social intimacy and the reactions of minor publics. These recent conflicts are familiar to most Canadians because they circulated through national newspapers and magazines and via online forums such as YouTube and blogs, thereby confronting large audiences with racial issues and introducing the possibilities of critical debate about the racial politics of everyday life. Operating in a much different fashion, the creative texts I examine in this book engage smaller audiences and probe the social intimacies of race over a longer period of time. Joy Kogawa's novel *The Rain Ascends,* for instance, is an extended meditation on social guilt that forces the reader into an intimate relationship with the narrator, despite the reader's ethical and political reservations. Unlike a news story that summarizes a crime or an event, the confessional format of this novel means that the reader must endure the narrator's rambling and often-contradictory accounts and memories, and as a consequence may develop a fuller understanding, if not actual empathy, for Kogawa's narrator and, by extension, those unable to relinquish the privileges of whiteness. Continuing in a literary vein, Souvankham Thammavongsa's poetry also examines the overlooked desires of minor publics, but focuses more specifically on the struggles for representation by highlighting how formal devices such as metaphor are used to render minor lives illegible and seemingly inconsequential. The theatrical performances, performance art, and photographs I discuss in this book use visual strategies to explore feelings of awkwardness, discomfort, commonality, and alienation that constitute the affective conditions of social intimacy. As these creative interventions illustrate, art, literature, and theater occupy a different place within minor publics than do social texts and debates. While the former confronts us with the absence of social intimacy and our own unhappy reactions to this dilemma, the latter stages scenarios in order to investigate social discomfort in a variety of ways, dismantle individual and collective resistances, and make us want to desire social intimacy. Read collectively, these social and creative texts not only identify the resistant feelings that stand in the way of social intimacy, but they also force us to reexperience and repeatedly consider these anxieties in hopes that we may eventually understand and overcome them.

In Flux, Roy Miki's latest collection of essays on Asian Canadian literature, explores Asian Canadian as a racialized category produced in relation to institutionalized frames and destabilized through creative language acts. Reading this literature within the shifting frames of nationalism and globalization, he puts forward the understanding of *Asian Canadian* "as a limit term that lacks a secure referential base but rather is constituted through the literary and critical acts that are performed under its name" (*In Flux* xiii–xiv). Miki's approach to *Asian Canadian* as a flexible term whose meaning is generated through performance bears the marks of his work as a writer and critic of experimental poetry, and is a reading strategy that has been foundational for Asian Canadian literary studies. In a similar fashion, I interpret Asian Canadian publics as malleable collectives, and choose to define their membership through participation in debates about Asian Canadian concerns rather than solely through claims to Asian ethnicity, heritage, or nationality. While I do not disregard assertions to Asian Canadian identity made on those more familiar grounds, I make room for other forms of affiliation that include participation within Asian Canadian conversations. In thinking about Asian Canadian publics in terms of identification and as an intellectual formation, I grapple with questions of recognition, legitimacy, and audience central to publics and underscore the relations of power that make Asian Canadian a minor formation. I pluralize *publics* because there are often multiple Asian Canadian publics in existence, having been galvanized through particular concerns, and these publics are not always in conversation, or even aware of each other. I employ the terms *dominant* and *minor* to differentiate between various kinds of publics, not to suggest that one is more or less significant than the other, but rather to indicate the complex relations of power at work.

It is precisely those structures of power—national, global, classed, gendered, racialized—within which dominant and minor publics are located that I explore throughout this book. More specifically, with respect to the $100 bill example, I interrogate the relations of power that permit a dominant public, one that imagines itself in this instance to be synonymous with a national community, to dismiss such controversies as minor and inconsequential.

Multicultural Fatigue

As a much-feted aspect of Canadian identity, the official policy of multiculturalism is a point of pride for the nation and often gestured toward as proof of the nation's genuine commitment to diversity. Historically, the federal government gravitated toward this position through successive legislative acts, first instituting multiculturalism as official policy in 1971, incorporating it into the Charter of Rights in 1982, and passing the Canadian Multiculturalism Act in 1988. By framing race in terms of rights to heritage and ethnic languages and freedoms from racial and religious discrimination, multiculturalism formally incorporates racialized subjects into the structures of citizenship without addressing how, to a large extent, the basic shape of citizenship is determined by the legacies of colonial law. The familiar complaint that multiculturalism is more effective as a mechanism that coheres the nation than as one that alleviates the often-difficult conditions of racialized lives is perhaps unsurprising given that Canadian multiculturalism emerged out of former Prime Minister Pierre Trudeau's attempts to address Quebec's separatist aspirations and preserve the unity of the nation. It was in response to the recommendations of the Royal Commission on Bilingualism and Biculturalism that Trudeau announced a new "policy of multiculturalism within a bilingual framework" that intended to ensure cultural freedom, preserve national unity, and provide "the base of a society which is based on fair play for all" (House of Commons Debates 8545). That multicultural policy in 1971 was never intended to disturb the colonial structure of Canada is a point conveyed by Robert L. Stanfield, leader of the opposition, who praises Trudeau's multiculturalism because it "in no way constitutes an attack on the basic duality of our country" (House of Commons Debates 8546). The deliberations in the House of Commons reveal that, as a policy for recognizing cultural diversity, multiculturalism always intended to incorporate ethnicity in limited terms and to conceptualize race through its difference from English and French cultures.

In addition to verbally delivering his remarks to the House of Commons, Trudeau tabled the federal government's detailed response to the Royal Commission on Bilingualism and Biculturalism and appended the document to

Hansard. The objectives for multicultural policy are outlined early in this document, and the limitations of multiculturalism's interventions within the sphere of the law explicitly stated:

> The law can and will protect individuals from overt discrimination but there are more subtle barriers to entry into our society. A sense of not belonging, or a feeling of inferiority, whatever its cause, cannot be legislated out of existence. Programs outlined in this document have been designed to foster confidence in one's individual cultural identity and in one's rightful place in Canadian life. Histories, films, and museum exhibits showing the great contributions of Canada's various cultural groups will help achieve this objective. But, we must emphasize that every Canadian must help eliminate discrimination. Every Canadian must contribute to the sense of national acceptance and belonging. (House of Commons Debates 8581)

For Trudeau, the governmental turn to legislation to rectify "discrimination" is not meant to address the affective dimensions of multicultural difference that lie beyond the reach of cultural policy and constitute a vaguely imagined collective responsibility. Three decades later, Statistics Canada's 2002 Ethnic Diversity Survey (EDS) returned to the problem of multicultural feeling by identifying a rift between multiculturalism policy and feelings of unbelonging, and noted that this affective condition is particularly acute for contemporary and second-generation visible minority Canadians who identify less with Canada than do their parents. As David Chariandy suggests in his reading of the EDS and of a *Globe and Mail* front-page news story about the survey,

> it's also possible that we have erred in assuming that the ideal of multicultural citizenship could entirely assuage the painful, affective legacies of diasporic displacement and racialization, or else adequately address the *material* obstacles towards security, social acceptance, and dignified labour that many visible minorities in Canada continue to face. . . . The shorthand way of putting all of this is that we have moved into a moment in which belonging has been revealed as a fiction. (828)

These waning feelings of belonging for racialized individuals have gone largely unnoticed by a dominant Canadian public. Instead of seeking to understand the discomforts of racialized minorities, the dominant public in Canada has become saturated by multiculturalism and now experiences what Smaro Kamboureli calls "multicultural fatigue," a form of exhaustion that "directly reflects the dominant society's comfortable assumption that multiculturalism, through implementation of the official policy and the proliferation of discussions and forums about it, has already fulfilled, if not exceeded, its mandate" (83). Rather than beginning national conversations about racialization, feeling, and collective belonging, multiculturalism policy has instead spelled the demise of these discussions for many individuals.

Although multiculturalism may have suppressed debates within a dominant Canadian public, it has also inadvertently produced thoughtful and provocative Asian Canadian critique that challenges the shape of a multicultural Canadian imagination. As the dominant force that sets the terms of racialization in Canada (by, for example, foregrounding markers like identity, culture, language, food, and heritage), multiculturalism makes difference visible as it attempts to homogenize it. Within a multicultural model of race and ethnicity, cultural difference is understood in singular terms and, consequently, narrow ways of being legible as, for instance, Chinese, Korean, or Filipino, exist. Excluded from a multicultural mosaic are the intricacies of colonialism, imperialism, migration, nationalism, and the Cold War legacies in Asia that produce multiple modalities of Asianness that undermine the simple fictions of national identities, such as large populations of ethnic Koreans in northern China, Zainichi Koreans in Japan, indigenous Taiwanese struggles, and competing identifications as Chinese by people from the People's Republic of China, Taiwan, Hong Kong, Singapore, and Malaysia. In this book, I focus on transnational, diasporic, and global structures of feeling in order to interrogate the limits of Canadian multiculturalism and imagine more capacious configurations of the "Asian" and "Canadian." My goal is to trouble reified understandings of the *Asian* by investigating the transnational flows of Asian affects, memories, bodies, and capital that move through, shape, and often pause within the Canadian nation-state. In this way, the Asian may be recognized as a subject rather than as merely a racialized adjective for *Canadian.*

Sociologists Jeffrey Reitz and Rupa Banerjee analyze the affective dimensions of difference or first- and second-generation immigrants and present compelling arguments for broadening a Canadian project of multiculturalism to include affect. Through their examination of the EDS, they deduce that children of immigrants feel a weaker sense of belonging than do their parents, despite the fact that the economic obstacles (such as unemployment and low earnings) that this younger generation faces are not nearly as daunting. While they may not confront material hardships to the same extent as their parents, for this second generation, "experiences of discrimination and vulnerability remain, slowing the social integration of minorities. Furthermore, these effects may be intensified for the children of immigrants, whose expectation of equality may be greater than was the case for their parents" (Reitz and Banerjee

34). The disillusionment of second-generation immigrants reminds us that we need to consider "how power shape[s] the production of sentiments and vice versa" (Stoler 12), because neglecting to critically examine the long-term affective and material effects of racism means that multicultural citizenship can only ever be an insincere promise.

In *The Minor Intimacies of Race*, I contend that, in order to create social intimacy within collectives, a widespread sense of curiosity about how race and power operate on a daily basis must exist. As Ann Laura Stoler notes in her study of colonial intimacies, *Carnal Knowledge and Imperial Power*,

> struggles over who is a citizen or subject, who is exempt from marriage laws, to whom pass laws apply, who can live where, who can travel and be issued a passport, whose children have access to which schools, who is incarcerated (where, in what conditions, and for how long) make up the micronodes of governance that impinge on and give distinct shape to the quotidian conditions of people's personal and family lives. (xxi)

Stoler explores the everyday intimacies of the Netherlands Indies in the late nineteenth and early twentieth centuries by focusing on colonial sexualities and domesticities. Her project unseats colonial categories of knowledge, and thus serves as a useful methodological example for those of us working on race in the Canadian context. In this book, I also turn to intimacy in order to undo classifications, but do so in order to critique racial categories central to multicultural governance. Moreover, *The Minor Intimacies of Race* focuses less on the kinds of intimacy produced by sexuality and more on forms of intimacy or shared knowledge that exceed the nation-state's mode of multicultural recognition, even as they are produced in part by them. In order to understand the affective dimensions of racialized life, I analyze how Asian Canadian subjects turn to other social formations such as diaspora, transnationalism, and globality, concentrating on the productive dimensions of social intimacy and, more specifically, on how it "builds worlds; it creates spaces and usurps places meant for other kinds of relation" (Berlant, "Intimacy" 2). Our multiple and conflicting attachments to these social spaces and formations are crucial forms of intimacy that, as Lauren Berlant describes in her summary of Jürgen Habermas's bourgeois public sphere, are "a public mode of identification and self-development" ("Intimacy" 3). At stake in my pursuit of the kinds of social intimacies absent from multicultural rhetoric and policy is a desire to make public the quotidian aspects of Asian Canadian subjectivity.

The recent Canadian currency debates call attention to how the circulation of racialized images, the flows of local and global capital through national economies, and individual and collective attachments to the symbolic, economic, affective, and social dimensions of the Canadian nation-state are mediated by race. As well, these struggles over national currency index broader issues of racial logics, representation, and, I want to emphasize, feeling. To gain further insight into the Canadian public's affective attachment to its national currency, I direct attention to related debates that preceded by a few months those about the racializing of Canadian currency. In May 2013, many Canadians began to speculate that the new $100 banknote smelled like "sweet, rich and wonderful" maple syrup (Sherrett). Some people were convinced that the bill was scented with this iconic Canadian odor and that the smell was heat activated, while others believed that the maple leaf on it was actually a scratch-and-sniff patch (Beeby, "Are Canada's $100"). The possibility that the bill had been deliberately scented with the odor of maple syrup as a new security feature was largely framed as an intriguing one ("Sniff Test"), and I stress how sharply this reception contrasts with the later reactions to the proposed Asianizing of Canadian currency. This rather unusual visceral public response to the perceived odor of Canada's new currency—claims that the bank denied—disappeared fairly quickly (as did the later outcry over the whitening of the bill's female scientist). These mixed public responses to the $100 banknote for its images and smell enact persistent national anxieties about how legitimacy, representation, and security are tied together, particularly where economic and symbolic value are concerned. More precisely, the affective reactions to and heated disputes over the $100 bill underscore how the banknote mediates social imaginaries and economic systems as it circulates as a form of national currency within global economic systems.

The contested relations to the figure of the Asian and its contingent place within the Canadian imagination stage in affective terms what John Erni calls the "politics of being 'included-out'" (2). Through his reading of legal cases that demonstrate how Hong Kong law is used to deny permanent residency to unwanted applicants even when they meet the requirements of Hong Kong's Basic Law, Erni explores the politics of partial inclusion that characterize national belonging and citizenship. Countering our firm but perhaps underexamined beliefs in national inclusion and the rights of citizenship, he recognizes the precarious nature of citizenship through an analysis of how "citizenship management has been practised *through* the state of general included-outness and this changes everything that used to be called politics. . . . This transformation, well evident today, can be described as a move away from the multiverse of restricted citizenship and border control to a general social economy around the instability of 'belonging' as such, as a structure of felt, lived, and often feared reality" (3).

In the Canadian context, the Asian scientist is a figure of partial inclusion that troubles the instinctive nationalism triggered by the smell of "secure, durable, innovative, syrup" (Newton), and, I argue, compels us to investigate how state powers and national identifications operate within transnational and global contexts. More than a simple and isolated instance of racism, the rejection of the Asian scientist from the banknote is part of a larger resistance to acknowledging the multiple and unrecognized flows of bodies and capital that have long circulated through Canada. I stress the importance of analyzing Canada as part of a global system rather than as a completely autonomous nation-state in order to understand the multiple and "different physiolog[ies] of power" at work (Cheah, "Crises" 102). The desire to maintain the authenticity of the banknote—as a unit of value that can withstand the efforts of counterfeiters and legitimately represent the national imaginary—is part of a larger ongoing struggle over the politics of racial and national representation articulated within various publics.

The currency controversy locates the disputes over national identity in a form that indexes the circulation of symbolic and material economies in local and global contexts. I stress here that the $100 bill struggle is over the expression of value rather than value itself, and note that to ask whether banknotes should be racialized is very different from investigating the racialization of the national economy, labor force, or notions of value itself. At stake in these debates then is the question of how to represent value, because money, as sociologist Georg Simmel notes, is a symbolic form that is supposed to neutralize exchange: "Money can enter adequately into the relations that form the continuity of the economy only because, as a concrete value, it is nothing but the relation between economic values themselves, embodied in a tangible substance" (125). Simmel's philosophy of money perceives it as depersonalized and able to function as simply a unit of exchange. But for the banknote to function as money, as "the pure form of exchangeability" (130), it must retain nonspecific value. And while the appearance of the banknote may not actually affect the value of Canadian currency, the resistance to incorporating an Asian image onto the $100 bill suggests a change to its affective value and, moreover, a need for the surface of the bill to remain visibly nonracialized if it is to act as the standard of exchangeability.

Money may operate as an economic form of whiteness, but, as Marx reminds us, money "is the measure of value inasmuch as it is the socially recognised incarnation of human labour" (Marx 68). Even though money may strive to standardize exchange, this intention can never be completely realized given that money derives its symbolic value from the economy of which it is a part. Christine So argues that in an Asian American context, belief in money offers communities an illusory avenue into dominant America and while money has only symbolic value, "the act of exchange itself at the very least signals an albeit brief relationship between two parties" (4). The parties are unequal in practice, but the exchange is "based on equality, a presumption that in fact disguises the unequal class relations that exist" (4). So's study sketches out crucial differences between an idealized economy and the actual form these relations take, and when transposed into a Canadian context, her insights remind us that we need to historicize our understandings of exchange and the economies within which they occur. More specifically, these differences between symbolic value and actual exchanges ask us to scrutinize the process by which the labor of bodies—which in the histories of Asian migrants to Canada and the United States has often taken the form of tasks such as laundering clothes, building railroads, domestic labor, and prostituting bodies—is disavowed by a neutralized and unmarked form of exchangeability such as money. The $100 banknote makes visible the process by which Canadian money functions as absolute exchangeability and highlights how the history of racialized labor is part of this economy. Located in the very form of the $100 banknote—and by *form* I mean at once the appearance of the note, its social circulation, and the logic of currency—is a set of pressing questions about how to recognize and satisfy the competing histories and multiple debts embedded visibly and invisibly (for instance, the perceived smell of maple syrup and traces of the expunged Asian woman) within the everyday transactions that suture together local, national, and global economies and the fantasies of neutrality that underpin them.

Diasporic, Transnational, and Global Feelings

This book critiques understandings of race that have been produced through multicultural policies and ideologies by acknowledging that although the national is a crucial stage for identity formation, it is not the only or often even primary space in which racialized identities are formed. This is perhaps another way of saying that the racial imaginary exceeds the scope of a national symbolic or set of national identities even as the nation-state continues to exert undeniable force on its subjects. *The Minor Intimacies of Race* explores the affective dimensions of racialization by analyzing how Asian Canadian publics negotiate tensions between the national and the diasporic, transnational, and global. Without dismissing the significance of the nation-state's ability to make subjects legible in political and legal terms, we must also acknowledge the significance of racial affects that circulate beyond national borders. Lily

Cho eloquently reminds us that "we cannot, given the choice, choose not to be citizens. To do so would be to render ourselves refugees—a state that Agamben identifies as one that illuminates the limit of citizenship" ("Diasporic Citizenship" 103). Cho responds to the predicament of national citizenship by turning to diasporic citizenship because "diasporas function as a perpetual reminder of the losses that enable citizenship" (108). Other critics have used transnationalism and globality in a similar fashion to account for the exclusions that sustain national citizenship. In *Asian North American Identities,* Eleanor Ty and Donald Goellnicht invoke Asian North America as a category to address hemispheric experiences of exclusion and racialization. While conscious of the national specificity of struggles for recognition and justice, Ty and Goellnicht mobilize Asian North American as a category for the strategic political possibilities it offers Asian subjects through "coalition building and common identification" (2). Ty employs a similar approach in both *The Politics of the Visible in Asian North American Narratives* and *Unfastened,* using *Asian North American* as a term to emphasize the common histories of racialization experienced by Asian Canadians and Asian Americans. In these two monographs, she reads Asian Canadian and Asian American texts through the lens of globality to emphasize the social conditions produced by newer accelerated global flows and to analyze Asian North American agency and subjectivity. Moving these concerns in yet another direction, Roy Miki examines Asian Canadian writing for how it struggles with the forces of globalization in the 1990s, arguing that "these practices have the capacity to enable a rethinking of *nation* as a complex of heterogeneous global/local formations, not constituted solely as enclaves of identification but more generatively produced by or through negotiations across and within temporalities and boundaries" (*In Flux* 52). Ty, Goellnicht, and Miki approach the transnational and the global in different ways. For Ty and Goellnicht, the shared experiences of racialization in Canada and the United States produce transnational forms of identification and consequently make it possible to speak of Asian North American as a lived category. Miki is instead primarily interested in the transnational and the global as forces capable of transforming the racialized landscape of the Canadian nation-state.

Even as they turn to the paradigms of diaspora, transnationalism, and globality, these various critical projects illustrate how Asian Canadian subjects have historically been produced by the nation-state and its policies of migration and multiculturalism; Miki's project engages with the interfacing of the nation-state and transnationalism by putting forward nuanced critiques of the nation-state's ongoing processes of racialization whereas Ty's *Unfastened* focuses on literature that writes about the "unfastening" of Asian diasporas from nations. Both the competing desires to look inward and hold the nation-state accountable and to look outward and examine the global consequences of state policies for Asians have influenced my own thinking. However, in this particular project, I deviate from these paths somewhat by tracing how *Asian Canadian* circulates beyond national borders in an effort to understand first and foremost what is meant by *Asian* in the term *Asian Canadian,* and then to critique the Canadian nation-state. For similar reasons, I refrain from framing the texts in this book as politically resistant because I am not convinced that the nation-state, or North America more broadly, is the primary object of critique for many of them. Without dismissing this kind of national political project entirely, I see the writers and artists examined in *The Minor Intimacies of Race* as searching largely for publics willing to engage with diasporic memories, global migrations, and transnational racial identifications not often recognized by a national multicultural imaginary, and consequently understand critiques of a particular Canadian liberal imaginary as secondary rather than primary goals. These pursuits of social intimacy are an invaluable part of an Asian Canadian political project that interrogates how racialized subjects are formed, recognized, and made to matter for a range of local, national, and global audiences. In expanding our conception of political engagement to include the affective dimensions of debate and dialogue and examining how these forms of identification exceed the nation-state, these Asian Canadian cultural producers remind us that although the nation is one important stage on which subjects are racialized, it is not an isolated stage. For this reason, I analyze transnational circulations throughout Canada and other parts of the globe, including the United States, and critically examine how these identifications are produced and the work they perform. In this way, I investigate how transnational categories such as *Asian North America* are generated on an ad hoc basis rather than assuming that they exist in a permanent and enduring fashion. In order to grasp more fully how these processes occur, I contend that we must consider the marginalization of national subjects within the context of minor empires (a concept I explore more fully later in this introduction) and global systems of partial inclusion.

In considering the publics generated by these texts, it is necessary to take into account that the audiences they address vary considerably in terms of size, scope, and mood. Many of the artistic works I analyze only have the capacity to reach very limited audiences; for example, David Khang's *Mom's Crutch* and Cindy Mochizuki's *Bioboxes* are creative projects that reach a single participant at a time. In contrast, other texts such as the "Asians in the Library" YouTube video and its responses have amassed millions of viewers. The number of people who engage with these publics is undeniably important for understanding the potential political impact of Asian Canadian publics, but is not the only indicator. While the design of Khang's and Mochizuki's works means that fewer people are exposed to them, they impact their viewers deeply by opening them to transformative possibilities in a manner that is both startling and rare. By addressing individuals rather than collectives, these art projects begin to fashion their participants into social subjects that are self-reflexive, thoughtful, and accountable. The intense engagement demanded by these art projects complements the other kinds of affective labor undertaken by wider publics, such as those formed in response to *Maclean's* "Too Asian?" article or even the $100 banknote controversy that I have discussed at length in this introduction. Collectively, Asian Canadian publics that engage with art, literature, and debates in print and on social media reorient us by transforming social imaginaries and taking seriously the work of engaging audiences. This project intends to contribute to the valuable and illuminating critical conversations occurring in Asian Canadian publics by emphasizing how matters of address, affect, and audience shape the local, national, and global exchanges that constitute minor publics.

Historicizing Canadian Orientalism

I return once more to the example of the $100 banknote, and by extension social imaginaries with respect to race and national identity, this time in order to invoke the longer history of Asian Canada. After all, the 2012 debate pivoted around the suitability of an image of an Asian-looking female scientist rather than, as would have been the case less than a century ago, whether an Asian woman could be a scientist in Canada. Even though legal and political restrictions are no longer in place to prevent Asian Canadians from voting or entering into professional fields or educational or political institutions, these changes have not translated into a dominant public willing to fully embrace Asian Canadians as citizens in the same manner that it embraces "racially neutral," to return to the Bank of Canada's language, citizens. The skirmishes around the $100 bill illustrate that while post-WWII changes to the structures of citizenship are of undeniable significance for Asian Canadians, they need also to be accompanied by transformations to the social imaginary, and in particular to the affective bonds that influence how political promises of equal citizenship are realized. Minor publics examining race, which is how I characterize the discussions around the $100 banknote, illuminate the dissonances between the political discourses of citizenship and the lived experiences of racialized bodies, often by participating within the realm of the political without necessarily entering into the language of political representation or structure of electoral politics. Asian Canadian publics make room for the affective dimensions not included, or at least not foregrounded overtly, within the political structures of a dominant public. It is not possible to have extended conversations within a multicultural forum that explore the affective dimensions of racialization—even though brief engagements occur, prolonged investigations are not encouraged by these structures. These kinds of examinations do, however, take place within minor publics and often result in sharp insights into the racial unconscious of a liberal Canadian imagination.

The relatively easy erasure of the image of the female Asian scientist from Canadian currency speaks to the vexed ways in which Asians have inhabited Canada, materially and symbolically, over the past century and a half. We might read the traces of this expunged image in relation to the long history of Asians as a source of cheap labor even as they are refused Canadian citizenship, or to a related and ongoing fear of an Asian invasion, configured previously as incoming hordes of racialized bodies and now as wealthy Asians dominating local real estate markets. Because the current placelessness of the Asian within the Canadian social imagination is produced by complex histories of colonialism, cultural imperialism, and immigration, I situate the Asian as a persistent problem for the Canadian social imagination within a brief overview of the long twentieth century in Canada and what I call a *minor empire*.[3]

In his seminal study *Orientalism* (1978), Edward Said sketches out the development of Orientalism in Europe throughout the nineteenth century, and demonstrates how, as an invention of the Western imagination, the uncivilized and unscrupulous Oriental is a figure of alterity whose very existence legitimated the need for European colonialism. Said not only demonstrates how European power works through the misrepresentation of "Orientals," but also how these Orientalist beliefs structure Western institutions and produce forms of knowledge that have persisted for centuries. More recently, Asian American critics such as Jodi Kim, Lisa Lowe, Colleen Lye, and Jane Park have examined the transformation of Orientalist discourses within a U.S. context; to be more precise, they explore the Asian as an ambivalent figure for America, largely because the nation has remained economically reliant on the Asian even as it has continued to threaten the United States in social, political, and cultural terms. I return to Said's analysis to draw attention to the affective terms of Orientalism; more specifically, to explore how knowledge of the Orient and its facilitating of colonial expansion and exclusion was enabled by and orchestrated through affective responses vis-à-vis the Oriental other (i.e., desire, revulsion, and/or sadistic fascination regarding "despotic" cruelty and violence). Fear, anxiety, fascination, and other affective responses demonstrated by dominant publics to the Asian echo these Orientalist affects and link earlier discourses of the Orient with contemporary ones of Asia.

When shifting to the Canadian context, Canada's location within the histories of nineteenth-century European colonialism and twentieth- and twenty-first-century American imperialism further complicate how Orientalist affects, cultural representations, and dynamics unfold. As a former British colony currently under the influence of U.S. imperialism, Canada lacks the kind of imperial clout possessed by those European countries that Said describes. And while it is, as a minor empire, unable to express and regulate social relations in as straightforward a manner, Canada continues to be shaped not only by "the imperial and colonial scripts that have provided the templates for settler-society formations in North America" (Miki, *In Flux* 121), but also by its own imperial desires and versions of Orientalist discourses. In seeking to implement anti-Asian regulations, Canadian authorities (like those in other settler colonial countries such as Australia and South Africa) have maneuvered deftly between local, national, hemispheric, and transnational powers and contexts. For example, Canadian efforts during the late nineteenth and early twentieth centuries to enforce a "white by design" immigration policy were often necessarily covert because of the complex imperial triangulations of power at work. As historians Marilyn Lake and Henry Reynolds note, "The project of whiteness was thus a paradoxical politics, at once transnational in its inspiration and identifications but nationalist in its methods and goals. The imagined community of white men was transnational in its reach, but nationalist in its outcomes, bolstering regimes of border protection and national sovereignty" (4). Shaping the composition of Canada's population demanded intricate negotiations between various empires, countries, and international powers—such as the British, American, Japanese, and Chinese—that were each in different stages of formation.

During this late colonial period, Canada was caught between the imperative to respect the web of imperial allegiances and international treaties within which it was located, and its own desire to exclude racially undesirable bodies from its borders. In order to satisfy the conflicting demands of the British authority and its own local populations, the Canadian government explored various forms of discrimination capable of screening racialized bodies without explicitly declaring to the rest of the world its national desire for whiteness or the ethos of white supremacy. One such strategy was the passport, which, as Radhika Viyas Mongia explains, proved to be invaluable for controlling the movement of racialized bodies. According to Mongia's interpretation of the events surrounding the birth of the passport, the nation—as a particular relationship between people and territory—was not actually an entity that needed to be protected from the incoming waves of immigration, but rather was produced by raced migration (528). As a technology that "nationalizes bodies along racial lines," the passport's history demonstrates that racial discourses have long been central to the formation of both nation and state (529). The history of Indian immigration to Canada is a particularly illuminating case study as the migratory desires of these racialized British subjects necessitated that Canadian authorities formulate a strategy for practicing racial exclusion without naming it as such (550). Thus, what Partha Chatterjee calls the "rule of colonial difference," whereby the colonies existed as exceptions to the notions of truth, equality, and universality proclaimed by the queen, could continue uninterrupted (qtd. in Mongia 531). That this regulation of racialized immigration during the early twentieth century generated cohesive national bonds and what I call forms of social intimacy between white subjects is relevant when critically examining discourses of contemporary multiculturalism, race, citizenship, and immigration, and is a process that I explore in more detail later in this introduction. Mongia's analysis of the passport offers a useful lens for reading Canadian history over the past two centuries and recognizing that Canada's mediating position within various imperial triangles and its role as a minor imperial power produced the need for discreet forms of discrimination.

Despite the many objections to the passport system initially raised by the Indian government, India was eventually persuaded by other governments to institute the passport as a requirement for Indians traveling abroad. This acquiescence in 1915 to the passport as a formal means of regulating Indian mobility throughout the empire was prompted in large measure by the 1914 *Komagata Maru* incident, which saw a ship carrying 376 passengers (mostly Sikhs) depart from Hong Kong with the intention of eventually docking in Vancouver, British Columbia. As many critical investigations of this event reveal, the ship's attempt to anchor in the Burrard Inlet posed considerable challenges for the Canadian government.[4] While determined to prevent Indian immigration, the Canadian government was hampered by the need to maintain the illusion of equality among all British subjects, even though this was at odds with the obvious and deep inequality practiced in everyday life (Mongia 531). Hiding racist motivations behind covertly discriminatory laws was a common Canadian practice, as is evidenced by the example of the continuous-journey passage provision which was cited as the official reason for turning the *Komagata Maru* away (as the ship had made stops in China and Japan before entering the Burrard Inlet). The furor in response to the Canadian government's refusal to permit the ship's passengers to disembark, letting hundreds of people languish in the harbor for two months before the ship was escorted out by the Canadian military, was certainly one factor that prompted the Canadian government to embrace other exclusionary measures, such as the passport system.

The continuous-journey passage provision and the imposition of passports for Indian subjects are only two of many instances in which the state sought to practice racism without using an overtly racialized language. The 1907 Pacific riots, an anti-Asian protest that traveled from Bellingham, Washington, to Vancouver, British Columbia, also illustrate how strong racist feeling was interwoven with a refusal to directly articulate such sentiments. In Vancouver, the anti-Asian riots lasted for days, moving through Chinatown and toward Japantown (with the latter protected only by barricades that had been erected after it had been warned of the impending crowd [Price 58]), and became the subject of newspaper headlines around the world. Like the *Komagata Maru* incident that was to follow, the 1907 riots provide key insights into how power is structured and spoken; not only are these riots clear examples of the racist sentiments of a Canadian public, but they also make evident the government's consciousness of its own racism through its "general policy of not *naming* race" (Mongia 546). As historian John Price writes in "'Orienting' the Empire," the 1907 riots were propelled by a desire to assert Canada's identity as a white settler colony, but "took place in a transnational context in which the British Empire faced increasing challenges, particularly from the anti-colonial movements in India and China as well as from imperial Germany, Japan, and the United States" (55). While the inclination on the part of the government and the Canadian public was to limit all transpacific immigration, the manner in which these flows could be restricted was contingent upon the relations between Canada and the Asian countries in question. In the case of Japan, its imperial status and the existence of the 1894 Anglo-Japanese treaty meant that diplomatic language was required. Following the riots, Rodolphe Lemieux, minister of labour, was sent to Japan to meet with the British ambassador and Japanese government about restricting Japanese migration to Canada. Lemieux's report to the cabinet outlines the need to maintain more cordial relations with Japan and notes the inappropriateness of imposing an exclusionary head-tax policy on Japanese people similar to the one already in place for the Chinese (Price 65). In contrast, Chinese migrants were openly discriminated against, as their five-hundred-dollar head tax (the only one imposed on immigrants to Canada) attests. A range of strategies was deployed against migrants from India, Japan, and China in order to maintain, as was sung at the time, "White Canada Forever," with the measures differing in terms of how explicitly racist they were. At the same time, this desire to exclude nonwhite migrants was also shared by other countries; as Price notes, it became the basis for "an international Anglo-American alliance that was race-based. This vision and the policies adopted in this era were foundational in the consolidation of the Canadian state and in the articulation of an autonomous Canadian foreign policy within the British Empire" (53).

There are a number of seeds planted here that later sprout in the philosophy and policies of multiculturalism: the relation between the "multicultural" or migrant periphery and a dominant or white center; the language of belonging, whether as an imperial subject or citizen, and the unequal sets of rights that accompany it; the need to regulate racialized migration differently from "unracialized" migration, executed in a manner that balances foreign-policy concerns against domestic ones; and the migrant as not only a racialized and thus undesirable social body, but one that also acts as a cheap, and therefore necessary, source of labor. These multiple points suture together debates about nineteenth- and early twentieth-century migration with later ones about twentieth-century multiculturalism to suggest that, while their particular rhetoric would suggest otherwise, these discourses share an investment in the hegemony of whiteness. Without dismissing the genuine benefits that people have derived from multiculturalism in Canada, we must acknowledge that the uneven power dynamics that characterize Canadian-Asian relations in the past century continue to exist within liberal multiculturalism. Thinking about Canada in a premulticultural moment reveals the trajectories by which we arrive in the present, and also demands that we contend with the tenacious legacies of the past. Historicizing contemporary Canada in such a manner also underscores how a dominant Canadian public's response to Asian Canada is strongly influenced by global discourses about the figure of the Asian. In recognizing the larger global context that informs Canadian multiculturalism, we recognize the need for political strategies that grapple with the nation-state and the larger legacies of imperialism.

In addition to providing the background for my exploration of Asian Canadian publics, the sketch of Canadian Orientalism highlights the triangulated structures and dynamics of power at work in contemporary social formations. Unlike Said, who focuses primarily on representations of Asia by the West, I examine Asian Canadian publics that, partly by belonging to neither the Asia nor the West envisioned by Orientalists, complicate conversations about race and citizenship. In doing so, I take my cue from Said's comments in his preface to the twenty-fifth anniversary edition of *Orientalism* (xxii) on modern imperialism and the need to account for the pernicious impact of Orientalism on its subjects. Tracing a line of conquest that extends from Napoleon to ongoing struggles over oil in the Gulf, he comments perceptively on the shifting knowledges and languages produced about the other. Said uses a humanistic approach in *Orientalism* to "open up the fields of struggle, to introduce a longer sequence of thought and analysis to replace the short bursts of polemical, thought-stopping fury that so imprison us in labels and antagonistic debate whose goal is a belligerent collective identity rather than understanding and intellectual exchange" (xxii–xxiii). Like Said, I am similarly interested in revising the terms of engagement with Orientalism and undermining the fiction of an Asian-Western opposition. I attempt to do so by considering how Asian Canadian publics do not exist outside the boundaries of this knowledge formation, but instead are positioned differently within them. And whereas Said in his preface focuses on the possibilities of community for humanistic critique, I direct my investigation toward the critical possibilities of publics in order to understand how the constitutive roles of speaker and audience determine the shapes of publics.

The debates about the $100 banknote speak to the legacy of a twentieth-century Canadian Orientalism that manifests as a dominant public unwilling to engage in frank and sustained conversations about race. My wager is that if we remain cognizant of this longer history, examinations of this discussion and others like it can render visible the racialized dimensions of public consciousnesses. This book undertakes this work by engaging with Asian Canadian critical and creative contributions to contemporary discussions of multiculturalism, transnationalism, print and digital culture, diaspora, and international human rights, and focuses on the aesthetic, social, and affective dimensions of these dialogues. Asian Canadian publics remind minor and dominant publics of the necessity of considering not just what is said about race, but also how these things are spoken about and felt; in short, content, style, and affect shape how we enter into debates about politics, economics, and social and legal rights and how they play out on multiple scales and via interrelated formations. As sites of social intimacy, minor publics offer a sense of belonging to racialized individuals and collectives. This feeling of affinity supplements struggles for recognition and encourages critical investigations of the terms by which racialized subjectivity is generated.

Asian Canadian Publics, National Discourses, International Frames

The Minor Intimacies of Race approaches Asian Canadian as a heuristic category, one that enables a type of critical work, rather than as a sociological group. Put plainly, *Asian Canadian* is something of an oxymoron given that *Asian* has historically been synonymous with not being Canadian. The term *Asian Canadian* invokes the long history of exclusionism that has protected the whiteness of the nation even as it works to circumvent this legacy by engaging with the histories and relations that bind together the Asian and the Canadian. A careful examination of these terms reveals their different logics, with *Asian* signifying a displacement, a diaspora always imagined as rooted elsewhere, and *Canadian* claiming national fixity, a set of borders, and a banal kind of legitimacy. Unraveling each of these concepts further questions the real and imagined relations that suture together Asia and Asian diasporas, and how these formations are shaped by the particularities of the nation even as they continue to operate transnationally. The conflicting logics at work within the Asian and the Canadian are visible in the historical example of Japanese Canadian internment and repatriation during WWII, events that undeniably illustrate the precarious nature of citizenship for Asian Canadians. By imagining that the Japanese, and by extension the Asian, could easily be sequestered or expelled from Canada, the state asserted the fiction that the nation is autonomous and ahistorical by forgetting the Asian labor—material and ideological—that produced Canada. Enacting the Asian Canadian as a methodological approach brings these histories and legacies into conversation as it examines how they continue to generate each other.

While *The Minor Intimacies of Race* focuses specifically on Asian Canadian publics as self-directed spaces of discussion that also critique a dominant public, the national specificity of Asian Canadian as a formation must be understood continentally, even hemispherically, as national borders, though they constrain and circumscribe, are porous and problematic. Diasporic imaginaries, for example, also shape Asian Canadian publics by offering models of identification and mediating the normalizing pressures of the nation-state. Thus, the denial of Asian Canadian and Asian American as mutually exclusive categories can also be understood as a critique of nationalist epistemes. For this reason, I include as part of my discussion of Asian Canadian publics work by Susan Choi, an Asian American writer, and a YouTube video by former UCLA student Alexandra Wallace. I do so not as an act of national appropriation, but instead to draw attention to the Asian Canadian social imaginary as shaped simultaneously by what happens within Canada and as it imagines itself as part of a North American, and even global, public. The recent furor over NBA star Jeremy Lin and the racialization of his unexpected success is another example of transnational cultural phenomena that influence what it means to be read as Asian in Canada—in Lin's case, by expanding modes of conceptualizing Asian masculinity.[5] These various examples illustrate both the mobility of racial identification and the particularities of Canadian and American racial formations. Understanding the history of Asian Canada requires discerning the legacy of British colonialism and the ongoing influence of U.S. imperialism on the Canadian national psyche. At the same time, Asian Canada and Asian America remain part of Asian diasporas that extend beyond these particular national formations and form a collective subject that claims aspects of itself that are rejected by Canada and the United States.

In the chapters that follow, I sketch out some of the ways that Asian Canadian publics participate in conversations about contemporary North American cultural politics. I end with an examination of how these discussions shape and are shaped by international affairs. To briefly summarize the arc of my argument: I begin by examining the limitations of multiculturalism for understanding Asian Canadian subjectivity and considering how struggles for social intimacy are articulated through Asian Canadian performance art and literature. In chapter 2, I turn to print and online forums to examine the affective and logical dimensions of debate about Asians and how these discussions circulate transnationally. In the third chapter, I focus on the tension between nation and diaspora as affective, social, and political formations, and use literary and artistic examples to consider the extent to which they shape each other. Through poetry and zine culture, I examine in chapter 4 how the Asian refugee operates as a metaphor for the inhuman in discourses of national citizenship and international human rights. The book's conclusion again engages with poetry, this time to contemplate the limits of social intimacy for various publics. Throughout this book, I analyze a range of cultural examples that include literature, visual culture, theater, performance art, and YouTube videos to consider how minor publics respond to debates about race and, often more specifically, the figure of the Asian. In using these various cultural representations to trace the Asian as it circulates throughout local and global systems, I sketch out the conflicting and competing impulses that work simultaneously to shape social imaginations. These texts offer immensely useful entry points for thinking about the fleeting nature of memory, the persistence of racial trauma, and possibilities that exist for reconfiguring and reimaging social citizenship through various forms of art, literature, theater, and popular culture. Within the spaces of art, digital and print media, and literature, Asian publics critique dominant cultural representations and produce new ones. By selecting texts that use a range of media and address different scales and kinds of Asian publics, I examine the complexity as well as the multiplicity of these publics and their audiences as well as the particular conditions under which they are produced.

The chapters of this book also consider the constitutive ephemerality of these publics. These minor publics illuminate different affects that are part of race, but cannot quite be translated into social or political discourses without sacrificing crucial aspects of this knowledge. In addition to constituting a kind of temporality, the ephemerality of these publics indicates much about the relations of power within which they are located as well as the cultural grammars of nation, diaspora, and other forms of collectivity. To be more precise, Asian Canadian publics are ephemeral and last only for a short time, contra the long history of Asians in Canada I describe earlier. The texts analyzed in this book intervene within debates about race, citizenship, and sociality by highlighting a vulnerability peculiar to Asian Canadian publics, one produced when their concerns are made to seem insignificant and irrelevant to the interests of a wider dominant public. While other minor publics also risk marginalization, I believe that the style or strategies of marginalizing minor publics are unique to each. Each chapter of this book addresses a different form of ephemerality, and in so doing, considers the materiality of these particular publics. While the framing by a dominant public of Asian Canadian publics as trivial, fragile, unfinished, and lost threatens to dismiss their contributions and questions, I contend that it is precisely this very fleeting nature that equips these publics to produce insights into the racial unconscious and is also why minor publics can only ever be ephemeral. And while these publics may only ever exist temporarily, they transform the social imaginary by forcing us to engage with racial affect and our desires for greater social intimacy.

The first chapter of the book examines how the figure of the Asian is currently positioned within the project of Canadian multiculturalism in order to discern how differently racialized bodies experience affective and political citizenship. This chapter critiques the assumption that Asian Canadian publics demand recognition in multicultural terms by turning to two contemporary Asian Canadian texts that explore the unfinished nature of these conversations about race. The first part of this chapter uses Theatre Replacement's 2007 production *Bioboxes* to examine how the ideals of multiculturalism are reshaped through an Asian Canadian insistence on social intimacy. The second section of this discussion turns to Joy Kogawa's 1995 novel *The Rain Ascends* (rev. 2003) to consider what happens to a nation designed in multicultural terms when whiteness is denaturalized. What are the affective and political implications for citizenship when normativity, a primary mechanism for regulating difference, is disrupted? These texts, as they call for intimacy, demand recognition in different ways: the first forces the audience to be physically conscious of the racialized body with which it shares a confined space, and the second uses the genre of the confessional novel to compel the reader to witness the most mundane and personal details of the narrator's story. From the angles that Theatre Replacement and Kogawa provide, we recognize that the imperviousness of official discourses of multiculturalism to the feelings of racialized participants and the all-too-fleeting and transient nature of actual moments of multicultural interaction mean that multiculturalism is a necessarily incomplete project. By presenting multiculturalism in ways that unyoke identity and community, discourses and experiences, these creative texts gesture toward new social relations and alternative forms of political engagement for Asian Canadian publics.

The second chapter of this book extends the focus of my introduction—namely, how public discussions about race are often perceived to be trivial—to include recent print and online discussions about Asian students in postsecondary institutions in Canada and the United States. Unlike the other chapters of this book that focus on works of literature and art, this chapter examines controversial online and print journalistic texts that launched heated debates about the cultural politics of racial representation in postsecondary institutions. The firestorm ignited by these texts generated extensive publics, audiences far larger than those garnered by most of the literary and artistic texts I write about in this book. To understand the nature of the publics produced by Stephanie Findlay and Nicholas Kohler's "Too Asian?" article (2010) and Alexandra Wallace's "Asians in the Library" YouTube video (2011), I pay particular attention to how these texts and their respondents invoke logic and emotion as well as to how the technologies of print and the Internet lend themselves to different kinds of public participation. By reading the influx of Asian students akin to an invasion of postsecondary institutions, Findlay, Kohler, and Wallace rework the language of Yellow Peril and other kinds of Orientalist imagery within Canadian and American contexts. The circulation of shared Orientalist representations throughout Canada and the United States, and the ability of Wallace's YouTube video to generate fierce debate in Canada despite its American focus, illustrates the transnational nature of dominant social imaginations bound together by common anxieties about the Asian despite the significant differences in the national histories of higher education in Canada and the United States. At the same time, I engage with what I call an Asian North America—a minor public that comes into being through its reactions to this anti-Asian sentiment—for the pressing questions it raises about the politics of representation, citizenship, and recognition.

Chapter 3 reads works by Korean Canadian artist David Khang and Korean American writer Susan Choi through the lens of fragility in order to understand the complexities of diasporic publics as formations of feeling. I explore fragility in Khang's art through the brokenness of bodies and memories and in Choi's fiction through romantic misalliances; their projects speak to the geopolitics of feeling and the local, national, and global structures that shape delicate memories, racialize social intimacies, and formulate Asia as a site of alterity. Khang's art installation *Mom's Crutch* (2004) and performance art project *Wrong Places* (2007–14) and Choi's 1998 novel, *The Foreign Student,* underscore the need to spatialize discussions of postcolonial intimacies and affect by reminding us that diaspora is an affective formation whose participants are situated within diverse national contexts, and moreover, that this tension shapes global politics and possibilities. This chapter begins to contemplate what representations of Asia reveal about the likelihood of postcolonial intimacy, despite or perhaps because of the comparable historical and ongoing experiences of imperial practices that colonize public imaginations. On the one hand, Khang's *Wrong Places* and *Mom's Crutch* draw attention to the relative paucity of Korean War representations and the excess of 9/11 representations within the North American imagination, thus posing pressing questions about how these competing representations of war and suffering shape publics. By reminding us that structures of feeling are specific to places and generations, Khang's art foregrounds the fragility of feeling and remembering for a Korean diaspora. Choi's novel, on the other hand, explores historical intimacies between Korea and the United States that have been forgotten in the current moment by writing a budding romance between a Korean foreign student and a local American woman. The illegibility of this interracial couple within the American South of the 1950s speaks to the process of forgetting that characterizes contemporary American-Korean relations and the Korean diaspora as a formation. Here, Asian Canadian is an ephemeral public that illuminates the complex interplay between national and diasporic formations through subjects divided on the levels of affect, politics, and memory.

The final chapter of this book extends previous investigations into the ephemerality of minor publics by using the poetry of Souvankham Thammavongsa to understand the figure of the Asian refugee as a metaphor for the inhuman within human rights discourses. Her first two books, *Small Arguments* (2003) and *Found* (2007), offer mediations on the mechanisms of power that threaten to render certain lives lost and forgotten. I contextualize Thammavongsa's poetry by turning to her work in *big boots,* a now defunct Toronto-based zine united by feminist and racialized concerns. By recording the experiences and creative outputs of this minor public in print, this zine legitimates marginalized lives and interrogates the structures that constantly threaten them with erasure. I read the focus in *Small Arguments* and *Found* on everyday and neglected objects and minor lives, such as insects, newspapers, and a journal kept by the poet's father in a Thai refugee camp, through a similar lens. Thammavongsa's poetry draws attention to the structures of power that produce socially recognizable forms of life, as well as the larger polis to which they belong, by excluding bare life; the texts investigate how the legitimating capabilities of print are necessary in order for a logic of exception to be exercised and human rights discourses to operate. I also explore how *Found* and *Small Arguments* rely on metaphor to humanize both cockroaches and refugees. This poetic strategy is used to address the relations between the social and political, affect and human rights, poetics and social narratives, and to query how these tensions determine whether we experience things as noise or hear them as part of publics. The poems suggest that to be either a cockroach or the reader that recognizes the humanity of these subjects has everything to do with positioning and virtually nothing to do with actual feeling or ability, and moreover, that this project is distinct from one that aims to recognize the human rights of all individuals. The struggles undertaken by the subjects of Thammavongsa's poems illustrate the intertwined nature of national citizenship and the principles and narratives of human rights. *Small Arguments* and *Found* demonstrate that the national imagination is shaped by global events and discourses.

This book concludes by examining what I propose to be a temporality of racialized publics. Beginning with a discussion of poet and visual artist Roy Kiyooka's work and his influence on Asian Canadian creative and critical work, I outline a form of ephemeral intimacy that emerges within racialized publics and that might also potentially be extended to include dominant publics. Kiyooka's work operates as an Asian Canadian archive for how it historicizes racialized logics that are often at odds with racialized representations. I focus on Kiyooka's *StoneDGloves* (1997), which, as an experimental piece of visual art and poetry, explores the limits of aesthetic and social representation, a concern that is also, I argue, at the heart of Asian Canadian publics.

CHAPTER 1

National Incompletion

Awkward Multiculturalisms and Denaturalizing Whiteness

In this chapter, I interrogate Canadian perceptions of multiculturalism in order to contextualize the demands that two contemporary Asian Canadian texts, Cindy Mochizuki's section of Vancouver-based theater company Theatre Replacement's *Bioboxes* (2007) and Joy Kogawa's novel *The Rain Ascends* (1995, 2003), levy on the multicultural nation. In this instance, multiculturalism as a regulatory matrix becomes recognizable through the subjects it simultaneously imagines and fails to recognize in practice. The first part of this chapter uses Theatre Replacement's production *Bioboxes* to examine how an Asian Canadian insistence on social intimacy reshapes the ideals of multiculturalism. The second section of this discussion turns to Joy Kogawa's novel *The Rain Ascends* to consider what happens to a nation designed in multicultural terms when whiteness is denaturalized. What are the affective and political implications for citizenship when normativity, a primary mechanism for regulating difference, is disrupted? These texts, as calls for intimacy, demand recognition in multiple ways: the first forces the audience to be physically conscious of the racialized body it shares a confined space with, and the second uses the genre of the confessional to compel the reader to witness the most mundane and personal details of the narrator's story. By experiencing discourses of multiculturalism in ways that unbundle identity and community, these texts explore new forms of political engagement for Asian Canadian publics.

Mochizuki's and Kogawa's works interrogate familiar perceptions of Canada as a multicultural nation that values diversity, promotes tolerance, and demands equality for all citizens. Multiculturalism as policy and ethos poses something of a contradiction for Canada; more precisely, given the nation's perception of itself and the existence of a democratic political framework, how do we understand the need to legislate multiculturalism in Canada—first as policy in 1971, then as part of the Canadian Charter of Rights and Freedoms in 1982, and finally as an official act in 1988? In asking this question, my intention is to highlight the disparate production of citizenship, both in affective and political terms, for differently racialized Canadians, and to analyze how it is mediated by multicultural policies and attitudes. At the same time, I also consider how the language of identity enters into conversations about national identification and ethnic demands and shapes the political possibilities for visibly racialized participants. By drawing attention to the slippage between the kind of citizen imagined as being recognized as equal under the constitution, entitled to the democratic rights under the Citizenship Act, and whose linguistic rights are enshrined within the Official Languages Act (Government of Canada, "Canadian Multiculturalism Act") and the kind of citizen perceived as requiring an additional multiculturalism policy in order to participate fully and equitably within Canadian society, I suggest that the passing of such an act at the federal level underscores a profound disjuncture between the socially imagined and material practices of citizenship. As both a Canadian governmental policy and an ideology promoted within multiple countries, multiculturalism is an imperfect social model that has been critiqued, for example, as a model of inclusion, for reducing culture to diversity, and for misreading economic issues as cultural ones.[1] By joining this conversation, my intention is to explore the limitations of multiculturalism and understand how the logic of multiculturalism regulates social and political engagement in the current moment.

My concern lies with understanding how multiculturalism obliquely legislates identity in Canada and, more specifically, how this occurs unevenly and dissimilarly for disparate groups. The deeply ingrained assumption that identity is fundamental to collective politics is visible in a number of ways (such as, for example, a low-grade but widespread anxiety about national identity, a general cultural lack ascribed to whiteness, and a perception of ethnic populations as special-interest groups), and yet it is a mistake to believe that identity structures groups and nations in a similar fashion. Approaching the identity politics of visibly racialized groups as if they are analogous to national identity obscures how whiteness, neutrality, and normativity are conventionally equated and generate forms of identity typically unrecognized within discourses of multiculturalism. Given the historically different ways in which visibly marked and unmarked groups have been collectively framed, it is unsurprising that public participation, on the levels of speech, identification, and recognition, often look and feel quite different for each of them. Historicizing multiculturalism as both an ideology and federal policy that relies on misrecognition reveals how culture is used strategically to incorporate tiered forms of citizenship into the Canadian political machinery. By examining the implications of multiculturalism, I call into question the past and present shape of politics for racialized participants, and, furthermore, lay the groundwork for imagining a form of politics not necessarily contingent upon discourses of identity and community.

The particular strategies of recognition at work in multiculturalism have been critiqued as extensions of colonial strategies for managing ethnic populations. Eva Mackey, for instance, provides an overview of the project of nation building in the Canadian context that traces a colonial trajectory from early relations between Aboriginal populations and English and French settlers up to late twentieth-century multicultural policies. Throughout these phases of Canadian history, there is a consistent practice of superficial engagement with ethnic difference that upholds rather than challenges the status quo. One critical reading of multiculturalism would be to see it as providing an idealized social fantasy that circulates globally even though it is at odds with the nation's social and economic realities. As Himani Bannerji argues, there is a profound tension between the material realities of immigrant life and governmental policies and discourses of multiculturalism. She historicizes the emergence of multiculturalism by noting that immigrants were raising issues about matters such as employment, immigration policies, racism, child care, and language. These are challenges that are "endemic to migration, and especially that of people coming in to low income jobs or with few assets. Immigrant demands were not then, or even now, primarily cultural, nor was multiculturalism initially their formulation of the solution to their problems" (44). And it is within this social fantasy of Canadian multiculturalism as a national solution that Asian publics are imagined to be part of an audience seeking social recognition.

Theatre Replacement's *Bioboxes*

Theatre Replacement's Japanese *Bicbox* sounds like the ideal enactment of multiculturalism: onstage is a Japanese Canadian actor performing an immigrant narrative in a bilingual mode while the audience listens attentively. Except that in this particular staging, the actor and her single audience member are both *in* stage—a twenty-four by sixteen by sixteen–inch box that sits on the actor's shoulders—and the spectator is most likely preoccupied by questions such as: How should I position my knees? Where do I place my hands? Should I look away or stare into the actor's eyes? How is my breath? While these sorts of concerns about bodily negotiations are commonplace ones for people engaged in intimate acts in private places, they do not often shape public discussions of multiculturalism; both as a matter of government policy and as a national ethos, the province of multiculturalism is typically seen as constituted by rights, citizenship, and the preservation of culture. Dominant approaches to multiculturalism emphasize representation as a vexed problem that plays out in the law, on the level of government and politics, and on the national stage. By inserting intimacy into conversations about cultural politics, Theatre Replacement's staging of *Bioboxes* reminds us that we need to make explorations of feeling and affect part of our investigations of race, ethnicity, and culture. We need, in other words, to examine how we feel about bodies that are visibly marked as racially different, and, moreover, how we feel about *being* those bodies that are racially marked. By putting actor and audience within a cramped space, one that literally tries to get inside the immigrant's head, the performance compels us to contemplate how we can occupy a public that is intimately invested in racialized subjectivities and what kinds of conversations might subsequently emerge.

In January 2007, Theatre Replacement (an experimental theater company founded and codirected by Maiko Bae Yamamoto and James Long) created and produced *Bioboxes* for the first time, a series of six seven-minute-long monologues that explore everyday stories, multilingual realities, and issues of race and ethnicity. The scripts for this show are based on hour-long interviews with first-generation immigrants and are performed by bilingual actors of the same ethnicity. I am particularly interested in *Bioboxes*'s "Japanese box" (which was written and performed by Vancouver-based artist Cindy Mochizuki) given the kinds of questions it poses about race, publics, intimacy, and performances of the Asian. I note, however, that Mochizuki's was not the only enactment of Asianness, because *Bioboxes* also features Donna Soares's performance as the "Chinese" *Biobox*. Like all of the other boxes, this play engages with personal memories—all of the interviewees for *Bioboxes* were asked to bring three objects with stories attached that they could share with their interviewer. Yoshiyuki, a male international student and the subject of Mochizuki's *Biobox,* brought a bus pass, a charm, and a camera; he used these artifacts to speak at some length about being an avid photographer and the process of capturing and forgetting memories while traveling. Mochizuki reshaped Yoshiyuki's words into a monologue that explores, among other things, the desire not "to be a bird but . . . to be *like* a bird" (Mochizuki, "Japanese Biobox"), the struggle to pose appropriately and honestly in photographs, and the anxieties associated with speaking imperfect English, which she staged against an interactive set.

While this performance is really the product of multiple collaborations—between the performer and interview subject, performer and audience, and directors and performer—the collective nature of this project might be easily overlooked because the various subject positions are performed by a single Asian Canadian body. *Bioboxes*, then, is a site that encourages us to seriously consider the slippage between social performativity and theatrical performance, how racialized bodies register for different viewers, and precisely how publics make meaning. What audience exists for Asian Canadian bodies not performing familiar narratives of trauma (i.e., Hiroshima or Japanese Canadian internment), but the everyday stories of individuals? And beyond the actual theatrical performance, how do these performances continue to proliferate as stories about performances or memories of memories, and, consequently, open up ways of thinking through race, performativity, and social memory? What do the telling and consequent reimagining by a larger public that has not literally witnessed the performance, but has access to parts of it and representations of these representations, make possible?

The form of the *Biobox* performances emphasizes the critical importance of public address as it demands, even more so than most theatrical performances, that the audience be attentive and hopes that it will be emotionally engaged. Unlike conventional theater, this audience is not permitted the illusion of invisibility as performances are staged for a single audience member at a time, within a small box that the actor wears on her shoulders. The audience member is also given control of a card that tells the actor to switch between English and a second language and, in the Japanese box, is encouraged to pull on strings to unfurl photographs, much like a pop-up book. The face-to-face interactions of the *Bioboxes* make the audience member just as visible as the performer and both individuals are made acutely aware of precisely how their bodies inhabit this tiny stage. One critic speaking of her experience as an audience member states: "I was very aware of my face mirroring her face. I was trying to respond to the mood. When she started to cough and things became serious, I stopped smiling because it wasn't smiling time. I was performing as well" (Levin et al. 62). Moreover, although the audience is able to control the performance to a degree by deciding which language the performer will use, these are exercises of power for which the audience is held accountable. In the case of the Japanese *Biobox*, the audience can compel Mochizuki to switch back and forth between Japanese and English, but the audience must also look into Mochizuki's eyes as it exerts its desire.[2] While perhaps not quite dialogues (or perhaps the oxymoron *silent dialogues* might be appropriate here), these performances constitute moments of physical and emotional exchange between the actor and audience. And because they take place in quarters too intimate to permit the division into public and private space, the interactions demand a redrawing, if not absolute erasure given the relations of power, of the line that separates speaker and listener. As Kim Solga astutely notes in a discussion with other Canadian theater critics about *Bioboxes,* as an audience member watching *Bioboxes,* "you're hyper-aware of the spectatorial structure shaping your experience, and you're trying to get inside it, and you're having a dialogue with yourself at the same time as you're having a dialogue with the box about the problem" (Levin et al. 67).

Since the *Bioboxes* are performed in front of one audience member at a time, even though the show toured the country on three occasions (2007, 2009, 2011), only a limited number of people is ever able to see these performances.[3] And despite, or perhaps precisely because of, its insistently local nature, *Bioboxes* directs attention to how various publics come into being as a range of people encounter it. While the actual performance of the *Biobox* is quite intimate and idiosyncratic, much like a peep show (an observation that Laura Levin also shares [63]), any kind of a public attached to the *Bioboxes* is formed through the conversations that audience members have, either with each other or with those who have not seen the performance. At the same time, the Japanese *Biobox* reveals much about the

Figure 1. Cindy Mochizuki in Theatre Replacement's *Bioboxes,* 2007. Photo by Shannon Mendes.

terms of public address and orientation as well as the shared worldviews and common feelings that create social intimacies and are assumed to be at work in publics. The particular moment of public dialogue is key for understanding how utterances resonate for different audiences. Mochizuki has commented on some of the various ways that stagings of her *Biobox* performance have been read, noting, for instance, that some audience members have been moved to feelings of compassion for Hiroshima and, after March 2011, the Fukushima nuclear disaster, even though her piece does not make overt reference to either of these events (Mochizuki, "Discussion of Arts of Conscience"). The range of meanings generated through these performances is suggestive for thinking about how certain representations of Japan, and by extension Asia, resonate in more and less intimate ways depending on the circumstances of their stagings.

The collaboration between performer and interview subject raises issues of specificity and generality long familiar to Asian Canadian and Asian American studies, ones that include but are not limited to matters of generation, language, gender, and relation to the nation. The heterogeneous nature of Asian Canadian experience is apparent when we focus specifically on the Japanese *Biobox* as Asian Canadian theater and as part of ongoing conversations about Asian Canadian studies. It is, however, less easy to see the complexity of Asian Canadianness when the "Japanese" *Biobox* is positioned next to the five other ethnic *Bioboxes* (French, Chinese, German, Italian, and Serbo-Croatian) as these are more recognizable as performances of Canadian multiculturalism. In this panethnic (as opposed to pan-Asian) context, the singular performing body becomes less representative of *a* kind of difference and more representative of difference itself.

The Politics of Multicultural Recognition

In much of the critical discussion about multiculturalism, the desire for recognition by ethnic subjects and their subsequent misrecognition by others receives the lion's share of attention. Charles Taylor and Smaro Kamboureli both make significant contributions to this conversation; Taylor by arguing that identity is, to a large extent, shaped by the recognition of others, and Kamboureli by critiquing how the politics of recognition operate in Canadian law, media, and in Taylor's essay itself. To briefly recap, Taylor's landmark essay, "The Politics of Recognition," begins by tracing the development of recognition from ancient to modern times, noting that earlier and exclusive notions of honor have now been replaced with an inclusive sense of dignity. In the contemporary period, identity and recognition are sutured together in ways that seem self-evident and the misrecognition of individuals and groups understood as capable of "inflict[ing] a grievous wound" (26). But while the devastating consequences of withholding recognition seem to be generally agreed upon, there is much less consensus about how to properly grant it. Taylor outlines two dominant lines of thought with respect to this problem: first, a politics of universalism that emphasizes the equal dignity of all people, and second, a politics of difference that seeks the recognition of distinct identities. Responding to these contradictory political aims, Taylor argues, "There must be something midway between the inauthentic and homogenizing demand for recognition of equal worth, on the one hand, and the self-immurement within ethnocentric standards, on the other" (72).

In his essay on the Vancouver-based comedy troupe Assaulted Fish and multiculturalism, Christopher Lee builds on Taylor's and Kamboureli's arguments by productively resituating their insights into recognition within the contexts of Asian Canadian culture and critical practice. Lee analyzes demographic transformations that have occurred within Asian Canadian communities, noting that these changes have produced a shifting sense of cultural politics and made it difficult to clearly define either the multiple and often competing commitments of Asian Canadian communities or the political potential and meaning of Asian Canadian culture. We are therefore asked to imagine what Asian Canadian studies might look like without identity politics, or perhaps, even without Asian Canadians. "Recognition," Lee writes, "is about becoming attuned to the possibilities that can arise at the intersection between political and aesthetic imaginations and practices" ("Asian Canadian Performance" 106). In order to work through this juncture as it pertains to the relationship of Asian Canadian culture to politics as well as to the Canadian state, "Asian Canadian Performance and the Politics of Misrecognition" turns to Kamboureli's critique of multiculturalism as a strategy of containment. Noting that the goal of Asian Canadian critical practice cannot simply be an increase in either the numbers of Asian Canadians or the status of Asian Canadian culture, the essay advocates for a close examination of the framework of multiculturalism in order to determine whether it is capable of promoting social change. Lee draws upon the concluding section of Kamboureli's discussion of multiculturalism as a form of sedative politics, focusing in particular on her suggestion that the goal of multiculturalism should be "the mastery of discomfort" (Kamboureli qtd. in Lee, "Asian Canadian Performance" 109). The notion of resisting the politics of recognition is certainly a productive one for an Asian Canadian project, and the potential implications of unyoking Asian Canadian critique and culture are considerable.

I am deeply invested in the kinds of questions about Asian Canadian cultural politics that Lee raises, but find myself wanting to return to them from precisely the angle that he moves away from, namely, the "power of the negative—the ability of that which escapes rational forms of cognition and representation to act as the basis of community formation" (109). This question of what lies outside the rational language of representation and recognition also nags at the edges of Kim Solga's written response to Theatre Replacement's *Bioboxes*. In her short essay, Solga grapples with the discomfort that the performance produces in her; Solga struggles to understand what it means that, despite her efforts to be an ideal viewer, she is unable to make the leap and "not just ... 'watch' another immigrant story but ... bear witness to the struggle of its telling, the awkwardness of its hearing" ("Artifacting" 165). Solga's inability to be deeply moved by Mochizuki's performance deserves to be closely examined because she tries, within the framework provided, to be a "respectful" audience that acknowledges the importance of culture, heritage, and language. Indeed, she even opts to listen to much of the performance in Japanese, writing that

> I'm not entirely sure why I kept switching into Japanese. I think I felt bad that the character in the narrative, still so unsure in her English, should have to keep using it just for me. Or perhaps I sensed it would be somehow more respectful to hear the performance in its "native" language. In hindsight, I know I was wrong: my choice might have seemed somehow generous at the time but it proved unhelpful, provoked by my useless guilt as an English-speaking, native-born Canadian. Ultimately, the language barrier stopped me from experiencing Cindy's performance fully. Now I barely know enough of it to pass on. (161)

Solga provides us with an ideal enactment of what Charles Taylor calls the "recognition of difference," an act that he claims, when paired with the judgment of equal value, will lead to the transformation of ourselves provided that it is accompanied by "a willingness to be open to comparative cultural study of the kind that must displace our horizons in the resulting fusions" (73). And yet Solga's reflections clearly demonstrate a moment when the recognition of difference—demonstrated by a willingness to step into the box, listen to the monologue in an unfamiliar language, and participate in the performance—does not produce the kind of transformation that Taylor envisions.

I invoke Solga's response as a critique of Taylor's formulation, not in order to criticize her ambivalent emotions toward Mochizuki's performance, but to underscore the problem of multicultural recognition, at least as it presents itself to me. While my own thinking is deeply influenced by many of these provocative arguments about multiculturalism, I am still somewhat perplexed by the word *recognition* and am not entirely certain what it means to "recognize" the multicultural or where that leaves that which is unrecognizably multicultural. What kinds of spaces are left open for examinations of racialized lives and histories within dominant publics? How complex is that public dialogue? Recent conversations about government-issued apologies, redress movements, and matters of reconciliation and compensation demonstrate that there is considerable interest in historical trauma and racial injustice. And although occurrences such as media accounts of the ongoing Truth and Reconciliation Commission of Canada devoted to Aboriginal residential schools, the incorporation into literary canons novels such as Joy Kogawa's *Obasan* (with its exploration of Japanese Canadian internment), and the production of *Red Letters* (a musical about the Chinese Canadian head tax staged by Vancouver Asian Canadian Theatre in late 2010 and early 2011) address these events and keep these conversations active, the tendency to present racialized existences as shaped by large-scale historical traumas obscures the smaller emotions and routine conflicts that are experienced on a daily basis.[4] I wonder then whether there is space for other configurations and articulations of race and whether, within a public shaped by multicultural discourses of recognition and historical trauma, interest can be generated in the often mundane intimacies of racialized lives.

Racializing Publics

In her preface to *The Female Complaint,* her work on mass women's culture and intimacy, Lauren Berlant defines *publics* as spaces "constituted by strangers who consume common texts and things," noting that they are intimate because there "is an expectation that the consumers of its particular stuff *already* share a worldview and emotional knowledge that they have derived from a broadly common historical experience" (viii). Berlant's assumptions about emotional knowledge and publics, while they certainly seem to hold true, make me wonder where those with dissimilar worldviews and emotional knowledges are positioned within or in relation to a dominant public. That public conversations are shaped both by how participants are predisposed to feeling and what it is that they are feeling this way about is particularly pertinent when we try to understand how debates about race operate. Those that do not share the broad emotional orientation toward these "common texts and things" must either bracket their feelings and soften their criticisms in order to be part of this conversation or else find a minor public interested in exploring these emotions and worldviews. And while the language of social justice, cultural recognition, and liberal guilt is an invaluable part of discussions of race, it is easy to see how it can dominate and prevent other conversations—those interested in how race operates on the intimate level of the mundane and everyday—from taking place in the dominant public. The relegation of these kinds of intimate topics to private spheres or minor publics ensures that dominant publics implicitly remain sites of whiteness.

That the refusal to grant recognition, or at least the refusal to expand the terms of recognition, regulates public discourse about race becomes quite clear once we revisit Taylor's discussion of the politics of recognition and note its terms of operation. Taylor writes that the need for recognition occurs on two levels: "First, in the intimate sphere, where we understand the formation of identity and the self as taking place in a continuing dialogue and struggle with significant others. And then in the public sphere, where a politics of equal recognition has come to play a bigger and bigger role" (37). Although Taylor mentions these two levels in a relatively cursory fashion, really only making the distinction in order to declare that his interest lies in the latter sphere, it is a crucial division worth revisiting. From the vantage point of Asian Canadian critical practice, it is unclear how the intimate and public, or dialogue and recognition, can be separated and understood as distinct. *Bioboxes* acts as a critical interlocutor by offering a sense of what a public might look like if it refused those kinds of assumptions and made others—namely, that the quotidian aspects of racialized lives should be central to contemporary conversations about race and multiculturalism. Indeed, this performance enables Berlant's definition of an intimate public to resonate quite differently. If, to return to Berlant's point quoted previously, the intimate public is one in which "the consumers of its particular stuff *already* share a worldview and emotional knowledge that they have derived from a broadly common historical experience" (*Female Complaint* viii), then Mochizuki's *Biobox* makes the ordinary experiences of a racialized subject the "particular stuff" that its public consumes and, moreover, that binds it together.

While I appreciate that Solga's thoughts are influenced by theater and performance studies work on empathy and witnessing, I wonder whether the Japanese *Biobox* was ever really capable of pushing "audiences to feel against the grain of the self and toward the other in a profoundly ethical way" ("Artifacting" 165). She ultimately concludes that the performance is more successful at "enact[ing] the politics of *defining* a genuinely democratic act of theatrical witness" than it is at making audiences feel empathetic (166). I am, however, inclined to think of the goals of *Bioboxes* as being a little more modest in scope. That Solga concludes toward the end of her essay that Mochizuki's "story didn't matter all that much to me in the end" (166) does not seem to constitute a failure on anyone's part.

While it would, of course, be ideal if audiences had unanimously found themselves caring deeply about Yoshiyuki's memories, fantasies, and insights about being an international student, it is quite a feat that the performance even succeeded in making others conscious of Yoshiyuki's narrative and gave it a space, however minimal, within the wider social memory. Mochizuki's *Biobox* offers a close-up of the intimate details, feelings, minor fantasies, and memories of an everyday individual, and moreover, assumes that this mundane narrative will be of interest to others. While these assumptions hold more easily in the context of an Asian Canadian public than in a dominant Canadian public, I emphasize that neither public usually narrates Asian Canadian culture and experience by focusing on minor narratives. *Bioboxes* is unusual for performing the mundane everydayness of life and it is important that the production circulated within, and consequently generated, a range of publics. In doing so, the performance pushes for the inclusion of affect in discussions of citizenship and conversations about extraordinary as well as banal articulations of racism. To return once again to Berlant's work on the intimate public, she rationalizes that it is a valuable space for its participants—in her case, consumers of women's mass culture—because it "legitimates qualities, ways of being, and entire lives that have otherwise been deemed puny or discarded. It creates *situations* where those qualities can appear as luminous" (*Female Complaint* 3). And I would extrapolate that, in the instance of the Asian Canadian, the intimate public is a formation that lets us engage with stories and memories attached to "minor" lives without having to monumentalize them, and that this shift allows us to explore the pleasures of social intimacy.

Alternatively, when Mochizuki's *Biobox* is placed in the context of Canadian multiculturalism, instead of zooming in on an experience, the *Biobox* becomes a diminution of experience. By this I mean that Japaneseness is compressed and shrunk in order to fit into a frame with other equivalent forms of ethnic difference (and is able to represent, along with the Chinese *Biobox*, pan-Asianness). As part of a multicultural archive, the ongoing switching between English and Japanese reminds us that the initial impulse for official multicultural policy was biculturalism, even as the *Biobox* works to expand that linguistic register. Within a multicultural narrative, the six different *Bioboxes* might be read as parallel group identities, each defined primarily through the historical injuries inflicted by government and/or dominant society, and representative of the kinds of voices that can be heard within institutional and political settings. In his work on cultural memory, Andreas Huyssen writes that "the act of remembering is always in and of the present, while its referent is of the past and thus absent" (3–4).

This insight into how the present makes use of the past is necessary to bear in mind when sifting through the various responses to the memories presented in Mochizuki's *Biobox*. One of the reasons that I devote so much time to working through Solga's response to Mochizuki's *Biobox* is because I see her as wrestling with having made the right gestures, but not for having felt the expected emotions. In other words, as a spectator, she feels J. L. Austin's performative utterance twist for what it does not do, or, more precisely, what it does not make her feel. This is perhaps the predicament of multiculturalism as being both a sham and as producing shame in its subjects that Solga explores in her longer and more recent *Bioboxes* essay ("Meet Me").

All of this highlights the fact that the structure of multiculturalism is not designed to make encounters with minor lives in the present moment possible, and certainly not face-to-face (or knee-to-knee) intimate encounters that make us uncomfortably aware of the relations of power within which we are located. While, as Sara Ahmed argues, the promise of multiculturalism is happiness, its design actively works against the attainment of this goal: "Happiness is promised as a return for loyalty to the nation, where loyalty is expressed as 'giving' diversity to the nation through playing its game" ("Multiculturalism" 123). In "Multiculturalism and the Promise of Happiness," she argues that disappointment or the absence of happiness typically leads to a questioning of actions rather than of the ideals themselves, with individuals being more willing to attribute failure to personal shortcomings rather than to the impossibility of social fantasies. *Bioboxes* is a somewhat dissimilar approach to multiculturalism in this regard. Despite the promise of multicultural happiness that *Bioboxes* initially presents, the performances push us beyond what Ahmed describes as "the appeal of happy surfaces" (134). And to draw this out a little further, the Japanese *Biobox* gets under our skin, both in the sense that it permits us to understand race outside of the more familiar sociological definitions of race and in that it causes us to feel discomfort, and possibly even unhappiness.

Multiculturalism will only ever promise happiness and always shortchange the delivery if it does not broaden and complicate the work of recognition. Given that official history is saturated by the monumentalized histories and injustices that have supposedly been resolved, there is little space left over to take "small" memories seriously. At the same time, the manner in which the *Bioboxes* mobilize everyday memories and lives spotlights the relationship between intimate publics and political demands. In her reading of women's intimate publics, Berlant argues that these spaces are by nature "juxtapolitical" (*Female Complaint* 3), existing near but not in the realm of the political, because its members distrust the political. Memories of how racialized bodies and communities have been and continue to be treated are part of the reason that Asian Canadian and other intimate publics often feel compelled to search out alternate publics. However, even as we use minor public spaces in order to engage with our ideas and selves, we also need to push for a reworking of the dominant public by refusing to move the work of discomfort and minor narratives into "private" spaces. This kind of obstinacy is necessary if minor publics are to be more than simply publics that others do not want to engage with, let alone care about.

It is precisely this kind of refusal that I see Mochizuki performing through her *Biobox*. That there are competing representations of Japanese Canadianness and Asian Canadianness circulating within different publics is obviously no new insight. What is new and exciting is that her *Biobox* explores the affective and political dimensions of these representations, and demands that audiences take notice of how these two registers are often disconnected. Even though the *Biobox* performance speaks to at least two distinct publics, an Asian Canadian and a dominant public, it is still performed by a single body that speaks in a voice that is at once emotional, intimate, political, and multicultural; the simultaneity of this voice asks us how we might understand the intimate alongside more overtly articulated political demands. The *Biobox* pushes provocatively for a public capable of engaging with an embodied political voice and, more specifically, a racially embodied political voice. In his work on publics and counterpublics, Michael Warner notes that nonnormative bodies have always been carefully regulated in public spaces, and he cites as proof the examples of queer bodies criticized for flaunting their sexuality and women in the public sphere chastised for being too aggressive and therefore masculine, arguing that these bodies "disturb deep and unwritten rules about the kinds of behavior and eroticism that are appropriate to the public" (25). Similarly, racialized bodies are also implicitly encouraged to keep the intimate details of their existences to themselves when the dominant public seems uninterested. The boxing of the body gestures to this through the disciplining of the body in the performance space of the *Biobox* and by playing on the notion of thinking both within and outside of the box. *Bioboxes* pushes for a different orientation to bodies in order to make possible publics capable of both intimacy and social change, of speaking one on one while being cognizant of the larger structures that shape our interactions, and of responding to the affective and political registers of the everyday. By transplanting experiences and insights that are typically diminished within a larger public into a smaller space, this performance reconfigures the social acoustics of multiculturalism and lets racialized subjects make emotional demands that register—emotionally, cognitively, and politically—for a variety of publics.

Recognizing Whiteness

In my reading of *Bioboxes,* I claim that Mochizuki's performance makes us uncomfortably aware of how racialized subjects are recognized in multicultural terms. In order to extend this argument about the inaudibility of racialized voices within the framework of multiculturalism, I turn to Joy Kogawa's fiction to examine how discourses of multiculturalism produce particular kinds of affective citizenship through their inscriptions of race and, moreover, how they are positioned within national and global histories. My turn to Kogawa's fiction is inspired in part by recursive moves she has made in and to her own writing. For example, the publication of Kogawa's *Emily Kato* in 2005, a revision of her earlier novel *Itsuka* (1992), marks a momentous return to the Japanese Canadian internment and the subsequent redress movement. *The Rain Ascends,* Kogawa's novel that is the focus of my discussion here, was also revised years after its original publication. Released sixty years after the 1945 bombing of Nagasaki, *Emily Kato* also commemorates this anniversary. But in drawing attention to the historical through a reshaping of an earlier published narrative, *Emily Kato* acts as an urgent reminder of the need to repeatedly interrogate the modes and motivations of contemporary returns to history. The text underscores the need to mediate between the demands of the past and understandings of the present while keeping an eye fixed on the nature of national citizenship, global histories of imperialism, and the intersection of political and literary strategies of representation.

Kogawa's writing and rewriting of the narrative of redress, itself a return to narratives of internment, highlight the ongoing work of negotiation, both outside of the text with respect to the need of the redress movement to negotiate between the Japanese Canadian community, a body marked by complex and often contradictory impulses, and the Canadian government, and within the text as it revises its language and draws attention to the yet-to-be-attained closure. The textual work of narrative revision symptomatically gestures to a political reiteration of the demands for social justice circulated between Japanese Canadian communities and the Canadian government, and implicitly underscores how such negotiations are contingent upon the shifting terrain on which they are carried out. Kogawa's work highlights the difficulties of articulating mutually agreeable terms of justice, in part because such bargaining involves assigning value to lives and weighing the symbolic and material dimensions of citizenship against each other, and such findings are always relational even when they appear absolute. Kogawa's repeated return to internment and redress simultaneously suggests an inability to adequately articulate an impulse to justice within the paradigm of the Canadian nation-state, a strong investment in becoming recognized as part of this imagined national community, and a sense of frustration produced by the impossibility of expressing this desire within these terms. Symptomatic of this problem is the widespread recognition, celebratory even, that Kogawa's first novel, *Obasan*, received.[5] Publics as diverse as literary critics, public-school educators, and those involved in national politics have engaged with *Obasan* for its social and historical contributions but have not done so with Kogawa's subsequent work. This intensive engagement with Kogawa's representation of internment and relative dismissal of her later work (with the exception of a handful of scholars who have carefully thought through Kogawa's other texts)[6] suggests an impulse to respond with lofty affective reactions such as sympathy, which offer a pseudocathartic resolution to the wounding insistence of racism in the present moment. Connected to this is a desire to see Japanese Canadian redress as an event that effectively ended collective suffering, despite the sheer impossibility of such a feat. As Kirsten McAllister notes in her thoughtful study of Japanese Canadian memory projects, "The government's apology for this violation of rights was essential for redressing the past, but it did not and could not fully resolve the damaging impact" (17). Kogawa's repeated returns to both internment and its legacy, much like the ongoing Japanese Canadian memory projects McAllister analyzes, open up this historical moment to remind us that internment, like most moments of injustice, was not a singular event, but instead clearly part of an ongoing process of tiered national citizenship and global politics. For this very basic but fundamental reason, our responses to it need to be multiple, sustained, and always historicized.

I locate my discussion of Kogawa's *The Rain Ascends* within this larger historical context because such framing highlights matters of uneven citizenship, public participation, and race that are not immediately visible in initial encounters with the text. My desire to work through this text stems from two separate but interrelated problems that it poses: first, the question of publics as social formations and what it means to address an Asian Canadian pubic, and second, how to think about the work of racialization, especially as it relates to Asian Canadianness. This approach to *The Rain Ascends* may seem peculiar given that the novel makes no direct mention of either racialized bodies or historical events such as the Japanese Canadian internment. Instead, the plot of *The Rain Ascends* focuses on a middle-aged white woman slowly becoming emotionally unhinged as she struggles to come to terms with her father's history of molesting dozens of young boys, an act he engaged in repeatedly while occupying the position of Anglican minister. But it is precisely because Kogawa's novel avoids using more familiar ways of writing about race and Asian Canadianness that it lets us return to these matters and productively interrogate how we come to inhabit social imaginaries in particular ways, the emotional consequences of these locations, and the possibilities for conceptualizing these spaces differently.

Asian Canadian Publics

I return now to Warner's *Publics and Counterpublics* for its reading of the public and national citizenship as two distinct but overlapping spaces. Warner's focus is on a textual public created through the circulation of texts and the participation of its members in the form of responses to these texts. Unlike other social formations, textual publics do not have institutional frameworks to regulate and legitimate their existences or determine their memberships. Moreover, the terms of this kind of public, the question of what connects or shapes this larger body, are never entirely clear; consequently, Warner observes that "when people address publics, they engage in struggles—at varying levels of salience to consciousness, from calculated tactic to mute cognitive noise—over the conditions that bring them together as a public" (12). I complicate further Warner's ideas about the public as a site defined by participation by thinking about what such participation looks like and how we might understand the work of address and recognition within an Asian Canadian public. This is especially pertinent given the difficult and ambivalent relations that participants often have toward the term *Asian Canadian,* which has operated at various historic moments as a marker of derision, exclusion, collective identity, and coalition. At the same time, Warner's model of the textual public may well proffer a means of reconfiguring and therefore reentering the space of citizenship by allowing us to rethink the dynamics and significance of recognition. Tied to the complexities of recognition is the problem of what happens when a public is addressed but does not recognize it is being addressed. Might there be transformative work that occurs regardless and new possibilities generated for changing the shape of that public?

Thinking about Asian Canadianness in terms of a textual public recognizes it as dynamic and expansive, a site constantly reshaped as its participants engage in dialogue and witness other exchanges. And here, I note that Warner emphasizes multiplicity as well as reciprocity when he states,

> No single text can create a public. Nor can a single voice, a single genre, even a single medium. All are insufficient to create the kind of reflexivity that we call a public, since a public is understood to be an ongoing space of encounter for discourse. Not texts themselves create publics, but the concatenation of texts

through time. Only when a previously existing discourse can be supposed, and when a responding discourse can be postulated, can a text address a public. (90)

Formulating the public as a space shaped by circulation is key when reading Kogawa's work and understanding it as struggling to racialize Canadian whiteness and to produce a different social imaginary of Canadianness altogether. To read *The Rain Ascends* in this fashion requires positioning it as a response to Kogawa's other work, to conversations already circulating within Asian Canadian publics, and perhaps even as a text capable of being legible because of the texts that preceded it. Much of the criticism about Kogawa's other novels, *Obasan, Itsuka,* and *Emily Kato,* foregrounds how the texts grapple with historical injustice, Japanese Canadian internment, institutionalized practices of Canadian racism, and memories of betrayal. I position *The Rain Ascends* within those conversations as well in order to think about this novel that is ostensibly about the disgrace of the Reverend Charles Shelby, a white Canadian minister, and his family as also furthering our understandings of how socially marked bodies are located within public spaces. One of the shocks that Millicent, Reverend Shelby's daughter, receives occurs at the end (of the original version) of the novel when she realizes that by confiding in the bishop about her father's crimes, she has transformed them from a private family matter to a public affair. Millicent balks at the prospect of her father's crimes circulating in the public domain, and the text tells us that she "clutche[s] her throat in [her] mother's gesture of alarm, willing [her] hands to choke back a rising fear" and states "'You're going to tell everyone? You're going to make this public? You mean all this—all this that I've told you in confidence—as in a confessional...'" (209). In response to Millicent's outburst, the bishop claims that the needs of the victims, justice, and the Church require that these crimes be made public and that her father will only truly understand the implications of his actions once these matters are out in the open. Even though Millicent protests this route, arguing that the media attention and widespread scrutiny will help neither her father nor herself and might instead kill both of them, the bishop is firm in his belief that the public recognition of injuries is necessary. While this is the bishop's official position, the text introduces other ways of connecting social justice, publics, and reparations, always with the larger goal of personal and collective healing in mind. Indeed, Millicent's relation to her father's crimes and the question of responsibility is addressed further in the revised version of the novel. Released in 2003, Kogawa added a third section that explores Millicent's life six years after she tells the bishop about her father's crimes. Despite Millicent's fear that making her father's crimes public will kill him, he passes away before knowledge of his acts becomes widely known. Instead, it is Millicent who carries the burden of her father's guilt and is vilified by almost everyone she knows, even her niece, who likens Millicent's actions to "put[ting] the gun in his filthy hand" (222, rev. ed.). After bearing the public humiliation in Juniper alone and her remaining family having broken ties with her, Millicent finally sells the family home and moves to Ontario to become part of its Juniper Centre, where she finds "a new world, dense and sweet as honey and friendship" (192, rev ed.).

In an essay titled "The Future of Racial Memory: Forgiveness, Reconciliation, and Redress in Joy Kogawa's *Obasan* and *Itsuka*," Julie McGonegal suggests that *Obasan* and *Itsuka* reimagine the work of forgiveness as well as the work performed by the apology (or, in the case of the official government apology to Japanese Canadians, perhaps not performed). According to McGonegal, in Kogawa's fiction, forgiveness and reconciliation require that the conditions of remorse and restitution first be in place. I extend this reading of reconciliation and forgiveness to include *The Rain Ascends*, and in so doing suggest that Kogawa's efforts to renegotiate the terrain of forgiveness also require that we rethink how Japanese Canadians specifically, but perhaps also Asian Canadians more broadly, are racialized. Without reducing *The Rain Ascends* to an outright allegory of Japanese Canadian internment and racial wounding, I read Kogawa's exploration of the multiple psychic and social dimensions of sexual abuse as teasing out differently a thread already present in her earlier novels. Foregrounding such dynamics as performed by and on racially unmarked bodies produces a sudden visible racialization of these bodies and questions the terms and conditions upon which they are granted social legitimacy and political legibility. *The Rain Ascends* pushes us to rearticulate the terms of race and to recognize how racial wounding takes place within the Canadian nation-state and beyond.

Unmarking Race

In an essay published as part of *Broken Entries,* Roy Miki explores how race shapes the conditions of possibility for subjects, and how "[i]n the mundane and the daily, it acts out and re-presents what is expected, side-stepping confrontation and thereby appeasing the turbulent memory of violation" (31). He refers to the pressures to assimilate, be invisible, and be model citizens as particularly acute examples from the postwar period (31). Miki's insights into the limitations imposed by race reveal the complicated intertwining of silence, injustice, and community and give us a means of entering into Kogawa's *The Rain Ascends*. All of Miki's perceptive comments—about the Japanese Canadian social imagination as it inhabits the space of denial and wrestles with the model-minority myth—are equally applicable to Kogawa's *The Rain Ascends*. And yet, I wonder what it means that I want to use insights culled from the difficult situation of Japanese Canadian internment to explore the racially "unmarked" white body.

Bringing together these texts and discourses and reading them as participating in a common public allows us to rethink the logic that determines familiar discourses of race. *The Rain Ascends* opens up questions of ethical responsibility, complicity, and victimhood, matters also central to contemporary understandings of racialization as a kind of social injury. Kogawa's novel troubles the Christian paradigm of truth, confession, and reparative justice by exploring Millicent's frustrated desire for such a model: "I needed a repentant man. I needed him to cover himself in sackcloth and ashes and to beat his breast and wail, 'Lord, I have sinned against heaven and against Thee and I am not worthy to be called Thy child. I have abused and molested your children. I have betrayed a holy trust.' But Father had never made such lamentations. Never" (168). It is not easy for Millicent to relinquish this language of Christianity or its model of ethics because such a letting go requires that she both come to terms with her own feelings of inadequacy for being unable to recognize, prevent, and respond to these acts, and forge a new relationship to how matters of violation and value, humanity and betrayal affect all parties involved.

Thus, in the simplest terms possible, *The Rain Ascends* is a novel preoccupied with white guilt; it permits us to engage with the economy of emotions at work in narratives of social justice. But the reader's relation to past injuries is complicated because it is shaped by Millicent's complicity and, more specifically, her inability to relinquish her attachment to the injurer. Millicent tells us (or perhaps more accurately tells herself) as she eases her readers into the narrative that "[i]f Father could have publicly confessed, if he could have faced the consequence and quit the church, you might have been able to walk down the road with him, with pity, with love. But that never happened" (19–20). And later, she notes: "You can sometimes go for days without thinking about it. Or if you do, briefly, you sweep the thought aside, quietly under the carpet with the undisturbed dust of other imponderables, other better forgotten small burials, insect wings" (22). The emotional topography of the novel is a composite of what Sianne Ngai calls grander passions and minor or ugly feelings. Ngai contrasts the "potentially ennobling or morally beatific states like sympathy, melancholia, and shame (the emotions given the most attention in literary criticism's recent turn to ethics)" with feelings that are

> explicitly *amoral* and *noncathartic*, offering no satisfactions of virtue, however oblique, nor any therapeutic or purifying release. In fact, most of these feelings tend to interfere with the outpouring of other emotions. Moods like irritation

and anxiety, for instance, are defined by a flatness or ongoingness entirely opposed to the "suddenness" on which Aristotle's aesthetics of fear depends. And unlike rage, which cannot be sustained indefinitely, less dramatic feelings like envy and paranoia have a remarkable capacity for duration. (6–7)

And it is perhaps that possibility of indefinite sustenance that Millicent most fears, that she might have to inhabit forever this position of uncertainty and never be cleansed of the emotional burdens placed upon her by her father's heinous crimes. Less dramatic than shame, she skulks about for much of the text as a figure of dissatisfaction, one longing for the family's former glory and perhaps even envious of herself before she knew. What Millicent seems to desire for much of the narrative is to move toward a state of anger because rage eventually dissipates and can potentially be resolved, whereas the ambivalent relationship that she has to shame could last forever.

Millicent's desire for an easy outpouring of passion and subsequent catharsis contrasts sharply with the libidinal economy operating in *Obasan*, a novel characterized by a very different set of affective relationships. While there are certainly very strong and powerful feelings running through that text, they operate quite dissimilarly. If the unsatisfied impulse in *The Rain Ascends* is for catharsis and emotional explosion, *Obasan* is driven instead by enduring emotions and is a text marked by utter weariness. The obvious contradiction to this flattening of emotions occurs at the end of the novel when Naomi and Stephen are read their grandmother's letter that describes the horrors of Nagasaki following the American bombing. Coincidentally, this letter is described as "an outpouring" inconsistent with Grandma Kato's first letter, a "brief and emotionless statement" (*Obasan* 214). But learning about the experiences of her grandmother and mother does not offer Naomi a cathartic release, an end to the emotional limbo their absences produced in Naomi as a child; it instead signals a different relationship to lasting grief. Toward the end of the novel, Naomi tells us about a dream she has in which

> a small child sits with a wound on her knee. The wound on her knee is on the back of her skull, large and moist. A double wound. The child is forever unable to speak. The child forever fears to tell. I apply a thick bandage but nothing can soak up the seepage. I beg that the woundedness may be healed and that the limbs may learn to dance. But you stay in a black and white photograph, smiling your yasashi smile. (*Obasan* 222–23)

And, as Miki points out in his reading of *Obasan*, Naomi's response to the letter does not act as the novel's conclusion. Rather, a memorandum sent to the House of Canada and Senate asking that Japanese Canadians not be deported concludes the book, an ending that Miki reads as solidifying precisely this sense of weariness as "nothing has happened to change the social and political background to Naomi's experiences" (*Broken Entries* 116).

The contrasting emotional economies of *The Rain Ascends* and *Obasan* are important to note because of their social and political implications. Ngai argues in her theoretical work on ugly feelings that "art that produces and foregrounds a failure of emotional release (another form of suspended 'action') . . . does so as a kind of politics" (9). This is particularly suggestive for thinking about how guilt regulates public discussions about the practice of citizenship. Perhaps then what *The Rain Ascends* offers Asian Canadian publics is yet another reason to be suspicious of enjoinders to move beyond race, to "get over" the past, and to heal the wounds of history. The desire for a trajectory of release and resolution is also an attempt to write over the affect produced by racialization, a means of ignoring the precise ways in which the wound of racialization incapacitates, and how the wound continues to leak. This is neither a claim that movement is impossible nor is it a repudiation of my earlier attempt to build on McGonegal's reading of *Obasan* as a text concerned with forgiveness. It is instead a suggestion that as we undertake reconciliatory measures, we be attentive to how race shapes emotional economies and how fantasies of healing and closure contradict the dominant logic of race. For the Asian Canadian subject, race is simultaneously just, but also much more than, a marker of visible difference. Race is also the inscription of historical memory and a tool used to position people precariously within national and diasporic communities.

This is also where I see the novel as intervening in current conversations about multiculturalism and racial discourses, and, more specifically, as drawing attention to how the recognition of racialized difference relies on the nonrecognition of whiteness as a form of normative subjectivity within the context of liberal paternalism. This is particularly significant given that both *Obasan* and *The Rain Ascends* are stories about the breakup and breakdown of the family unit. Kogawa's novel racializes whiteness,[7] perhaps most simply through the racial dissonance between Kogawa, the author, and Millicent Shelby, her protagonist, which underscores the need to be conscious of how narrative perspectives are racialized. *The Rain Ascends* uses Millicent's voice as a white female protagonist to explore the complex feelings associated with personal and historic traumas as well as the limitations inherent in memory. More specifically, the novel uses the language of shame, guilt, mercy, and compassion to describe both Reverend Shelby's fall from grace and its impact on his family. Millicent's conflicting feelings and ethical dilemmas make visible our symbolic and material investments in liberal paternalism even as we understand that such forms of governance often injure rather than protect.

This novel provocatively extends critical investigations central to whiteness studies by taking seriously the task of imagining what it means to inhabit this subjectivity and, moreover, contemplating what the privileged burden of whiteness might feel like. In so doing, the text reveals much about the psychic structure of paternalism and the complex investments in it. Even though the power and privileges ascribed to whiteness have been, and continue to be, the subject of much critique and contestation, whiteness nonetheless continues to implicitly and explicitly structure race relations within a multicultural Canadian context by acting as the normative center around which difference constellates. The relational nature of social and political identities means that shifts in our understandings of whiteness also pose affective and structural consequences for the identities of nonwhite subjects.

I situate *The Rain Ascends* within my discussion of multiculturalism and Asian Canadian publics because of how the novel writes both the difficulties of marking whiteness and feeling Asianness. Because multiculturalism is a project that reifies particular forms of social difference, other forms of difference are largely rendered illegible for dominant publics. The difficulty of speaking about difference in more nuanced and complicated terms is highlighted through Kogawa's repeated rewriting of this novel (as well as many of her other literary works). I read this impulse to narrative revision as part of a broader desire to underscore the contingent nature of social interactions and, more specifically, to work through how public address influences the legibility of topics and subjects. The persistent rewriting, in often quite dramatic ways, of Kogawa's fiction not only emphasizes the continuous nature of dialogue, but also illustrates how discourses of ethics and justice register differently depending on how they are racialized. By writing transgression, guilt, and apology from the perspective of a white subject, *The Rain Ascends* allows these representations of emotion to resonate very differently than they do in *Obasan* and *Itsuka*, novels explicitly concerned with Japanese Canadian internment narrated through a Japanese Canadian voice. That the significance attached to utterances of pain and injustice shift considerably depending on the speakers and publics addressed underscores the inability of multicultural discourses to convey complicated social affects and relations. Thus, the very linear structure of multicultural logics discourages us from examining whiteness and visible racialization in dialectical terms.

At the same time, the constant revisioning of Kogawa's work is provocative for what it suggests about public anxieties about trauma, representation, and responsibility. If, following Phillip Wegner's study of popular literature and film from the 1990s, repetition is a means of understanding how history is periodized, then Kogawa's revisions are particularly productive for what they suggest about the limits of historical intelligibility for cultural moments that continually signal beginnings rather than endings. Drawing on the work of Alain Badiou and Slavoj Žižek, *Life between Two Deaths* argues that the historical significance of a moment such as 9/11 stems from the fact that it is the repetition of an "Event" begun in 1989 with the fall of the Berlin Wall and that this "second death" marks the imposition of a new world order. Thus, when Wegner notes that "the true meaning of this moment emerges only in repetition" (21), he claims that the meaning of a moment cannot truly be grasped if it is seen as a beginning. In light of Wegner's framing of history, I see Kogawa's fiction as enacting a pattern of repetition that is a series of beginnings incapable of generating meaning in the sense of Badiou's Event. It is a perpetual beginning in the way that Christopher Lee has suggested of Asian Canadian studies entering the academic institution—a series of firsts that always marks the newness of difference rather than the continuation of dialogues that historicize the production of difference ("Lateness"). And in this way, the ongoing process of emergence that Lee describes of Asian Canadian studies speaks to the singularity of difference housed within multiculturalism.

The containment of difference within a structure of multiculturalism is consistent with a broader impulse to examine internment and the Japanese Canadian redress agreement primarily for what they reveal about the nature of Canadian law and justice. While this is, of course, important to consider, locating these occurrences solely within the context of national history also runs the risk of overlooking multiculturalism's global conditions of production. For this reason, I argue for reading the unintelligibility of Japanese Canadian internment according to the terms that Wegner uses to understand the relationship between the alleged end of the Cold War and 9/11. Rather than representing closure for historic trauma, the end of internment and the signing of the redress agreement are transformative moments for existing relations between "Asia" and Western imperialism. The end of internment (whether it is understood as having formally come to an end when Japanese Canadians were no longer incarcerated or when they were able to return to the west coast) does not mark the conclusion of Asian subjugation; here, it is important to remember that the Canadian government ordered the closure of internment camps after the atomic bombs were dropped on Hiroshima and Nagasaki and Japan surrendered to Allied forces, but that Japanese Canadians were then given the option of dispersal east of the Rocky Mountains or being repatriated to Japan in 1945, after World War II had ended. This sequence of events compels a global reframing of Japanese Canadian internment for its suggestion that Japanese Canadian internment is terminated not because it is revealed to be unjust, but because the end of Japanese imperialism and American military occupation renders it unnecessary. While a shifting logic determined that Canadian citizens of Japanese descent were enemy aliens and justified the "repatriation" of these individuals to Japan as a reasonable measure, the military overcoming of Japan eventually prompted another transformation to the meaning ascribed to the figure of the Asian in Canada. The dismantling of the Japanese empire meant that Western power could be inscribed directly onto Japan and, consequently, that Japanese Canadians could be written through these power relations in less overt ways. And in a directly related vein, Japanese Canadians could be given the franchise in 1949 because "Asia" as an ideological site was being dominated elsewhere. Read from this angle, the rewriting of Kogawa's work over a twenty-year span can only be understood as an ongoing revision and never a repetition simply because the global order of American imperialism still has not yet come to an end in Asia. The ongoing presence of American military bases in Japan, despite considerable protest by Japanese inhabitants, is just one example of U.S. imperialism in contemporary Japan.[8] In this context, both the interminability of white guilt and the inability to represent closure for Japanese Canadian historic pain in a satisfying manner signal the fundamental contradictions that exist between national discourses of multiculturalism and the Western domination of "Asias" on a global scale.

At the same time that *The Rain Ascends* gestures toward a need to think about multiculturalism as part of a global production enacted on national stages, it also loosens the link between intimacy and the private sphere. Liberal paternalism as personified by Reverend Shelby is a form of authority that structures the public sphere along the lines of the private. For racialized publics, this shaping produces particular contradictions, ones that theorists Anne Anlin Cheng and David Eng comment on in their discussions of the landmark *Brown v. Board of Education* case in 1954. With the end of racial segregation in American public schools in 1954, the responsibility of upholding a cultural logic of race was increasingly relegated to the space of families. In this light, Eng asks that

> we might consider how the politics of colorblindness reconfigure whiteness as property to focus critical attention on the private structures of family and kinship as the displaced but privileged site for the management of ongoing problems of race, racism, and property in U.S. society. That is, in a colorblind age, the intimate sphere increasingly becomes a crucial site for a reconsideration and reevaluation of racial conflict organizing not just the private domain but the public sphere as well. The current evisceration of a political and public language to address social inequality across both realms reveals only one part of a historical process that Lauren Berlant identifies as the incredible "shrinking public sphere," a process solidified by the neoconservative Reagan-Thatcher revolution of the 1980s. (6)

By teasing out Eng's line of thinking in relation to *The Rain Ascends*, we can begin to analyze the complex consequences of a public-private continuum. What space exists for racialized intimacies if, on the one hand, debates about race are displaced onto domestic spaces, but on the other hand, liberal paternalism regulates the public according to the logic of familial space? Within the space of the novel, the reader is compelled to recognize the absence of harmony between law, justice, and whiteness. By posing these sorts of questions in Millicent's voice and using them to rethink her position in relation to her father's formerly firm authority, we can ask what happens when, to borrow a term from Ann Cvetkovich's work on lesbian archives, "feeling queer" means feeling white and nonnormative?

If, as I have argued earlier in this chapter, visibly marked racialized bodies are encouraged to keep intimate details to themselves, Kogawa's novel poses an important question about what happens when those same details are shared, but by a body marked as white. *The Rain Ascends,* much like Mochizuki's *Bioboxes,* disrupts racial formations by turning attention away from identity categories and instead interrogating the cultural logics and processes that produce them. This reorienting has significant implications not only for the representation of both Asianness and whiteness, but also for the larger critical framework of multiculturalism. If whiteness can no longer be read in terms of neutrality and invisibility, then multiculturalism must find other ways of negotiating the always contingent and complex positionings that shape social dialogue. For multiculturalism to invoke responses other than a now familiar and cynical disdain in either dominant or minor publics, a public rethinking of the global politics and local aesthetics of Canadian multiculturalism must occur.

CHAPTER 2

Transnational Triviality

Print and Digital Asian North American Publics

Between the end of 2010 and the beginning of 2011, two texts ignited fiery debate about race in Canadian and American postsecondary institutions. The first was "Too Asian?," an article published in the print and online versions of *Maclean's* (which bills itself as Canada's national magazine) in November 2010. In it, Stephanie Findlay and Nicholas Kohler use anecdotal evidence to examine how race relations within Canadian universities contribute to the reputations of specific schools and the overall climate of postsecondary institutions. Their central claim is that many high school students avoid attending universities perceived as "too Asian" because that would require sacrificing social aspects of their university experiences in order to compete for grades. Asian students are characterized as focusing solely on their academics and as consequently "alienating their more fun-loving peers," a representation that reinforces the model-minority myth (Findlay and Kohler). Four months later, a then UCLA student named Alexandra Wallace released "Asians in the Library" (2011), a YouTube video in which she airs her grievances about Asian students at UCLA who lack "American manners"; of particular interest in this video is her annoyance at the "hordes" that descend into her apartment complex on the weekends (referring here to the family members that visit the students) and her description of rude Asian students who talk loudly on their cell phones in the library and annoy students who are trying to study. Asian publics objected strongly to these texts for how they racially stereotyped Asians and framed them as perpetual newcomers in Canada and the United States; clearly visible within many of these reactions are deep feelings of alienation, anger, and frustration at the persistence of white privilege and the ongoing racialization of Asians. The *Maclean's* controversy triggered debate in newspapers, on the radio, and in online forums, inspired teach-ins throughout the country, and produced open letters, one of which accused the magazine of "reinforcing a long and deeply ingrained history of anti-Asian racial anxiety that has led to bigoted profiling and discrimination of Asian Canadians" (Canadian Coalition, "Open Letter"). This particular open letter, written by Canadian community and university groups, demands reparations in the form of an apology, antiracism policies, and employment-equity programs to address the racial stereotyping perpetuated by media outlets. While the reaction to "Asians in the Library" was generally quite similar, a number of responses also took the form of satirical social media commentary. YouTube parodies such as Jimmy Wong's "Ching Chong! Asians in the Library Song" and Clemchan17's "Asians in the Library—The Guy She Saw Speaks Up" engage with Wallace's video by mocking her description of the family hordes and performing her racial stereotypes by, for instance, affecting Asian accents, using her offensive and nonsensical phrase *ching chong,* and, in the case of Clemchan17's video, wearing a large calculator in his shirt pocket. These responses to "Too Asian?" and "Asians in the Library" use strategies such as humor, physical gestures, political action, and argumentation to critique the structures of racialization that have shaped Canada and the United States for the past century and that continue to influence the public spaces of print and digital media.

This chapter centers on the common feeling of Asianness as it circulates throughout transnational debates about "Asians in the Library" and "Too Asian?" to consider the kinds of Asian publics it creates. Feeling Asian in North America and identifying as such are two distinct matters that often overlap in conversations about Wallace's and Findlay and Kohler's texts. As Yoon Sun Lee observes of the Asian American everyday, "Paradoxically, while the everyday as a set of practices can provide the experiential basis for a group's solidarity, the everyday as a structure does not result in a conscious sense of identity" (19). Lee's valuable insight into the difference between the small and banal moments that constitute the Asian American experience and the abstractions required to formulate an Asian American identity is extended in a transnational direction when we investigate how Asianness is imagined and enacted in "Too Asian?" and "Asians in the Library." These texts underscore how anti-Asian racism in North America offers a point of common identification without necessarily resulting in a shared identity.

Even as these debates map the continuities between Canadian and U.S. contexts, they also attest to significant differences that are signaled perhaps most clearly by the fact that Wallace's YouTube video went viral in the span of about twenty-four hours whereas the controversy about the Findlay and Kohler article was neither as immediate nor as intense. The contrasting shapes and scales of these debates indicate that while Asian North America exists as an affective formation, the particularities of rhetoric, media, and national contexts influence how these affective identifications are articulated and can be mobilized. The almost instantaneous outpouring of emotionally charged commentary about "Asians in the Library" highlights how, as a less centralized and more flexible form of communication than print media, online platforms such as YouTube reach larger audiences and invite greater levels and more immediate, but not necessarily more thoughtful, forms of participation. In social media forms like YouTube videos, the voices, physical gestures, and bodies of participants are rendered visible and the affective dimensions of participation made central to the publics they foster. As media theorist Henry Jenkins notes, "A participatory culture is one which not only lowers the barriers to participation but also creates strong social incentives to produce and share what one produces with others. Arguably, many people are taking advantage of the distribution platform YouTube provides, in part, because they feel the emotional support of a community eager to see their productions" (116). At the same time, to push Jenkins's observation further, these debates about "Too Asian?" and "Asians in the Library" invite us to also scrutinize how the act of participation is shaped by national structures of racialization and local debates about race. Rather than producing a more authentic connection, social media produces additional representations of subjects that work with, against, and alongside those created in print and within the guiding racial logics and social structures of places. By drawing attention to the specificity of anti-Asian racism, these texts encourage us to examine what circulates transnationally under this umbrella of Asian North American.

The debates surrounding "Too Asian?" and "Asians in the Library" make us conscious of the racialized systems that shape representation, citizenship, and recognition for dominant and minor publics. What I call Asian North American publics—transnational minor publics reacting to anti-Asian sentiment—emerge through common structures of feeling, but these shared sentiments do not necessarily translate easily into cross-border political projects. While Asian Canadian viewers may cringe when watching Wallace's video and identify with the Asians she complains about, this does not necessarily mean that they will take part in politicized actions such as, for example, joining in solidarity to protest for Asian American rights in the United States. The transnational relationship instead is more akin to what John Ellis calls "mundane witnessing," a term he coins to describe the kind of everyday witnessing demanded by media of its viewers that imposes new forms of social responsibility. Through the act of witnessing both quotidian and major news events via media, people and events are made to seem familiar even as they remain distant, and thus they "hover in an uneasy space between that of civil inattention and personal acquaintance. This is a new state of everyday knowledge which could be summed up as being 'known unknowns'" (85). Without necessarily inciting viewers to political action, mundane witnessing requires that we reflect upon what we have witnessed, feel for those who have experienced it, and understand how we are located in relation to these events (86). For Canadian viewers of "Asians in the Library" or U.S. readers of "Too Asian?," a sense of distant familiarity underscores both the sameness and difference of anti-Asian sentiment on the other side of the border. The political work of these publics occurs on the level of transnational identification and, more specifically, in the crucial insights into racialized structures of feeling that they offer. As a form of distanced witnessing, watching or reading texts like these "carries with it the sense that seeing brings with it a set of social implications and an emotional commitment" (Ellis 86), and understanding these obligations is necessary for beginning to conceptualize and undertake political action that spans North America. The *Maclean's* article and YouTube video function similarly to the art and literature I examine in other chapters of this book because they all permit engagements with racialization as a mundane and everyday phenomenon that extends beyond national borders. "Asians in the Library" and "Too Asian?" differ, however, in terms of the size of the audiences that they command and the vernacular language they use, and for inspiring more direct forms of political action (such as open-letter campaigns and teach-ins) within the nation. These various creative, journalistic, and digital texts, along with the competing and conflicting publics they foster—small, large, thoughtful, reactionary, angry, or melancholic, to list just a few ways of describing them—simultaneously shape the social reality of what it means to be and to feel Asian in North America. These are important minor publics that call attention to the constant and complex power dynamics that minimize Asian Canadian and Asian American concerns as inconsequential ones.

In juxtaposing "Asians in the Library" and "Too Asian?," my aim is to examine the affective and political possibilities of Asian North America as a cultural formation and understand how and when it takes the shape of a public responding to anti-Asian feeling. In their respective stagings of a desire to maintain institutions of higher learning as sites of whiteness, the texts showcase the complexities of public address and recognition—what audience is addressed, what audience is believed to be addressed, and how it is addressed—at work in national and transnational conversations about race. The anxiety produced by the racialization of North American postsecondary institutions by Asian students is a shared concern, but Wallace's video is much more explicit about her feelings than Findlay and Kohler's article, which hedges its argument in the language of meritocracy. These texts presume audiences that share their views on the perils of Asian students, but the responses to them suggest that more complex racial anxieties and attachments to whiteness are at work within dominant publics. The critiques of "Too Asian?" and "Asians in the Library" constitute some of the more vocal and heated debates about race, representation, and the figure of the Asian that have occurred recently within North America, and I situate them squarely on a continuum that includes other less contentious, more mundane struggles with racial anxieties. It is this wider, messy, and slippery series of shared Orientalist representation that I seek to draw attention to for what it reveals about the transnational dimensions of social imaginations bound together by the discomforting figure of the Asian and contestatory desires to challenge that representation.

Similar to the conversations about representation and Canadian currency I discuss in my introduction, many responding to "Too Asian?" and "Asians in the Library" saw these texts as trivial and isolated instances rather than as part of a wider and deeply entrenched pattern of discrimination linked to the longer project of transnational whiteness that structures North America. Unsurprisingly then, the debates about "Too Asian?" and "Asians in the Library" also emerged and disappeared relatively quickly from the attention of the dominant public, despite the pressing questions about race, social citizenship, and transnational imaginaries they pose. According to *Know Your Meme,* a website devoted to viral videos, the Internet interest in 'Asians in the Library" spiked quite dramatically in March 2011 (D.D., "Asians in the Library: Viral Videos"). The bulk of the responses to Wallace's video (which took the form of responding YouTube videos, online posts, and newspaper editorials online and in print) emerged in March 2011. A few of these responses called for a more sustained engagement with the issues that "Asians in the Library" raised. For example, a blog post titled "thoughts on a. Wallace & asian am response" expressed a greater interest "in using instances like this to build critical consciousness around race than getting back at individuals like AW" (qtd. in Asakawa). In the case of "Too Asian?," there was a similar flurry of online blog postings and comments on websites, the establishment of a Facebook page, and exchanges published in online and print newspapers, but these were also supplemented with other forms of action such as teach-ins and a boycott of Rogers Communications that look a little more time to mobilize. A collection of essays titled *"Too Asian?" Racism, Privilege, and Post-Secondary Education* (Gilmour et al.) that addresses this event was also published in 2012.

These controversies are, however, familiar to many Asian Canadians and others interested in race relations in North America, and this discrepancy between dominant and minor publics is part of the reason that I use these texts as case studies to anchor my discussion. This chapter locates "Too Asian?," "Asians in the Library," and the outrage of Asian publics within longer transnational histories of race, power, and knowledge in order to complicate the presentist and nationalist lens through which the Asian Canadian is frequently viewed. These ongoing debates demonstrate how whiteness as a formation in Canada and the United States is often produced through its relation to the figure of the Asian. In the late nineteenth century, for example, North American responses to Asia—configured simultaneously as flows of unwanted migrants and as an untapped market to be penetrated—gave rise to borders and immigration laws in Canada and the United States. In an effort to curtail the migration of Asian bodies that would sully North American claims to whiteness, borders around the Americas were hardened even as British and American empires sought to expand into Asia. As historian Kornel Chang notes of the Pacific Northwest, the "border emerged from expanding imperial relations and struggles to demarcate the boundaries of a 'White Pacific' in which race and empire was instantiated in and through space and geography" (13). Chang's study of the Canadian and U.S. borderlands analyzes the transnational flows of capital, bodies, and ideas between Vancouver and Seattle in order to argue that "the Pacific Northwest, rather than being a spatial-geographical given, was animated by border-crossings of various kinds" (13). This century-long North American project to construct whiteness both against and through Asia finds contemporary expression in moments such as "Too Asian?" and "Asians in the Library" that recast Asian/non-Asian binaries in new and familiar ways. Read from this perspective, the trivialization of Asian anger reveals much about the structures of feeling and representation in dominant publics, and, more specifically, how the erasure of Asian subjectivity is necessary in order to affirm whiteness.

The current terms of anti-Asian sentiment are historicized by Jeet Heer's introduction to *"Too Asian?"* in which he positions the "Too Asian?" debates alongside earlier, comparable controversies such as the 1979 *W5* controversy that erupted when the Canadian Television network (CTV) news program *W5* (similar to the U.S. program *60 Minutes*) reported on how foreign students were taking spots in universities that should have been allocated to Canadian students. Much like the more recent "Too Asian?" debates, CTV used the categories of "Canadian" to refer to white students and "foreign" to mean those of Asian heritage, even though "all the nameless and exoticized 'foreigners' in the *W5* episode were Canadian citizens or landed immigrants" (Heer, "Introduction" 3). It is worth noting that there are certain similarities and lines of continuity that connect the reactions to the *W5* and "Too Asian?" incidents on the part of Asian and dominant publics. The initial protests over the *W5* controversy also failed to generate much uptake. Anthony Chan describes the incident as sparking the anger of students who spoke publicly, wrote letters, and distributed pamphlets in order to protest the piece. When these efforts failed to produce substantial support, the Ad Hoc Committee Against *W5* turned to picketing and demonstrating. By December 1979, the protest had grown and "united the Chinese community regardless of occupation and political persuasion" (Chan 171) and eventually received the support of politicians and 20,000 people who signed a petition protesting the program. CTV issued a statement of regret that the Ad Hoc Committee found inadequate. On April 16, 1980, CTV finally issued a public apology that acknowledged the program was racist. The anti-*W5* movement eventually became what now is the Chinese Canadian National Council for Equality.

It is perhaps unsurprising that the assumed whiteness of postsecondary culture and national identity in all of these cases produced angry outbursts by Asian Canadian publics. In the "Too Asian?" situation, these reactions were dismissed as unfounded, overtly by journalists such as Barbara Kay and Margaret Wente (writing for *National Post* and the *Globe and Mail,* respectively), and more subtly by *Maclean's,* which expressed regret if some had felt offended by the piece, but not for the article's content or style. These exchanges demonstrate how dominant publics dismiss as illegitimate or irrelevant the concerns of minor publics responding to moments of racialization. The risks of trivialization are further courted by the tone and location of the debates over "Too Asian?" and "Asians in the Library"; much of this conversation took the form of heated online debates that might be perceived simply as instances of "flaming" instead of as part of a wider repressed conversation. Without putting too fine a point on it or reproducing their racism by quoting them, much of the online response generated by "Too Asian?" and "Asians in the Library" was reactionary and expressed negative, sometimes even hateful, feelings and opinions. This is particularly true for "Asians in the Library," which resulted in misogynistic comments and death threats directed toward Alexandra Wallace. While the openness of the Internet to potentially all users means that anyone with Internet access can participate in the conversations, I read these kinds of vitriolic posts (many of which were made by anonymous users) as gesturing toward the difficulties of being heard and thus as expressions of anger and resentment by people who feel excluded from politics proper. In using these emotional responses to underscore what is excluded from the parameters of legitimate debate, my intention is not to defend them, but rather to render visible the racialized nature of publics and the deeply entrenched structures that produce them. While the publics generated by "Too Asian?" and "Asians in the Library" emerged separately, they participate within a larger, though not necessarily coherent, conversation about Asians, Asian Canadians and Asian Americans, and social imaginaries.

The conflicts over the *Maclean's* article and YouTube video reformulate familiar anxieties about Yellow Peril within the contexts of educational institutions in North America. But when exploring the transnational circulation of anti-Asian sentiment, the national contexts in which these debates erupted must also be taken into account given the differences between their narratives of racism and education. Much of "Too Asian?" is structured as a comparison between Canadian and American higher education, with the U.S. story being held up as the Canadian telos. Findlay and Kohler describe how U.S. admissions policies have been revised to maintain racial quotas, whereas university admissions in Canada have traditionally been based on grades, noting, "Likely that is a good thing. And yet, that meritocratic process results, especially in Canada's elite university programs, in a concentration of Asian students."[1] This shared anxiety about Asian students displacing white students from universities is pertinent for locating "Too Asian?" and "Asians in the Library" within wider debates about the racialization of higher education in North America, and for understanding how, despite their very real historical differences, U.S. racial discourses (particularly those connected to affirmative action) shape the Canadian imagination in often palpable ways.

"Merit," *Maclean's* response to the "Too Asian?" controversy, states that the article's title was not intended to be offensive but rather meant to gesture toward a National Association for College Admission Counseling panel held in 2006. The title "Too Asian?" confirms U.S. affirmative action admissions policies and racial caps as both a subtext for the article and a scenario the authors hope Canada will avoid. But Findlay and Kohler's reference to the American discussions of Asian students is, according to historian Henry Yu, a deliberate misreading of the U.S. context for the challenge there actually had to do with attracting rather than excluding Asian American students: "Except for a few exclusive universities in the 1980s and 1990s, no school in the United States wanted fewer Asian-American students; in fact they were considered prize students to be recruited, as the 2006 article indicates" ("Parable of the Textbook" 18). "Too Asian?" projects a doomsday scenario based on an erroneous interpretation of the American history it turns to, a fantasy about the figure of the Asian moving across the Canada-U.S. border even as real bodies are denied entry. The authors also lament the absence of open discussion about race and postsecondary institutions in Canada, a shortcoming they see as contrasting sharply with the American situation; they claim that because of meritocratic admissions policies and the absence of dialogue about this issue, "race is defining Canadian university campuses in a way it did not 25 years ago" (Findlay and Kohler). But in comparing racial debates within dominant Canadian and U.S. publics, "Too Asian?" overlooks how Asian publics have also engaged in those conversations and, moreover, how race has always defined Canadian campuses for Asian publics.

Through a shared anxiety about the inassimilatability of Asians within postsecondary institutions, "Too Asian?" and "Asians in the Library" rework all-too-familiar panics about Yellow Peril. In "Too Asian?," irrational fears about race relations on Canadian campuses becoming similar to those in the United States are aired without careful consideration of the radically different national histories of education, equity, and accessibility. Here, racial representations and racial logics guide the interpretation of material realities, even when those realities strongly resist such readings. I frame this tension between these national histories of race relations and transnational anxieties about the Asian in terms of what Denise Ferreira da Silva calls "the (socio)logic of exclusion," a term she uses to argue for an understanding of race that positions it "within the larger field of production of meanings of the *racial* as a modern category of being" ("Towards a Critique" 422). In her examination of the strategies of power or "analytics of raciality" that produce racial difference, Silva maintains that the category of racial difference is premised on the relation between "place (continent) of 'origin,' bodies, and forms of consciousness" (422) and that it fundamentally informs how modern social spaces are inhabited and understood. Within contemporary formulations, race is primarily understood in terms of racial difference, but such an approach obscures the political-symbolic processes that produce it. Connected to this formulation of racial difference is a logic that relies on race as a supplement in order to produce modern subjects and concepts such as universal justice; in other words, racial injustice is a necessary prerequisite for universalism. Seen from this angle, the racial demands to be recognized as "a form of power whose most crucial accomplishment is to inscribe itself in the bodies and souls of its subjects" (Silva, "Towards a Critique" 427) and as one whose major effect "*has been to produce* universality *itself*" (427; italics in original).

In clarifying the difference between moments of racist exclusion and the racial as a central logic of modernity, Silva's work helps us to navigate the nationalist and democratic discourses of territory, rights, and citizenship that Findlay and Kohler's article and Wallace's YouTube video implicitly invoke. By seeing the increasing number of Asian postsecondary students as tainting the kinds of social promises universities make, "Too Asian?" and "Asians in the Library" demonstrate how the racial continues to operate as a political-symbolic logic.

The current reliance on international students to help balance university budgets is a newer development in the transnational flows of bodies, knowledge, and capital that construct "Asia" and "Canada" as spatial imaginaries and material realities. Nationalist and capitalist logics crisscross through these histories of race and postsecondary institutions, as evidenced by multiple kinds of anti-Asian sentiments directed toward Asian Canadian and Asian American students as well as Asian students studying in Canada and the United States. Inspired by Kuan-Hsing Chen's critique of imperialism, colonialism, and globalization that uses Asia as its entry point into these conversations, I see these older and newer forms of race and racism within North American colleges and universities as working "not only to blur the new colonial structure emerging in global capitalism but also to purge the old colonial subject and to provide theoretical justification for reconfiguring the global hegemonic order" (12). The triangulated relations between Asia, Canada, and the United States are marked by uneven flows of political, economic, and cultural capital and the simultaneous presence of older colonialisms and newer imperialisms. Analyzing the Asian within Canadian and U.S. higher education involves teasing apart the national, imperial, and global capitalist logics and structures to grasp how they sometimes, but do not always, cohere.

While nondomestic undergraduate students are a valuable source of revenue for cash-strapped institutions given the high tuition fees they pay (often three times as much as domestic students in Canadian universities), the increasing numbers of these international students also generate feelings of resentment within local populations that feel beleaguered and excluded from the institutional, social, and imagined space of the university. The multiple and often contradictory relations of power at work within postsecondary institutions are visible, for instance, in the lure of North American schools, which is tied to some extent to American soft power (and Canada's lesser degree of soft power) and America's status as a superpower. It is, however, the growing economic power of Asian countries such as China and Hong Kong, Japan, Singapore, India, and South Korea that funds the studies of international students, and indirectly funds North American postsecondary institutions. At the same time, the global dominance of English as a hegemonic language contributes to the appeal of American, Canadian, British, and Australian universities as destinations for international students, even as the influx of these students also threatens dominant representations of these nations as privileged spaces of whiteness. By reading "Too Asian?" and "Asians in the Library" for their understandings of Asian Canada and Asian America as well as of Asian students in Canada and the United States, we unravel the dominant public's investments in the sometimes cohesive, sometimes conflicting logics of nationalism and global capitalism and see how they influence the limits of public feeling.

Triangulated Orientalisms

Wallace's and Findlay and Kohler's strong reactions to the presence of Asians in North American institutions of higher education indicate a desire to maintain these sites as spaces of social privilege for white students; this territorial impulse belongs within a larger formation that also includes liberal discourses that link education with principles of freedom and equality, and colonial projects that seek to civilize the non-Western world. The anti-foreign-student sentiment that "Too Asian?" and "Asians in the Library" espouse is not at odds with the rhetoric of global thinking and attempts to attract international students (for the revenue and networking connections they bring) that characterize North American postsecondary institutions these days, but rather is indicative of how an Asia-West binary continues to determine how the global is approached and publics structured.

As critics of area studies remind us, the term *Asia* originated in order to distinguish Europe from the rest of the world; within the academic field of Asian studies, Asia is an object of knowledge approached from the perspective of the West and assumed to be both bounded and foreign (Cheah "Universal Areas" 38; Sakai 790). Naoki Sakai traces this pervasive understanding of Asia as a non-Western entity through the example of postwar Japan and its strategic reconstruction via U.S. policies that promoted cultural nationalism in Japan. During negotiations for Japan's surrender, the crucial issue for Japan was maintaining its national body in the form of private-property rights and the emperor system. The new constitution drafted under the Occupation administration largely transformed the emperor into a figurehead that represented Japanese unity:

> The most ironic and interesting aspect of the postwar relationship between the United States and Japan can perhaps be found in the fact that the United States

effectively continued to dominate Japan by endowing the Japanese with the sense of Japanese tradition and the grounds for their nationalism. It is through the apparent sense of national uniqueness and cultural distinctiveness that people in Japan were subordinated to US hegemony in East Asia. (Sakai 809)

Sakai invokes this overview of postwar Japan to illustrate how "Japanese nationalism itself could accommodate US imperial nationalism, or even be an organ thereof" (809) and to argue by extension that Asia and the West are internal to each other's formations. This critical move undermines the West as a "mythical construct" (789) that is produced largely through the opposition of an imagined Asia. The understanding of Asia as a fundamentally non-Western and bounded area informs notions of Western normativity, citizenship, and public participation. The Asia and West binary imagines these spaces as homogenous, a configuration that deliberately neglects the racial, social, and religious diversity of the West: "It is precisely because it effectively disavows its diversity, as if its interior were congenitally homogenous, that the West as a social imaginary is called for in the first place" (Sakai 796). While Sakai's analysis focuses primarily on the Asia and West opposition as it informs scholarly knowledge, his point is also pertinent for understanding the shape of academic institutions and wider publics. The debates around "Too Asian?" and "Asians in the Library" speak to collective investments in perceiving the West as a distinct and homogeneous space despite overwhelming evidence that "Asia" has long existed within it.

The debates generated by "Too Asian?" and "Asians in the Library" are instances of publics negotiating the terms of social citizenship within Orientalist legacies. In Habermasian terms, the public operates as a sphere of dialogue through which private citizens participate in the governance of the nation. While the public as a forum for rational debate devoted to the needs of the common good is an attractive vision for many, this form of governance is predicated upon a colonial structure. As Edward Said details in *Orientalism,* colonial and bourgeois worlds are imagined as having logical interiors and irrational exteriors. Orientalism legitimated European colonialism by extending the scope of Western rationality and framing Oriental subjects as incapable of such thought, a racial politics that continues within current understandings of publics. Instead of making the state accountable to more individuals and communities, imagining the public as a forum for rational critical debate implicitly enshrines a white Western subject as its ideal participant and minimizes racialized participation. The emotional reactions to "Too Asian?" and "Asians in the Library" challenge this tension between publics, nations, and imagined Asias by querying what constitutes legitimate public participation.

Thinking through the affective dimensions of these debates requires attention to their national specificity and the particular technologies used to mediate these publics. The terms of dialogue offered by print and digital media permit public debates about race to unfold in multiple ways and to circulate far beyond their initial sites; as the Canadian reactions to "Asians in the Library" demonstrate, local and transnational debates about Asians alike prompt Asian Canadian critiques of whiteness and social citizenship. Although only "Too Asian?" is a Canadian text (in the sense of publication and likely the authors' citizenship), "Asians in the Library" also captured the attention of Canadian viewers and generated vigorous debate throughout North America. That a YouTube video produced by a university student in California was able to create as much, if not more, heated discussion about Canadian racial politics than an article published in a Canadian magazine underscores the transnational nature of social imaginations via, on the one hand, dominant publics anxious about Asian invasions and racialized publics that respond to this positioning, and on the other hand, the different kinds of publics created by print and social media.[2]

At the same time, I want to emphasize that even though Asian stereotypes circulate throughout North America and can even be read as producing a unified North America through their anti-Asian sentiment, this is not the same as suggesting that this is a uniform space. Although Canadian and U.S. histories converge at multiple points, they still remain distinct. For example, racial dynamics in the United States are conventionally narrativized in black-white terms, but on the west coast of North America (and especially in a city like Vancouver), much racial anxiety has been directed toward the figure of the Asian. While African Americans (and to a lesser extent, Hispanic Americans) tend to be the primary recipients in the United States, population numbers, immigration histories, and governmental policies during the past century, to name just a few reasons, have meant that much of the racial hostility in Pacific Canada is directed toward Aboriginal and Asian peoples. This curious erasure of black Canadians from imaginings of national identity is explored in much depth in *The Blacks in Canada,* a project that traces the beginnings of black Canada to seventeenth-century slavery in New France. Robin Winks uses historical details (such as the consistently small percentage of Canada's total national population that blacks have comprised, often around 5 percent) to sketch out a story of indifferent racism against black Canadians (482). This is a narrative with significant implications for understanding the various registers that constitute social dialogue, and the affects and emotions that come into play in order to racialize communities. In *After Canaan,* Wayde Compton adds to this discussion of North American racial dynamics by suggesting that we might read Vancouver in particular "as a kind of inverse of US racial trends, a place where racist whites most feared Asians rather than blacks, and blacks rather than Asians took the place of the so-called 'model minority'" (103). At the same time, Canada and the United States are also bound together as a hemispheric formation through indigeneity, which operates as yet another dimension of a North American racial unconscious.

The debates around "Too Asian?" and "Asians in the Library" direct attention toward how particular forms of technology construct publics and circulate racialized representations, both reinforcing and challenging existing social discourses about the Asian. According to Michelle Henning's analysis of older and newer forms of media, "remediation should be considered in terms of changes in social relations and in the manipulation of physical 'stuff' rather than as a property or tendency of new digital media. From this perspective, remediation cannot be separated from human social practice and especially from working practices and the exchange of commodities" (50). Remediation in technological terms reworks the possibilities of social dialogue by introducing new avenues for minor publics to explore relations between participants and to reflect upon shared knowledge. By highlighting the Orientalist structures that shape technological forms, Asian Canadian publics question the regulation of citizenship norms within public spheres. How do these technologies rework conceptions of community, citizenship, and subjectivity as they facilitate new and ongoing dialogues? And how might particular media introduce different circuits and potential public formations for Asian subjects? These are crucial issues because print and online forums widen the possibilities for public critique, but admittedly do so at the same time that they open the floodgates for inflammatory comments.

The section for readers' comments in the online *Maclean's,* for example, includes much outraged commentary from both sides of the debate and insofar as it rehearses a range of arguments about assimilation, multiculturalism, equity and equality, and the yoke of political correctness, it reminds us of the wider context from which "Too Asian?" emerges. "'Too Asian?' Talkback," a Facebook page created a few days after *Maclean's* published "Too Asian?," is a useful archive that makes these historical dimensions even more visible. Most of the earlier postings on the page are directly about "Too Asian?," and these take the form of, for instance, links to and repostings of articles and YouTube videos about "Too Asian?," publicity for upcoming debates such as the TalkBack forums at the University of Toronto (2010), Ryerson University (2011), and the University of British Columbia (2011), a Beyond Too Asian discussion at McMaster University (2011), and video clips of politicians such as Barbara Hall (chief commissioner of the Ontario Human Rights Commission, detailing a chapter in *Maclean's* history with respect to race, human rights, and censorship and Olivia Chow (member of Parliament, New Democratic Party) discussing her motion to condemn *Maclean's* article and demand an apology. Later postings continue to update users of the status of this conversation as it also directs their attention to Asian Canadian theatrical productions and the apology of a Fox Network television host for his racist comments about U.S. president Obama, encourages people to vote in the federal election, and publicizes the anniversaries and commemorations about the *Komagata Maru*, Tiananmen Square, and the Chinese railroad workers in Canada. This Facebook page also has postings about "Asians in the Library." In collecting together all of these threads, "'Too Asian?' Talkback" makes visible the thickness of this discourse about Asians and underscores the importance of situating the racialized rhetoric of *Maclean's* "Too Asian?" within a wider historical pattern.

National Protectionism and Print Culture in Canada

In "Too Asian?" and "Asians in the Library," Asian students are perceived as invading the space of postsecondary education and threatening dominant social power and privilege. While the framing of Asian Americans and Asian Canadians as model minorities has historically been used to discipline other racialized groups, most notably African Americans and black Canadians,[3] "Too Asian?," with its description of Asian students as "strivers, high achievers and single-minded in their approach to university," demonstrates how model minorities can also undermine the racialized status quo and become a form of Yellow Peril. Because institutions of higher education are valued for their ability to instill social values, disseminate specialized cultural knowledge, and produce professional classes, the supposedly overwhelming numbers of Asian students and the racial imbalance they create on Canadian campuses pose considerable long-term social and economic implications. In keeping with the spirit of the kinds of criticisms historically used to limit Asian immigration to Canada, "Too Asian?" furthers the belief that Asians are incapable of assimilation. Findlay and Kohler's description of Asian participation within campus life—low in terms of participation within student government and high for Asian clubs—as a kind of "balkanization" positions Asians as perpetual outsiders to national norms and culture, and reinforces the belief that these students usurp resources only to further their own interests. This line of argumentation is often invoked to justify the exclusion of the Asian from the public sphere; in such a formulation, the Asian is seen as unwilling, and perhaps incapable, of participating in the governance of the nation because she or he refuses to set aside her or his own private desires.

That an influx of Asian students is responsible for social degeneration (in this case because it has necessitated the imposition of higher academic standards) is a curious but persistent argument about the dangers that accompany foreign subjects, and its placement within the pages of *Maclean's* magazine is worth considering in light of the historic relationship between cultural industries and Canadian nationalism. In his book on white civility and the nation-building project, Daniel Coleman examines popular writing such as poetry, novels, and journalism circulated between 1850 and 1950; through his reading of this literature, he sketches out Canada's development as an independent nation and explains how "certain racial forms such as Britishness and whiteness were formulated as fundamental to the national narrative and these racial forms came to be contested" (36). Although Coleman's study stops in 1950, this intertwining of whiteness and nationalism continued in the postwar period through governmental interventions into Canadian cultural production even as it underwent significant transformations. Between 1949 and 1963, four different federal commissions were established to examine the arts, letters and sciences (Massey Commission, 1949), radio and television (Fowler Commission, 1955), magazine publishing (O'Leary Commission, 1961) and bilingualism and biculturalism (Laurendeau-Dunton Commission, 1963). These commissions came out of a desire to make Canadian cultural industries competitive in a marketplace long dominated by British and US forces, in part because of colonial copyright laws. The sale in the 1950s of Canadian publishing houses W. J. Gage and Ryerson Press to American buyers spelled out the dire need for federal support if these industries were to survive the onslaught of U.S. cultural imperialism. Government subsidies began to flow in response to the commissions' findings and were crucial to the promotion of Canadian cultural nationalism; in the case of book publishing, for example, the establishment of the Canada Council and a granting structure helped grow a national literature.[4]

Much like the book-publishing industry, Canadian magazine culture has struggled against a steady flow of American print material since the nineteenth century. The need to stave off American cultural imperialism shaped the history of *Maclean's* magazine; emerging first as *Busy Man's Magazine* in 1896, what would eventually become *Maclean's* magazine voiced "the Canadian national voice of the time—decidedly British and imperial" in an effort to ward off U.S. publications (Martin and Sarfati). This crisis became even more pronounced in the postwar period as Canadian magazine publishers had to contend with the presence of Canadian editions of American magazines, a change introduced a few years earlier. The Royal Commission on Publications was critical of how U.S. publications dominated the Canadian magazine market and suggested various measures that would make it less attractive for foreign magazines to enter the country. This federal commission was followed up by a Senate committee led by Senator Keith Davey in 1969 and then by an Ontario Royal Commission on Book Publishing in 1973; the findings of these reports when paired with the suspension of *Saturday Night* magazine in 1974 provided much of the impetus for Bill C-58 (Martin and Sarfati). Passed in 1976, one of the changes that Bill C-58 made was that the taxes paid on advertising in non-Canadian-owned publications could no longer be deducted, a protectionist move designed to reduce the profitability of American magazines and discourage them from the Canadian market so that Canadian magazines could compete with their American counterparts (Acheson and Maule 468). More specifically though, this change was aimed at shifting advertising revenue from *Time* magazine and *Reader's Digest* to *Maclean's* in hopes that the latter would become a Canadian weekly news magazine (Litvak and Maule 73, 82).

The perception that magazines (and books) are key vehicles of nationalism and that print culture, like other Canadian cultural industries, require sheltering in order to compete with foreign forces are tenacious beliefs that continue to be visible, for example, in the description of the Canadian Periodical Fund, which "provides financial assistance to Canadian print magazines, non-daily newspapers and digital periodicals to enable them to overcome market disadvantages and continue to provide Canadian readers with the content they choose to read" (Government of Canada, "Canada Periodical Fund").

Read in this context, the publication of "Too Asian?" in *Maclean's* reinforces *Maclean's* brand of nationalism with its protectionist tendencies.[5] Foreign interests, whether they take the form of American cultural imperialism at the beginning of the twentieth century or Asian populations in the twentieth-first century, threaten the existence of the Canadian nation as a community imagined as, on the one hand, independent and, on the other hand, white. The historic interweaving of print culture and national identity embeds anxieties about the foreign into the structure of Canadian communications outlets as it also conveys them on the level of content. That "Too Asian?" was published both in the print and online versions of *Maclean's* is pertinent given how communications technologies shape the possibilities of participatory citizenship. While the print version of "Too Asian?" continued to circulate in its original form, backlash to the article prompted *Maclean's* to edit and repost the online version with the more benign title "The Enrollment Controversy." These online changes illustrate how audiences shape publics through the pressures they exert. Although print publics are also structured through this kind of dialogue, the temporality of the Internet has crucial implications for how readers' reactions resonate and, consequently, how public demands are expressed. Key here is that while many assumed that the digital age would spell the demise of print (analogous to a belief that globalization would cause the decline of nationalism), in the case of *Maclean's,* the move to an online format strengthened its purpose as a disseminator of Canadian culture; by reaching a wider readership, the Internet has extended the life of the print magazine. Even those not part of *Maclean's* regular readership were drawn into this debate, many engaging quite passionately, and thereby generating the impression that the magazine has its finger on the pulse of Canadian news.

"Too Asian?" and its multiple respondents illustrate the deeply contradictory and firmly entrenched nature of anti-Asian discourse. While the desire to police national limits against foreign threats is central to the article, its very rhetoric demonstrates the difficulties of even identifying the foreign with any kind of precision. The article elides complex histories of racialized subjectivities and the nation to reduce this debate to one about the need to protect Canadian higher education from Asian intruders. And yet, the very problem caused by the academic success of Asian students within a meritocracy is that these students threaten Canadian ideals by embodying them. Moreover, as Findlay and Kohler describe the problem of Asians in Canadian universities, the increasing numbers of these students threaten the balance of power by transforming model minorities into the status quo. "Too Asian?" addresses the impossible desire to protect the nation from the very threat that constitutes it by constructing Asia as a space of containment that is physically within yet ideologically outside of the nation.

Silencing Racialized Publics, Imagining Citizenry

Not only does the debate about "Too Asian?" amplify historical anxieties about race and nation within the context of the contemporary moment, but it also opens up new avenues for thinking about citizenship and public engagement. More specifically, many of the critiques of "Too Asian?," including member of Parliament Olivia Chow's, which took the form of proposing a motion in the House of Commons of Canada that would ask *Maclean's* to apologize for its story, took issue with the article for assuming that *Asian* and *Canadian* were mutually exclusive categories, or, to phrase it slightly differently, that race negates citizenship. The furor about this article underscores the very real manner in which public spheres operate as crucial sites of legitimation for democratic societies.

Hence, it is not surprising that Barbara Kay, columnist for *National Post,* chastised Jeet Heer for his op-ed (which reads the anti-Asian sentiment in "Too Asian?" as reminiscent of the anti-Semitism of Ivy League universities in the 1920s) and demanded that he apologize for calling *Maclean's* racist. According to Kay, Heer was irresponsible in drawing this parallel because although anti-Semitism is a genuine problem, "no comparable, sustained phenomenon—'anti-Asianism'— exists." She interprets Heer's critique of white privilege as betraying a "racism-hunting reflex" and defends the desire of white students for a more social, less studious, and less Asian campus as "social pragmatism, not racism." As Kay and Heer push for very different analyses of "Too Asian?" (and, by extension, of race in the current moment), they demonstrate how publics imagine and exercise national citizenship differently. While Heer frames anti-Asianism as part of a larger pattern of racism that extends back over the past century, Kay reads racism in much narrower terms and reserves the term for only the most egregious and explicit instances. In calling for tighter restrictions on the use of the term *racism,* Kay discourages public discussions of race that would promote self-reflexivity and accountability. I read this struggle to regulate the terms *race* and *racism* as indexing the importance of the public sphere as "the prime institutional site for the construction of the consent that defines the new, hegemonic mode of domination" (Fraser 8).

This eschewal of race as a topic for the general public is consistent with the historical fashioning of the bourgeois public sphere. Nancy Fraser writes that the public was intended "to be an arena in which interlocutors would set aside such characteristics as differences in birth and fortune and speak to one another as if they were social and economic peers. The operative phrase here is 'as if.' In fact, the social inequalities among the interlocutors were not eliminated, but only bracketed" (10). Although Fraser refers specifically to eighteenth-century public spheres, this process of bracketing social inequality continues in the racial politics that informally regulate dominant publics. The refusal to discuss race in a critical and sustained fashion functions as a form of domination and enforces a form of soft censorship on racialized populations. Moreover, the reluctance of dominant publics to interrogate how the mechanics of race are central to conceptions of national citizenship indirectly promotes an understanding of experiences as isolated, rather than collective, incidents. Ghassan Hage describes this phenomenon as it plays out in the Australian context in his tongue-in-cheek preface to *Against Paranoid Nationalism.* He comments ironically on the strong backlash against antiracist culture, writing that there are people who "might have occasionally demeaned, inferiorised, treated insensitively or excluded people they have pictured as belonging to a tribe other than theirs, but [that] obviously I cannot apply the slur 'racist' to them when they have such an established record of hating the very sight of the word" (x). Hage's wry comments are instructive for reading the exchange between Heer and Kay as he addresses the peculiar fact that in the current social climate, there is often more resistance to calling comments racist than there is to actual racist behaviors themselves. And in this way we are reminded of Balibar's insight that race relations theory *"naturalizes not racial belonging but racist conduct"* ("Is There a 'Neo-Racism'?" 22; italics in original).

The discussions of publics, citizenship, and race prompted by "Too Asian?" took another provocative turn a few months later when Alexandra Wallace posted her YouTube video entitled "Asians in the Library" (Wallace). As is typical of many YouTube video blogs, this one opens with Wallace sitting in front of the camera and addressing the audience. She is an attractive college-aged student with long blonde hair and is wearing a tank top, physical details that were the target of much commentary in videos, blogs, and Internet forums that responded to her video. Wallace vents her frustration at being unable to study for her final exams at UCLA because of the Asian students that answer their cell phones in the library. To illustrate this disruption, Wallace parodies an Asian student on her phone by saying with a faux Asian accent, "Ooooh, ching chong ling long ting tong, ooohhhhh." Immediately preceding this impersonation, Wallace tells the camera that this violation of library etiquette is just one of the many ways in which she finds the Asians that "UCLA accepts into our school" troubling. These Asian students are always accompanied by their extended families who cook and clean for them, but they never "teach their kids to fend for themselves" or "their manners." While Wallace's is a brief video, not even three minutes long, and in many ways is typical of YouTube videos that feature individuals ranting about particular issues or even just pet peeves, this video went viral in a manner that most others do not, capturing the attention economy of YouTube in an unanticipated way. Within a week after Wallace's video was posted, it reached five million viewers and multiple video responses appeared, many of them also garnering thousands of viewers (Rivas). Jimmy Wong's "Ching Chong! Asians in the Library Song," for instance, boasts over five million views and landed him an interview with NPR's *All Things Considered* host Melissa Block. Wallace took down her YouTube video a few days after she first posted it, but since other users reposted it, it continued to spark debate. Despite the fact that Wallace's video is specifically about the American situation—her comments directly target what she perceives to be an influx of Asian UCLA students—it generated Canadian responses as well.[6]

In "Too Asian?" and "Asians in the Library," the Asian is framed as an unsolvable problem of difference for a non-Asian audience. The latter, however, produced backlash (from its intended and unintended viewers) provocative for what it demonstrates about persistent Orientalist affects present in publics and the license certain minor publics felt in formulating their responses. Many respondents commented in online forums while others wrote articles for major publications and student newspapers. Still others took to various forms of social media such as YouTube to produce their own videos, some of which parody Wallace by modifying her script (and some users even don blonde wigs for their performances); others responded more directly by outlining their criticisms; and a few even sing and rap their reactions. Wallace issued two different apologies, and in the midst of all of this, UCLA's chancellor also took to YouTube to express his dismay at Wallace's comments. The university, however, never took any formal measures to reprimand its student. An editorial published in the *New York Times* addresses this issue within the context of the First Amendment. The editorial paraphrases parts of a blog post by Eugene Volokh, a UCLA legal scholar, that suggests that Wallace's comments are protected by freedom of speech and that they do not constitute harassment against Asian students. Volokh argues that Wallace's video should instead be seen as part of the university's function "to debate major decisions about social and other policies—to build consensus and the foundations of community. To assure worthwhile debate, it's necessary to protect some worthless, even hurtful, opinion" ("Editorial: The U.C.L.A. Video"). The editorial is useful both as an explanation of why the university did not take legal action against Wallace and also for clearly outlining how the video is positioned within a model of the public sphere.

In "Too Asian?" and "Asians in the Library," the Asian marks the limits of the dominant public's tolerance. Conversations about these texts touched on familiar hot buttons such as stereotyping, and consequently produced waves of liberal guilt, outrage, discomfort, awkwardness, and dismay. But in addition to generating feelings conventionally associated with racialized topics, these exchanges also made their participants feel vulnerable and exposed in a manner that few other issues do these days, because the discussions veered beyond the limits of our socially scripted dialogues about race and risked speaking offensively. Beyond delimiting the affective parameters of this cultural moment, "Too Asian?" and "Asians in the Library" reveal how the specter of Asian publics haunts the dominant public and influences how it speaks. "Asians in the Library" and its responses, for instance, offer self-conscious performances of whiteness that denaturalize the historic linkages between whiteness, invisibility, and normativity and throw into relief how the terms of speaking (as part of either a dominant or minor public) are implicitly racialized and shaped by the media they use. Unlike the careful and nuanced examinations of white liberal guilt or investigations into the promises of multiculturalism for whiteness that

Joy Kogawa's novel *The Rain Ascends* and Theatre Replacement's *Bioboxes* undertake, two artistic texts that I explored in the previous chapter, the conversations about "Too Asian?" and "Asians in the Library" reveal sharper emotions and more immediate reactions unmediated by time or artistic processes as they circulate for thousands of people.

Given the almost tediously familiar nature of the sentiments expressed by Wallace, I am hard-pressed to believe that the actual substance of her comments in "Asians in the Library" was solely responsible for generating the performed feelings of public outrage. In analyzing the responses to Wallace's video, I find a letter written by UCLA's Asian Pacific Coalition quite insightful—more specifically, a small yet telling rhetorical question about the public nature of Wallace's comments embedded within the coalition's detailed response: "Her decision to state such culturally insensitive remarks via a forum as public as a Facebook [sic] video is disturbing. What gives her the audacity to record such a video?" (Asian Pacific Coalition, "In Response"). This minor point, almost a throwaway one in the context of the letter that outlines objections to Wallace's ethnic slurs and calls for an apology from Wallace, disciplinary action by UCLA, and collective action from UCLA's sizeable Asian American and Pacific Islander student community (which constitutes nearly 40 percent of the university's student population), reinforces my suspicion that many viewing Wallace's video were more upset by the ease and openness with which overtly racist notions could be expressed in a public forum. As an illustration of what can be and is said within a dominant public and, moreover, how those utterances can be injurious without being seen as formally constituting injury, Wallace's "Asians in the Library" reveals how social citizenship operates with respect to the figure of the Asian.

Wallace's video returns us to the problem of engaging publicly with race and racism by highlighting the importance of audience. "Asians in the Library" begins by addressing an audience that it presumes an intimate association with; this is evidenced by Wallace's caveats that she is not known for her political correctness, that her comments are about strangers rather than friends, and that "you guys are not the problem." Wallace's assumption that she is confiding in a sympathetic audience exemplifies how one of the privileges of whiteness is to be imagined as universal, transparent, and rational, and this returns us again to Silva's theorization of racial logic. In Silva's framework, the racial, the nation, and the cultural are key concepts, and while they work in tandem, they also operate in different ways:

> (a) the racial produces modern subjects as an effect of exterior determination, which institutes an irreducible and unsublatable difference; (b) the nation pro-

duces modern subjects as an effect of historical (interior) determination, which assumes a difference that is resolved in an unfolding (temporal) transcendental essence; but (c) the cultural is more complex in its effects because it can signify either or both. (*Toward a Global Idea* xxxvii)

In this formulation, the racialized subject is neither modern nor of the nation; temporally and spatially, the racialized body always operates as the outside to the nation.

Positioning Fraser's and Silva's work alongside Habermas's notion of the bourgeois public sphere asks how these insights might be reconciled differently by those interior and those exterior to the nation and, consequently, how we might understand one's potential participation within the publics that shape how the nation is governed. Fraser's critique of Habermas's public for bracketing inequality can be linked productively to the tolerance of racism discussed by Silva and other critics such as Hage, Balibar, and Wallerstein. The rational tone required to participate within the public sphere reaffirms the centrality of the modern rational subject that Silva argues is deliberately, rather than accidentally or occasionally, colored as white. If racism is necessary to universality, then the practice of bracketing social inequalities must occur for dominant publics to exist. As Silva points out, "[O]nly by reading modern representation against the grain does one learn that the particular temporality attributed to European bodies and social configurations results from how the racial, the signifier of globality, produces both self-determined and affectable consciousness" (*Toward a Global Idea* 168). Thus, it is not just that race and globality are necessary preconditions for the transparent and universal subject to exist, but also that the repeated sacrifice of the racialized body is required and overlooked (Silva, *Toward a Global Idea* xi–xii).

To return to "Asians in the Library," instead of successfully appealing to a like-minded audience, Wallace's video garnered contempt from Asian publics (that were clearly not her target audience) as well as non-Asian ones. While self-identified white users made a variety of arguments through their video responses, most were quick to condemn Wallace as racist and parsed her comments for their fallacies. Several video responses were also peppered with derogatory comments, many quite sexist, about how Wallace was unintelligent. One video titled "Re: UCLA Racist Rant" (K. Anderson) features three young non-Asian women who complain that they are embarrassed by Wallace and state that as "American girls," they do not want to be perceived as possessing similar values; however, they also note that they are uncomfortable with the sexist remarks that have been directed toward Wallace. The videos assert their strong desire to disidentify with Wallace by explaining her comments as the shortcomings of an individual rather than as indicative of whiteness as a social formation. While the refusals to identify with Wallace are understandable given the offensive nature of her comments, these public disavowals still provide valuable insights into the social intimacies operating within these publics. Because Wallace's comments frame the racial subject as exterior to the nation even as it is central to Western modernity, I read these rejections of her views as attempts to deny or suppress the central logic of race and modernity. Much of the discomfort stemming from "Asians in the Library" emerges from the inability to ignore the social logics and realities that bind together race, universal subjectivity, and social citizenship.

These debates about "Asians in the Library" illustrate how the power of whiteness comes from its association with normativity and that this combination produces its invisibility. As Richard Dyer writes in his analysis of filmic representation, the "property of whiteness, to be everything and nothing, is the source of its representational power" and that "white domination is reproduced by the way that white people 'colonise the definition of normal'" (45). Whiteness resists specificity by appearing "to fall apart in your hands as soon as you begin" analyzing it, quickly crumbling explorations of class, ethnicity, or race only solidify by way of comparison with nonwhite bodies (46). In the early twentieth-century U.S.-Canadian context, the slipperiness of whiteness was produced deliberately. Immigrants reconceptualized themselves within their new environments by "fixing on their whiteness, intensifying their racism," and "abstracting their ethnicity" (Harris qtd. in Chang 92). Whiteness became a category that European settlers could assimilate into, but Asian migrants could not.

Although the equation of whiteness and universality creates the illusion of invisibility, moments such as "Asians in the Library" reveal the cracks in this fantasy by directing attention to the conflicting strands that compose whiteness. But instead of dismantling whiteness, the disavowal of Wallace by other self-identified white respondents curiously upholds white privilege in a manner suggestive of Robyn Wiegman's analysis of white privilege in the U.S. South. She examines white power and identity in a post–civil rights era, noting that while overt displays of white supremacy are no longer acceptable, white supremacy itself continues to exist. By distancing themselves from displays of white supremacy, the townspeople of Laurens, South Carolina, produce an opposing form of whiteness that disaffiliates them from segregationist politics without actually relinquishing white power and privilege. Consequently, these new white subjects "can now join efforts to undo civil rights reform without recognizing their activities or opinions as participation in the contemporary reconfiguration of white power and privilege" (120).

Without dismissing the possibility that many respondents may actually disagree with Wallace's views, such framings of whiteness enable us to also understand the rejection of more conservative and somewhat anachronistic forms of whiteness as a necessary and strategic maneuver that preserves the privileged invisibility of whiteness. Part of the problem that "Asians in the Library" presents is one of style; by explicitly naming its racial anxieties and making visible an investment in white normativity, the video alienates its intended audience. The open declaration of her beliefs is at odds with the kind of silence Barbara Kay advocates in her response to Jeet Heer about "Too Asian?" and is typical of how Orientalism tends to be practiced within contemporary liberal democratic societies. According to Wiegman, the inability to claim universality as a social injury is seen to minoritize whiteness, and is an act that lets whiteness reclaim universality without necessarily reforming it (135). But by neglecting to unyoke white privilege and universality even temporarily, Wallace performs a dated form of whiteness that makes us overly conscious of how the material realities of the racialized everyday contradict the rhetoric of social change and progress.

Remediating Feeling and Thinking

Analogous to how the language of race and the performance of whiteness have changed over the past century while racial logics have remained intact, new media technologies introduce alternate means of articulating national, racial, and cultural identities as they continue to be informed by Orientalist logics. The use of social media and other online forums by publics responding to "Asians in the Library" and "Too Asian?" simultaneously demonstrates the possibilities for social change introduced by this technology and draws attention to the larger social narratives that shape the Internet. As Wendy Chun reminds us, William Gibson's *Neuromancer* initially imagined cyberspace as requiring that users plug their consciousnesses into a virtual reality and leave their physical bodies behind, a fictional premise that shaped understandings of the Internet when it was actually invented ("Orienting Orientalism"). Gibson's reworking of the Cartesian dualism gave rise to the belief that the Internet would offer a space free of race and gender, but the absence of physical bodies on the Internet has not actually eradicated either these symbolic bodies or those social logics. Instead, as Internet theorists such as Wendy Chun, Lisa Nakamura, and Mimi Nguyen argue, racialized discourses are reworked rather than erased as they travel between "real" and virtual spaces via Internet representations of the Asian body; the newness of this technology reinforces the oldness of racial logics and expands Orientalist practices. The emergence of digital media has also meant that the computer has become a dominant metaphor for memory. Given that it operates as a site of storage that can be easily erased, it is not difficult to see the appeal of computer memory as a model for social memory. When we contemplate the history of race relations in North America, erasing these memories or storing them within an archive that can be forgotten about seems like an ideal way to, as Anne Anlin Cheng would say, "get over" racialized grief.

The exchanges between Wallace and her respondents demonstrate that there is never an outside to the logics of race, gender, and sexuality, and consequently, that the Internet is not a disembodied virtual space. This is illustrated in a disturbing fashion when Wallace's critics subject her to a misogynistic Orientalist gaze and threaten violence. In "Orienting Orientalism; or, How to Map Cyberspace," her essay about race, sexuality, and power in cyberspace, Chun describes how narratives of cyberspace rely on Orientalizing others in order to produce pleasure for users (4). Through readings of William Gibson's *Neuromancer,* Mamoru Oshii's *Ghost in the Shell,* and Marty Rimm's Carnegie Mellon report on pornography consumption on the Internet, Chun demonstrates how narratives of cyberspace rely on Oriental sexuality to structure it as a space to be explored, and, moreover, how *Asian* has emerged as a pornographic category ("Orienting Orientalism" 29). At the same time that narratives of cyberspace uphold the binary logic of alterity, they unfix Orientalism from its more familiar representations, as evidenced by some Asian mail-order bride sites that include photographs of white women from the former Soviet Union. This act not only underscores the stereotype of Asian women as submissive and dependent, but also enlarges the category to include all economically disadvantaged women within Orientalist fantasies. Made apparent here is that "[t]hose who produce Oriental websites that include these 'other' white women on their sites assume that the desire for submission, rather than a certain aesthetic preference, drives desire for Asian women" (Chun, "Orienting Orientalism" 29). In demonstrating the flexibility of Orientalist discourse, these mail-order bride sites preserve the desire to dominate while revising the meaning of whiteness within it. Similarly, the sexist responses to Wallace return to an Orientalist script of alterity, but substitute gender for race as a site of inferiority, thereby reinforcing the logic of Orientalism even as they also seek new objects for it to regulate.

Haunted Publics

Read collectively, the debates around "Too Asian?" and "Asians in the Library" illuminate the complex discourses of whiteness and Orientalism at work in print and online publics, and demonstrate how they transgress national borders while upholding the logic of national protectionism. By making visible the structures of racialized feeling within North America, the reactions to "Too Asian?" and "Asians in the Library" illustrate how Asian Canadian publics function as phantom publics for dominant publics. In using the term *phantom publics*, I highlight how Asia is not only a construction used to ground the West, but also that it operates as a racial unconscious. But even as Asian Canadian publics ground dominant publics, they also move in other ways that, while shaped by this discourse, are not wholly produced by it. While the discursive apparatus of the West only imagines Asia in relation to itself, Asia continues to exist outside of those terms of representation; similarly, Asian Canadian publics also exist outside national borders. Asia exists as a "real" entity and in discourses other than Western Orientalist representations, even as it constantly negotiates these representations. In the same way, the Asia and West binary shapes the responses to "Too Asian?" and "Asians in the Library"; many appear quite conscious of this condition as their critiques of Orientalism also acknowledge the impossibility of getting outside of it. The reactions to these anti-Asian texts limn the Orientalist discourses that shape the social imagination and reveal much about how Asian Canadian publics negotiate the limits of what can be said and heard.

The *Maclean's* and YouTube controversies illustrate a continuum of publics that include those organized predominantly in Habermasian rational terms and more affective ones that operate primarily as spaces of emotional exchange. The debates render visible complex emotions and logics that range from careful and rational to angry and bewildered. The print conversations, on the surface at least, operate in more logical terms, guided both by the structure of the grammatically correct sentence that demands that a single idea be expressed at a time and the time-consuming process of editing and revision required by print publication. In contrast, social media commentary, particularly videos, tends to be freer to express the emotions that led to its creation. But even as I assert these broad divisions, I recognize how forms such as e-mails, blogs, and online magazines complicate my argument because many of these are as carefully constructed as articles appearing in printed newspapers and magazines. My earlier discussion of Jeet Heer's blog, for instance, reads his written commentary as rational and logical but does not investigate its affective dimensions or how its virtual publication exerts a shaping force. Also, at least two YouTube videos posted in response to Wallace go against the grain of the majority of the other videos by using "Asians in the Library" as an opportunity to address the deeper problems with race in a nuanced fashion. Slam poet Beau Sia performs a piece that takes seriously Wallace's racial anxieties and engages thoughtfully with her fears. Blogger and philosopher Cori Wong also interrogates race in a nuanced fashion by considering how visibility functions as one, but not the only, marker of difference ("Think for a Change"). It is worth noting, however, that this video is not just a response to "Asians in the Library" but part of a series of YouTube pieces designed to provoke critical thinking. At the same time, as a thirteen-minute video, it is quite long by YouTube standards, a length that the poster notes is both too long for YouTube and too short in terms of the work it needs to undertake.

Because many of the responses to "Asians in the Library," made by both Asian and non-Asian individuals, were brief, highly emotional addresses that often did not rely primarily on logic to structure their videos, they exercised a provocative aspect of participatory media. Unlike the imbalance in print media, which has large readerships and small numbers of authors, social media promises to be more democratic by creating a scenario in which all viewers are potentially authors (Hartley 131). For minor publics, this is an important forum that offers new speaking possibilities for subjects long constructed by the West as marginal, uncivilized, and nonuniversal. Read alongside the investigations into cultural politics offered by works of art and literature, these print and digital publics constitute valuable sites for examining and reworking the limits of political engagement and social participation.

Key here is that Asian publics claim public recognition through nonrational means. To return to Fraser's critique of Habermas, discussions of public participation must account for style as an informal mechanism that enforces inequality. Fraser takes issue with Habermas's claim that the public is a place where inequalities are bracketed because such a premise actually upholds existing power relations. Instead of pretending to create a space unsullied by power dynamics, "it would be more appropriate to unbracket inequalities in the sense of explicitly thematizing them" (Fraser 11). By paying attention to these matters of participatory style, we can understand how the affective economy at work in allegedly disinterested and rational debates as well as the cultural logics that regulate heated exchanges are means by which publics regulate participation and limit conversations about the common good. The turns to reason and emotion are provocative as both immediate reactions to the texts and as persuasive strategies used to address publics. This continuum of emotional and rational publics is flexible and these various forms—written, verbal, print, and social media—enact discursive pressure by introducing new performative modes. For example, many responses by self-identified Asians to "Asians in the Library" return to an Orientalist script, often parodying and at other times critiquing it. These videos, while reactionary to a degree, merit consideration for magnifying social inequalities and generating a public that refuses to pretend that inequalities can be bracketed.

Public participation is also regulated to some extent by the kinds of collectives that publics imagine themselves to be part of. For instance, cemented by Benedict Anderson's work on nationalism is the now commonplace perception of print as producing nations as communities, an insight reinforced by Canadian book and magazine history. This framing of print culture differs markedly from the rhetoric that heralded the dawning of the age of the Internet for its democratizing potential. This becomes especially clear if we turn to *Imagined Communities* for its examination of invented communities, specifically as they pertain to nations, which it notes is "both inherently limited and sovereign" (B. Anderson 6). Fantasies of community cohere people who often have little in common in terms of everyday reality by promoting belief in "a deep, horizontal comradeship" (B. Anderson 7). Print technology, whether it takes the form of, for example, the novel or newspaper, is key to circulating understandings of a national community that believes itself to be free and fraternal despite its obvious power inequalities. The construction of community via print already participates in the creation of hierarchies by privileging languages more easily translatable into written form in order to create newer "languages-of-power" (B. Anderson 45). Print communities are structures premised on inequality but which base their self-imaginings on self-regulation and fraternity.

In sharp contrast to the self-consciously bounded spaces of nations, the Internet is largely represented as an endless universe. The opening up of virtual terrain through social media platforms such as Facebook, Twitter, and YouTube was initially framed by many in utopian terms as the emergence of cyberdemocracy and perceived as promoting a collectivity quite unlike the imagined communities of print. Much of the excitement surrounding the Internet stemmed from a belief that the increased dissemination of information was an equalizing and democratizing change. YouTube is a pertinent example because it was launched in the aftermath of 9/11, a moment "defined by an impulse towards self-fashioning and authenticity on the one hand, and the impact of a traumatic mass-experience on the other hand, which reached its audience through visual channels—primarily television—and prompted an explosive self-dissemination" (Banita 95). And yet, as other technocultural critics remind us, claims that the Internet offers the means to freedom are simply untrue on many levels. Instead of promoting political representation and inclusion, technoculture in practice often exacerbates economic inequalities. Morozov addresses this danger when he warns against cyber utopianism, an uncritical belief in the liberatory potential of the Internet, which attributed recent global political struggles against autocratic governments to the spread of technology rather than to the efforts of the people who mobilize it. The nomination of the Internet for the 2010 Nobel Peace Prize (led by a public celebrity campaign) epitomizes this

Western tendency to limit politicized readings of cyberspace to democratic ones (Morozov 20). In addition to turning a blind eye to the use-value of the Internet for other ideological agendas, such utopic turns overemphasize the politicized dimensions of social networking tools, Internet search engines and other technological forms, and neglect their capitalist aspects (Morozov 21). As I have argued previously in this chapter, the Internet is not free of racial, gendered, and sexualized representations, and it is an Orientalized space as well.

As these brief sketches of print communities and online democracies demonstrate, these formations imagine public inclusion differently, with the former emphasizing shared identity and the latter privileging access and equality. Anderson and Morozov partly attribute the failed inclusivity of these collectives to their relations to capitalism, whereas my own interest lies in extending these critiques to include racial formations. Much has been written already on race in relation to nation, work that historicizes the political and ethical challenges posed by ethnicity to the nation.[7] By resituating race and nation within a conversation about print and digital publics, we see how media technologies produce modes of imagining and feeling collectively.

In *Imagined Communities*, Anderson explores the relation between temporality and nationalism. Perceiving of time as homogeneous and empty rather than as simultaneous is "a precise analogue of the idea of the nation, which also is conceived as a solid community moving steadily down (or up) history" (B. Anderson 26). In the imagined community of the nation, print promotes the idea that all citizens experience events collectively. Yet race intervenes within this social fantasy by introducing a temporal disturbance. This disjuncture between national and racialized time is scrutinized by Homi Bhabha who, through a reading of Frantz Fanon's "The Fact of Blackness," ponders the notion of belatedness "that does not simply make the question of ontology inappropriate for black identity, but somehow *impossible* for the very understanding of humanity in the world of modernity" (236–37). Bhabha claims that Fanon refuses to either be the Other to whiteness or to be made part of a dialectic that will produce a more just form of universality. While Bhabha's meditations focus on the problems of modernity rather than nation, his thoughts are still pertinent for understanding how race is understood as existing outside of homogeneous, or what he calls immediate, time. Bhabha uses the dissimilar temporality of postcoloniality to critique claims that modernity is a moment of immediacy. He argues instead that in postcolonial modernities, the "cultural inheritance of slavery or colonialism is brought *before* modernity *not* to resolve its historic differences into a new totality, nor to forego its traditions. It is to introduce another locus of inscription and intervention, another hybrid, 'inappropriate' enunciative site, through that temporal split—or time-lag—that I have opened up ... for the signification of postcolonial agency" (242). Although we might want to quibble with Bhabha as to whether race is actually by definition outside of modern time, his analysis still obliges us to contemplate how the shared identity that underpins community and is circulated through print makes a curious kind of room for the racialized figure that is neither located completely outside of this space nor within it, at least not at the same time as is whiteness. The print nation inscribes the racialized figure as part of a shadowy past that is loathed for the futures it forecloses. In this temporal nonspace, the racialized figure is jettisoned from the now of the nation and becomes part of a past that eludes the national narrative as well as a future that the public does not work very hard to realize. And here we might think about how the reinvigoration of old forms of racism through newer discourses holds onto the Asian as a figure of anxiety and foreboding.

With Anderson's model of the nation as a print community in mind, an analogous connection between democracy and the Internet can be recognized, particularly as these social formations and technologies imagine race. The triangulation of race, nation, and print reveals competing temporal logics that deepen formal and informal differences by representing white citizens and racialized bodies as being out of sync with each other. The now of the nation is a spatial moment inhabited by whiteness but haunted by phantom racial publics. Similarly, within the democratic Internet, thinking about race involves confronting ghosts—namely, visibility and secrecy—that are central to the practice, but marginal to the ideologies, of technoculture. In a moment when most questions are often answered by Google searches, widespread access to information has transformed and even produced additional forms of social anxiety as public secrets function as new loci of vulnerability. While the electronic dissemination of information means that it is nearly impossible to keep secrets any longer, Jodi Dean suggests that they continue to exist ontologically. The conflation of the individual with her database and digital identity, for example, turns the individual into the public secret that she is simultaneously afraid will be revealed and afraid is too insignificant to merit revelation (Dean 1). Dean's insights demonstrate how the Internet, as a space where information can be freely accessed, can exaggerate inequalities rather than further the goals of democracy. This concept of public secrets resonates quite differently when positioned within the context of racial discourses, and most immediately invokes a historic obsession with passing. The preoccupation with revelation and visibility signals a desire for racial certainty, but is impossible to realize given the way race has been codified. Formulations such as the "one-drop" rule, which promote an understanding of individuals as racialized if they possess any racial heritage, further "the gap between what the body says and what it means, since it became increasingly difficult to read the signifier, let alone the signification" (Chun, "Introduction" 18). Approached in these terms, the physical body becomes an archive used to affirm, rather than explore, the truth of racial categories, with surface markers like skin, hair, and facial features scrutinized for the secrets they may inadvertently betray.

Resituating the notion of passing within the context of the Internet complicates the tenets of democracy. While freedom of speech is a much-touted right in American-style democracies, the freedom to not speak might perhaps be seen as a cornerstone of cyberdemocracies. Dean's insights about the social anxieties stemming from public information and revelation are pertinent as race functions as a public secret troublesome because it has not been revealed. The absence of physical bodies in cyberspace does not mean that race, gender, sexuality, and other corporeal systems cease to regulate power or the representation of virtual bodies. Far from operating as an ideal site of abstract citizenship, on the Internet "all kinds of bodies and their doubles—digitized, prosthetic, virtual, textualized—are circulated, exchanged, and performed in the electronic market because bodies do matter, at least when it comes to asserting social hierarchies and variously hegemonic cultural logics"; moreover, knowledge of this does not effectively disrupt how bodies are publicly ordered (M. Nguyen, "Tales of an Asiatic Geek" 189). To produce a racially neutral space, the social and economic relations that determine difference would need radical revisioning. Not reading the Internet as an extension of offline social systems only sidesteps potential social intimacy.

The different rhetorical strategies of "Too Asian?" and "Asians in the Library" suggest how race is a technology used by print communities and technocultural neodemocracies to produce different publics. Print encourages a rational tone, and the responses to "Too Asian?" and "Asians in the Library" that appeared in newspapers and magazines, while not all uniformly calm and devoid of spectacular feeling, tended to present clear and articulate objections to the anti-Asian sentiment in the original pieces. These print debates direct attention to the terms one must adhere to in order to be heard by and as part of the nation, and reinforce that one cannot be heard if she or he is not part, however marginally, of this shared community. Similarly, Habermas's idealization of the public sphere as a space of careful and logical deliberation that legitimates the democratic processes of the nation can also be understood as disciplining its participants. In contrast, many of the online responses did not shy away from expressions of anger, frustration, and annoyance, and numerous comments left at the *Maclean's* site, the "'Too Asian?' Talkback" Facebook page, and YouTube videos made in response to Wallace suggest that conflict is actually what coheres collectives. These responses push the parameters of racial discourse and inadvertently work to heed Chun's more generalized advice that we should negate racism by making "race do different things" ("Introduction" 28).

Without idealizing participatory media, I suggest that the YouTube pieces and Internet postings reformulate race when they invoke a context other than the rational space of the nation-state; at the same time, I recognize that these online spaces are also particularly vulnerable to vitriolic expressions of racism as evidenced by vicious comments left in response to YouTube videos and in online forums. Nonetheless, many of the performances that address the anti-Asian sentiment of "Asians in the Library" call to mind Paul Gilroy's analysis of music as "encapsulat[ing] the playful diasporic intimacy that has been a marked feature of transnational black Atlantic creativity" (16). Black music is understood here as an ethical form that productively critiques social relations and motivates listeners to demand justice. Because the politics of fulfillment and transfiguration are simultaneously expressed in this art form, Gilroy uses black music to address promises made by modernity as well as those that exceed its logic and consequently are unsayable. The desire "to conjure up and enact the new modes of friendship, happiness, and solidarity that are consequent on the overcoming of the racial oppression on which modernity and its antinomy of rational, western progress as excessive barbarity relied" (Gilroy 38) that is found within black music also finds expression, I argue, in many of these YouTube responses to "Asians in the Library." Performing a collective response to an enduring racial logic, these videos remind us that diasporic imaginings are often the consequence of being squeezed outside of the parameters of the nation and being unsayable within the terms of modernity. While undoubtedly offensive and hurtful to many Asians and non-Asians, men and women, these texts also express the feelings of rage and frustration that intimately bind together racialized publics, but all too often escape clear and coherent articulation.

The inexpressibility of race poses grave consequences for racialized publics. Although the recent debates surrounding Asian students on university campuses merit careful consideration in and of themselves, they are also symptomatic of the more general climate of postsecondary institutions. Situating "Too Asian?" and "Asians in the Library" alongside recent allegations about the systemic racism of university hiring practices makes the urgency of equity issues on North American campuses painfully clear.[8] And in these sorts of instances involving formal complaints, the language of confidentiality and climate of heavy silences turn any attempt to speak about these matters into acts of speaking out. These kinds of obstacles in matters of equity suggest that while an individual may feel the impact of systemic racism, proving discrimination within the dense and often circuitous logic of the legal system is not an easy feat. The slippage between familiarities and intimacies—with racism, for example, functioning as an issue that everyone is aware of but not necessarily intimately versed in—often translates into the difference between communities and publics with their varying degrees of collective cohesion and commitment. Controversies like "Asians in the Library" and "Too Asian?" turn Asian Canadians and Asian Americans into mundane witnesses for each other that "feel something of the emotion of others and have a sense that we are engaged in a difficult process of understanding that is shared by others" (Ellis 86). As an affective formation, Asian North America reframes the dominant public's disinterest, boredom, anxiety about being uninformed, and social awkwardness as transnational strategies that softly shape fleeting conversations about race (with litigiousness operating as a strong strategy) and that pose serious consequences for how we inhabit local and global spaces in the contemporary moment. By underscoring the complex and conflicting structures of feeling and communication that shape racial politics in Canada and the United States, these debates generate new ways of thinking about social intimacy and cultural citizenship.

CHAPTER 3

Diasporic Fragility and Brokenness
Korean War Legacies and Structures of Feeling

In "I=You," her essay on digital identity politics, Kara Keeling explores difference within collective identification via an examination of cinema, an advertising campaign, and digital storytelling. Introducing her argument with Audre Lorde's words about women of color feminism as the "house of difference" and a turn to Brent Hayes Edwards's insights into diasporic *décalage,* which he describes as "a changing core of difference; it is the work of differences within unity, an unidentifiable point that is incessantly touched and fingered and pressed" (Edwards qtd. in Keeling 55), Keeling proposes "I=Another" as "an equation in which difference functions in and as the index" (57) for thinking about how identification and disidentification operate within racialized collectives and diasporic formations. She reads *The Fourth World War,* a documentary film that positions antiglobalization struggles in places such as Argentina, South Korea, and Palestine as part of a global collective protest, as producing a "we"—what I would call a *public*—through "a collectively forged faculty of hearing" that begins to break down the divisions between subjects (73). Although Keeling's examination is grounded in examples taken from black cultural studies, these insights into collective identity can productively be transposed onto the field of Asian diaspora studies. As a formation that coheres together generations of people and cultures dispersed throughout the globe, diaspora offers a language of belonging and shared understanding for those who identify as part of it; diaspora is, in other words, one means of creating an intimate public. And yet, given that narratives of diaspora generate their affective power by bringing together generations of people who continue to share a collective identity, what discursive space exists for difference and, more specifically, for recognizing competing registers of diasporic affect and sentiment within Asian Canadian publics? Keeling interprets *The Fourth World War* as leaking various stories into each other in order to produce "in the film's viewers a common sense of solidarity, a desire for an alternative globalization, and an intuition that its achievement is possible through sustained struggle" (70), and I wonder if a similar public exists in an Asian Canadian context, one capable of embracing diasporic *décalage* and still being moved affectively and toward forms of social and political action.

In this chapter, I turn to Asian Canadian and Asian American art and literature to engage with differences in relation to diasporic memory and sociability, focusing specifically on how Asian North American publics are formed through their relation to an imagined Asia, and how this informs their locations within North America and as part of a transnational network. In order to think through these social negotiations, I rely on two primary examples. I begin with installations by David Khang, an Asian Canadian visual artist, to work through the transnational circulation of affect for a Korean diaspora. Khang's work is provocative for what it suggests about the resistance from various publics to racialized feelings in the aftermath of global war, whether they are tied to 9/11 or the Korean War. My other point of departure is *The Foreign Student* (1998), a novel by Asian American writer Susan Choi that explores the illegibility of the Korean War within the American South. While Khang's and Choi's works explore common questions about the meaning and memory of the Korean War, they situate them within different temporal and spatial circuits, thereby underlining a range of ways for conceptualizing the Korean diaspora as a social formation. In my discussions of Khang's art and Choi's fiction, I sketch out an ongoing conversation about social intimacy and shared worldviews for minor publics caught between diaspora and migration.

As this chapter engages with Asian diasporas as they circulate throughout Canada and America, it extends the discussion from the previous chapter about how an Asian social imaginary moves across the Canadian-U.S. border. There are, however, two crucial differences between the chapters worth underscoring. First, chapter 2 scrutinizes the reactions of Asian Canadian and Asian American publics to the anti-Asian sentiments of dominant Canadian and American publics. This anti-Asian sentiment circulates beyond national borders, galvanizing minor publics into existence and pushing them into a hemispheric conversation. While this chapter also explores how an Asian Canadian social imaginary is shaped, in part, through its dialogue with Asian America, this particular conversation about Asian diasporas does not emerge in direct response to the anti-Asian feelings of dominant publics. Without dismissing the need to remain cognizant of the important material and symbolic differences between Asian diasporas in Canada and the United States, I take as my point of departure for this chapter diasporic conversations as they circulate within and beyond national borders. To return to my framing of *Asian Canadian* as a heuristic category in my introduction, as the *Asian* in *Asian Canadian* always operates as a term that defers belonging within *Canada* and is imagined as part of a diaspora that exists elsewhere, this chapter investigates how the logics and affects of diaspora shape Asian Canadian publics. Second, the chapters differ in their examinations of popular and "high" cultural examples. Whereas the previous chapter explores Asian Canadian publics as they emerge through print and digital media and interrogates conversations occurring on the Internet and in newspaper columns and magazines, this chapter uses art and literature to understand diaspora and migration as differing, but overlapping, social formations. And while Khang and Choi focus specifically on the Korean diaspora to probe collective identities fostered through memories, both firsthand and "prosthetic," to borrow a term from Alison Landsberg, I contend that their artistic engagements also have striking implications for Asian diasporas as forms of public intimacy. Their creative work questions diasporic investments by critically examining what it means to identify or want to be read as Korean outside of Korea, thereby drawing into public view the fragility of diasporic formations.

The Art of David Khang

Image 1: A black-and-white photograph of an Asian woman sitting at a desk, books in the foreground and a crutch leaning against a wall in the background. This image has been reproduced and affixed onto multiple pairs of underarm crutches just below the pads.

Image 2: Two juxtaposed images of an Asian man holding North and South Korean flags while clad in a military uniform and standing in front of a framed newspaper clipping.[1] These images are taken from two different projects by Vancouver-based artist David Khang, and are ones that I find my thoughts drifting to repeatedly after hearing Khang give an artist talk to my graduate seminar in the fall of 2010.[2]

Figure 2. David Khang, original black-and-white photograph, circa 1970, used in the *Mom's Crutch* installation. All photos by David Khang.

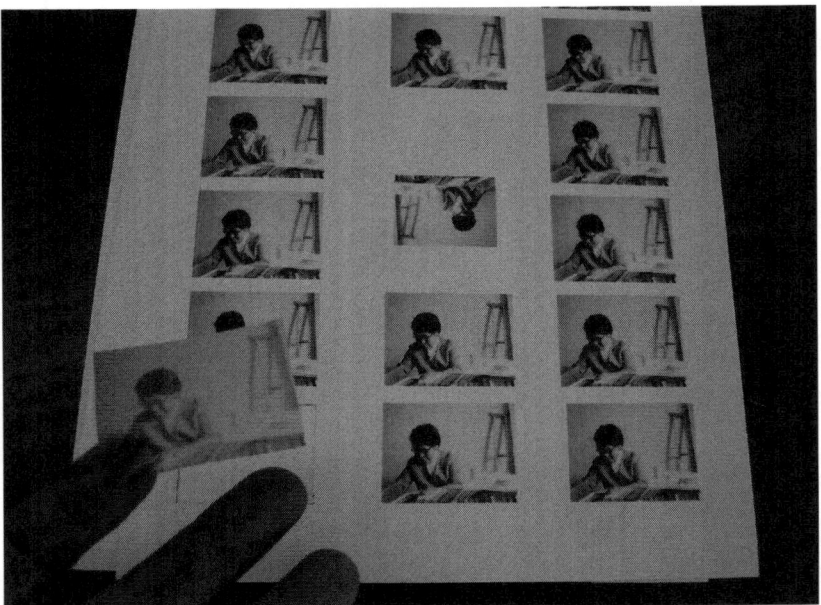

Figure 3. David Khang, 2003. Image made into stickers for the *Mom's Crutch* installation. All photos by David Khang.

Figure 4. David Khang, 2003. Stickers attached to crutches for the *Mom's Crutch* installation. All photos by David Khang.

Figure 5. David Khang, 2007. *A Wrong Place (Greening the DMZ)*, 2007. Green Line, Nicosia, Cyprus. All photos by Bill Greene.

Khang's narrative of the first project, *Mom's Crutch* (2004), stays with me in a particularly persistent fashion, resonating in the way that moments of unexpected intimacy often do. And in addition to its emotional residue, this project also leaves me with a set of provocative questions about the stylization of racialized feeling in particular places and the relation between racialized affects and the dominant cultural grammars of spaces and generations.

The first image is of Khang's own mother. He found the photograph after she passed away, coincidentally after having a dream in which she "appeared happy and well. Oddly enough, her legs were amputated at her knees, and she was calmly and deftly balancing herself on a pair of crutches" (Khang, *Mom's Crutch*). This found image then became the basis of an art project in her memory, one Khang initially envisioned as taking the shape of a roomful of crutches. When enough crutches could not be found to mount such an installation, this idea was discarded; instead, following a suggestion made by Harrell Fletcher, Khang opted to take "a quieter, more ephemeral approach" by turning the image into small stickers that he affixed onto the crutches that he had already amassed (Khang, *Mom's Crutch*). The crutches were returned to the secondhand stores they had originally been found in, and the project will be considered complete when the next owners of the crutches see the stickers. The potential formation of a public through the circulation of this image, a small yet deeply personalized gesture that makes possible intimate connections between strangers, is an idea that I am deeply moved by. I am even more intrigued by this open-ended art project because it was begun in the United States while the events of 9/11 were unfolding, and given this timing, I cannot help but be struck by the radical differences between the forms of grieving, both in terms of technique and scale, undertaken by Khang and the American nation-state.

In the photograph of Khang's mother, she sits at a desk, surrounded by books, and looks down. While not a posed portrait, the image nonetheless invokes the genre and idealizes the subject in a similar fashion because the mother working contentedly at her desk is a serene figure that is simultaneously maternal and a model minority. In gazing at the sheet of stickers bearing the mother's image, I am confronted by the multiplicity of Asian subjects that we potentially can feel for. In fixing these images onto crutches, Khang takes what Sara Ahmed calls the "stickiness of emotions," the ability of emotions to "'stick' as well as move" (*Cultural Politics* 4), quite literally; the gaze of an artistic son mourning his mother is shared with anonymous viewers who are invited to explore their own potential attachments to this image. This art project, by making mobile the image of Khang's mother via a number of crutches, poses intriguing questions about collective feeling and prosthetic memory that are particularly useful if we ask them in relation to diaspora. According to Alison Landsberg, prosthetic memory is a form of social memory that individuals possess even though they have not undergone the actual experiences. In using the crutch, a basic prosthesis, as a key component in this project, *Mom's Crutch* queries how these memories move and, in turn, are able to move us. In relocating this image from its original location in the archive of family photographs to a secondhand store that sells crutches, the found photograph becomes a potential catalyst for memory work in other subjects while still carrying the traces of its own memories. As Walter Benjamin notes of a photograph of nineteenth-century photographer Dauthendey and his model, "the spectator feels an irresistible compulsion to look for the tiny spark of chance, of the here and now, with which reality has, as it were, seared the character in the picture; to find that imperceptible point at which, in the immediacy of that long-past moment, the future so persuasively inserts itself that, looking back, we may rediscover it" ("Short History" 7), I also find myself looking at *Mom's Crutch* and feeling inexplicably connected to it. In his piece "A Short History of Photography," Benjamin begins to work through his seminal concept of the aura, defining it as "a peculiar web of space and time: the unique manifestation of a distance, however near it may be" (20), a move that asks how we are positioned in relation to the photograph as both viewers of art and witnesses of history. *Mom's Crutch* provocatively asks what it means to share our attachments and memories, and transform them into the basis of new and complex forms of diasporic subjectivity.

The second image is taken from *A Wrong Place: Greening the DMZ*, a performance that is part of a series of site-specific performances called *Wrong Places* (2007–12) that struggle to expand the linkages between memory and place while still holding onto the particular histories of regions and their political struggles. First performed in 2007 in Nicosia, Cyprus, the project engages with the condition of divided nations. Here, Khang sutures together representations of the Republic of Cyprus and the Turkish Republic of Northern Cyprus with those of the Republic of Korea and the Democratic People's Republic of Korea in order to bring into sharp relief their common histories of division, colonialism, and military occupation. While Khang acknowledges the deep differences that distinguish these nations, his position is that we need "only to take a leap of imagination, [in order to] . . . juxtapose these two places together 'wrongly'" (Khang, *A Wrong Place* 2007a). He invites us then to contemplate what these comparisons might mean in "an era of global mobility" by asking, "how do historically specific sites 'travel'? Is there a 'right' place to be situated?" (2007a). Jarring loose memory from meaning and place, all five of the performances that currently constitute *Wrong Places* encourage us to see the historical patterns that connect global spaces and consequently reinterpret postcolonial relations as we leap.

Because *Mom's Crutch* is such an emotionally tenacious piece for me, I cannot help but notice in retrospect just how different the tenor of my response is to both *A Wrong Place* and *Wrong Places* as a whole. I am, in fact, profoundly disturbed to realize that while the images from *Wrong Places* push me in all kinds of intellectual directions, they do not provoke any visceral reactions even though they raise pressing issues of social justice, political representation, and ideological violence. Taken together, these two projects are highly suggestive for thinking about the complex formations of publics, particularly for racialized participants, and how we are able to feel for and within them. I route this discussion of postcolonial intimacies and the problem of "Asia" as a site of alterity through these art projects because *Mom's Crutch* and *Wrong Places* speak to the geopolitics of feeling and the local and global structures that shape memory. Moreover, the levels, scales, and styles that *Mom's Crutch* and *Wrong Places* use to address their publics underscore the need to spatialize our discussions of postcolonial intimacies and affect, and locate them within particular histories and geographical contexts if we are to understand how imperial knowledges continue to shape global politics and possibilities. I share Diana Brydon's hope that "a strong sense of global entanglements can potentially create a new vision of community" (1002) and it is in this spirit that I turn to Khang's art, hopeful that it can help us work through the nature of our shared histories, competing and overlapping desires, and global entanglements.

In Lisa Lowe's influential and much-cited essay "The International within the National," she notes the tendency in the United States to represent Asians within either a national or a global frame, even though it would be much more appropriate to simultaneously draw on both. The persistent portrayal of racialized immigration to America as a recent phenomenon, for example, demonstrates an amnesiac tendency with respect to the long history of American imperialism in Asia as well as other parts of the world. Lowe works against understandings of Asian immigration that employ such singular focuses by reminding us that Asia has long since occupied multiple positions in relation to the United States; since the end of WWII, for example, Asia has been viewed as a threatening international economic and military competitor and served as a source of cheap labor used to power the American domestic economy (Lowe, "International" 35). Given this protracted yet neglected history of Asian exploitation by America, one that occurs irrespective of borders, Lowe "asks that the 'newness' of Asian immigration be 'de-reified,' that the history of new racialization be connected with the older one, and more importantly, that it be connected with the history of struggles against that racialization" (Lowe, "International" 45). Clearly, then, Asia and the United States exist in a prolonged and disavowed state of intimacy.

We would be wise to heed Lowe's suggestion to be conscious of how Asian American relations always unfold on various terrains at the same time, especially when engaging in debates about current American imperialist practices and working through the possibilities of postcolonial resistance. I am particularly interested in her proposition that we connect together new and old struggles against racialization, but wonder how such a feat might be accomplished, especially given the affective dimensions of such an undertaking. What do representations of Asia reveal about the likelihood of postcolonial intimacy, despite or perhaps because of comparable historical and ongoing experiences of imperial practices that colonize public imaginations? I turn to Khang's projects in order to begin dissecting this problem, in part because *Wrong Places* and *Mom's Crutch* draw attention to the relative paucity of Korean War representations[3] and the excess of 9/11 representations within the North American imagination; moreover, these competing representations of war and suffering shape public understandings of loss more broadly. For this reason, *Mom's Crutch* with its images left for strangers to notice is a powerful intervention in new and old racializations. The project uses ephemeral and vulnerable personal memories to transform strangers into an intimate public, and although the stickers as material signifiers lack permanence, the contributions they make to the politics of global feeling are potentially quite lasting. Circulating in the aftermath of September 11, this project puts on the table pressing questions about how we remember, what it is that we feel, and how we might engage in intimate dialogues about racialized lives, ones that need to be asked if we are to move outside the kinds of pathologizing racial discourses that saturate the present moment.[4] Khang's other project, *Wrong Places*, pushes this line of investigation in a somewhat different direction by drawing attention to etiquettes of remembering and the tendency to naturalize commemorative practices as belonging to particular places, an act of claiming that requires that we disregard the comparable nature of postcolonial experiences. *Wrong Places* interrogates the territorialization of memory through its representations of the 1945 Korean partition and the Korean War (1950–53) as essentially emotionally indecipherable events—albeit for distinct reasons and in different ways—for Koreans in Korea, the Korean diaspora, and Canadian and American publics. Both projects speak to the place of racialized subjects within local and global cultural memories under American imperialism: *Mom's Crutch* by asking how we might mark racialized lives lost not as a consequence of 9/11, but nonetheless still in a post-9/11 moment; and *Wrong Places* by demanding that we finally take notice of and responsibility for the affective, social, and political aftermath in North and South Korea. In this fashion, these art projects query whether it is possible to care about minor lives that exist outside imperialist narratives of loss and, if so, what might come of such feelings. *Minor lives* here is used as a term akin to what Ann Cvetkovich calls "small dramas," those which "draw attention to how structural forms of violence are so frequently lived, how their invisibility or normalization is another part of their oppressiveness" ("Public Feelings" 464). *Mom's Crutch* and *Wrong Places* demonstrate the range of ways in which subjects are rendered invisible, forgotten about, and positioned outside the limits of public feelings as figures the dominant public can neither feel for or with.

Public Structures, Public Feelings

Both of Khang's projects highlight the structures of feeling that shape how we feel loss, as overwhelming in the case of *Mom's Crutch* and nearly absent in *Wrong Places,* thereby getting at the problem of being outside the dominant emotional culture of a particular place. In his brief essay in *Marxism and Literature,* Raymond Williams sketches out how sentiments, affects, and emotions provide structures of feeling for generations. While these cultural feelings often refuse dominant representation, Williams reminds us that "they do not have to await definition, classification, or rationalization before they exert palpable pressures and set effective limits on experience and on action" (132). By analyzing active social negotiations and the connections between emergent and dominant cultural forms, "Structures of Feeling" draws to our attention the range of relations that exists between felt and formal meanings and beliefs and values (132). Williams's concept provides a vocabulary for working through ideas about feeling, racialized representations, and intimate publics generated by Khang's work, and this is especially valuable since the art projects reveal how feelings are, to an extent, specific to places. As a piece that explores grief, *Mom's Crutch* demonstrates that some diasporic and North American individuals and collectives inhabit similar emotional spaces. This is important because while *Mom's Crutch* mourns Khang's mother rather than those that perished as part of September 11, the piece diverges only in terms of who it feels for, not for what it feels. *Mom's Crutch* then expresses emotions that are still intelligible within the emotional landscape of post-9/11 North America even though it directs these feelings to different ends.

If *Mom's Crutch* indexes the presence of common feelings shared by diasporic and nondiasporic subjects, then *Wrong Places* can be seen as performing a contradictory kind of work as it recognizes affective differences in a manner that suggests that emotions cannot simply be extended across the Pacific. *Wrong Places* illustrates Williams's insight that "no generation speaks quite the same language as its predecessors" (131), while expanding it to include geographic differences. It is perhaps useful to note that in his brief essay, Williams provides a more detailed explanation of the sentimental differences between generational structures of feeling, writing that it is

> a particular quality of social experience and relationship, historically distinct from other particular qualities, which gives the sense of a generation or of a period. The relationships between this quality and the other specifying historical marks of changing institutions, formations, and beliefs, and beyond these the changing social and economic relations between and within classes, are again an open question: that is to say, a set of specific historical questions. (131)

This is key when thinking about *Wrong Places* and the potential for postcolonial intimacies; for while experiences of conflict in various communities and nations might be comparable, structures of feeling are site specific. Consequently then, what kinds of diasporic, national, and intranational conversations can take place given how cultural grammars shape exchanges within publics dispersed in both temporal and spatial terms? Khang poses this question when, for instance, he draws parallels between Korean and Cypriot partitions in the first site-specific performance held in Nicosia. And a similar question is asked in the second iteration of *Wrong Places,* albeit from another angle, as the performance uses Martin Luther King Jr.'s landmark speech to underscore very different dimensions of the Korean conflict. "I Have (Had) a Dream" (performed in Edmonton in 2008) puts African American civil rights into dialogue with Korean history and politics as the American presidential elections that culminated in an Obama victory were then under way. The third and fourth versions of *Wrong Places* take place in Santiago, Chile (2008), and Montreal, Canada (2010), and gesture toward the 1973 coup d'état against President Allende, the 1970 October Crisis (triggered when members of the Front de libération du Québec [FLQ] kidnapped the British trade commissioner as part of an effort to further Quebec separatism), and the varying degrees of collaboration between military and government in all three countries. And the fifth version staged in Mexico City in 2012 references the 1968 student uprising and massacre that occurred at Tlatelolco Plaza, Mexico City, just prior to the opening of the summer Olympic Games. The project is still potentially in process as Khang remains open to the idea of performing *Wrong Places* in additional spaces and inserting more histories into this conversation. It must be noted that, in the very form of the *Wrong Places* project as performance art, Khang already underscores the slipperiness of memory and the challenge of sharing feelings across generations and throughout space. The ephemerality of the performances, ones that only exist momentarily and then afterward as traces in photographs, videos, and the memories of those that observed them, frustrate attempts to preserve moments and histories. In his reflections on the work of conceptual and performance art in the late 1960s, Nick Kaye writes that the "fundamental aspects of live performance, including engagements with 'real time' and 'real space' and the simultaneous presence of performer and viewer, became aligned to experimental art's critical interrogation of the terms and conditions under which visual art takes place" (175). Similarly, Khang's *Wrong Places* engages with the specificity of memory work by asking how memories shift depending on when and where they are encountered, and, moreover, how the artist's body as a repository of historical and racialized traces is read differently in these particular sites.

While the five performances that compose *Wrong Places* offer ways to enter into dialogue about how the lingering experiences of colonialism, imperialism, and national conflict are felt on multiple levels and scales, not all audience members wholeheartedly embraced these openings. While it is difficult to gauge the responses of audience members for a host of reasons (Who is measuring these responses? How are facial expressions and comments being interpreted? Might one facial expression that seems to indicate displeasure actually be a sign of deep thought? And what about changing responses as perhaps initial reactions give way to other feelings?), Khang's observation that responses included individuals seeming amused, perturbed, angry, and contemplative but not actively engaged are nonetheless worth taking into account as they note the presence of both interest and resistance ("Re: Images"). The range of audience reactions signals the complex nature of the negotiations that shape postcolonial exchanges and the uneven global intimacies produced as a result. *Wrong Places* can therefore be read as a working through of what Lowe astutely phrases as "the particular loss of the intimacies of four continents" ("Worldliness" 141). In her essay "The Worldliness of Intimacy," Lowe provides a compelling overview of nineteenth-century global relations as they unfolded under colonial rule and moreover explores various meanings historically attached to the term *intimacy*; namely, spatial proximity, bourgeois privacy, and cross-racial alliance. I am especially interested in her third reading of intimacy with its emphasis on the colonial desire to disentangle existing cross-racial intimacies because they threaten bourgeois domesticity:

> The repeated injunctions that different groups must be divided and boundaries kept distinct indicate that colonial administrators imagined as dangerous the

sexual, labouring and intellectual contacts among slaves, indentured, non-white peoples. The racial classifications in the archive arose, thus, in this context of the colonial need to prevent these unspoken "intimacies" among the colonized. ("Worldliness" 136)

Because the need to forget the link between earlier colonial endeavors and ongoing imperial practices is built into liberal structures, "[t]he affirmation of the desire for freedom is so inhabited by the forgetting of its conditions of possibility that every narrative articulation of freedom is haunted by its burial, by the violence of forgetting. What we know as 'race,' 'gender' and 'nation' are the traces of modern liberalism's amnesia" ("Worldliness" 140). This structure means we participate in daily acts of both remembering and forgetting imperial violence, even as we struggle for social justice.

By rehearsing part of "The Worldliness of Intimacy," my intention is to bring Lowe's argument about the deliberate foreclosure of intimacy into conversation with her earlier thoughts about the need to make visible connections between new and old, and national and international racializations, and use these insights to examine *Wrong Places*. By weaving together poetry, photographs, military apparel, and other signifiers connected to the Korean demilitarized zone with those of the FLQ crisis, Chilean coup d'état, and the Cyprian division, Khang's performances underscore how pursuit of postcolonial intimacy requires complex negotiations with site-specific social memory and structures of feeling. As he moves through the streets of Nicosia, Edmonton, Santiago, Montreal, and Mexico City while bearing traces of the Korean partition, Khang encourages the remembering of conflict and promotes a communion of feeling. It is a call to reframe our perceptions of ourselves and each other as comrades struggling against ongoing histories of imperialism, and it hopes that we will be moved by the spectacle of another's suffering and loss. While the ethics of such a reimagining are compelling, it is not easy to see precisely how we, as a global audience, might begin to undertake this kind of work. How are we—meaning both those that identify and do not identify as Korean—to move from wanting to actually remembering conflicts, seeing them as part of the present, and feeling with other people? In the case of Korean history, this is a particularly tricky proposition given the relative dearth of Korean War representations and that lengthy histories of invasion and imperialism have produced very specific kinds structures of feeling in North and South Korea, shaped to some extent by their conflicting political ideologies. As many critics have noted, Japanese colonization was replaced at the end of WWII by an American occupation and this U.S. military presence still has not left Korea. As Grace Cho notes in *Haunting the Korean Diaspora,* the successive colonial regimes played significant roles in shaping a civil war that in 1950 became "a conflict taken up by Cold War superpowers, and for the United States, this would be an important moment in its long-term commitment to war.... The Korean War set into motion a massive migration in which millions of people fled in search of safety" (9).

This problem of cultural and racialized knowledges generated in and with respect to Korea is one that *Ends of Empire* (J. Kim) also takes up, approaching it through the lens of Asian American cultural texts that respond to the Cold War. Also drawing on Lowe's influential essay "The International within the National," Jodi Kim locates Asian migration to the United States within the larger context of American Cold War imperialism, reading Asian arrivals as the result of American displacements and suggests that the tangled imperialist production of devastated Asias and American havens "inspire dreams of the ultimately unknowable, of what might and could have been had 'you' never been there, and 'we' never been here" (12). According to J. Kim, American imperialism produced a tripartite structure consisting of the United States, racialized minorities within the United States, and subjugated nations positioned respectively as colonizer/imperialist, internal colony, and neocolony (16). The beginning of the Korean War was a key moment in U.S. foreign policy as it helped alleviate economic woes that had troubled the West since the 1920s (26). While the millions of Korean civilians killed during the Korean War and problems with postwar development are serious consequences, there are also numerous other effects that the country has had to reckon with for the past half century. And precisely because these devastating outcomes are necessary to empire—indeed, they act as its conditions of possibility in many ways—they are costs that largely have been forgotten by the North American public. Yet J. Kim, like Khang, refuses to minimize these losses and demands that we be conscious of the imperial logic at work by asking: "What does it mean to want to represent or 'remember' a war that has been 'forgotten' and erased in the US popular imaginary, but has been transgenerationally seared into the memories of Koreans and Korean Americans, and experienced anew every day in a still-divided Korea?" (J. Kim 34). She repeatedly emphasizes the centrality of these events for Koreans and the Korean diaspora they produced, and points out that the forgetting of this war is particularly egregious given that (1) the United States was instrumental in developing this conflict in Korea, and (2) that the war is far from officially over. Without taking away from J. Kim's necessary and provocative question, I wish to reformulate it slightly in order to focus on the consequences that this forgetting has had for relations between Koreans in Korea and the Korean diaspora. If the Korean War is largely a forgotten war, how exactly does it shape memory or structure feeling? And if J. Kim asks us to consider what it means that the Korean War is at once an event that was formative and traumatic for Koreans and the Korean diaspora it produced (J. Kim 143), and utterly bereft of meaning for most North Americans, I emphasize that this latter group also includes many Korean North Americans. While the war has, indeed, been seared into Korean diasporic memory on one level, it is still a memory that is difficult to actively remember on another.

Site-Specific Affects

To think about the phenomenon of a diaspora disengaged in a certain way from its own historic moment of production,[5] I turn my attention to *han*, an emotion that has been claimed as uniquely Korean by many people. In her essay on Korean Americans in the aftermath of the Los Angeles riots, Elaine Kim describes *han* as "the sorrow and anger that grow from the accumulated experiences of oppression" (215). *Han* refers to a common and familiar cultural affliction that is recognized by Koreans as having serious outcomes, and when those are fatal, "it is called dying of *hwabyong*, a disease of frustration and rage following misfortune" (E. Kim 215). More often though, *han* seems to be a persistent condition characterized by repressiveness and without the possibility of an explosive and therefore cathartic resolution (Chu 97). For E. Kim, the condition of *han* takes on a new sense of urgency during the uprisings that occurred as a response to the Rodney King verdicts, as this charged racialized context rudely awakened Korean immigrants to the realities of American inequities and made them feel this familiar condition of simultaneous rage, frustration, and oppression. The destruction of Korean businesses and property and the absence of police protection served as a "baptism" into becoming American (E. Kim 219), and contradicted American claims that the United States was unlike all other countries because it practiced absolute equality. One particularly intriguing aspect of E. Kim's argument is the implication that the more serious problem for Koreans was not the actual social inequality, but rather that many had been made vulnerable because they believed that America was truly democratic and thus different from South Korea. The Los Angeles riots were a moment in which Koreans "had to learn . . . that, as in South Korea, protection in the US is by and large for the rich and powerful" (E. Kim 219). This interpretation of the disillusionment of Koreans suggests that *han*, as a structure of feeling, can and does travel from Korea to North America. At the same time, however, it offers a limited circuit in that only certain generations can actually feel *han*. E. Kim's essay focuses on what the charged racialized tensions reveal about the supposed impossibility for Koreans to become American and how these individuals continue to experience *han,* thus perhaps demonstrating a different way that the international operates within the national.

In a sense, Khang's *Wrong Places* reverses this scenario to present the peculiar challenge diasporic Koreans confront when they try to feel Korean, at least in the way that they might imagine a previous generation feels. As a structure of feeling, *han* is glaringly inaccessible for the offspring of Korean immigrants. And yet, while subsequent generations might not feel *han* proper (an absence of feeling that gestures to a host of other differences that distinguish generations as well as Koreans in Korea from a Korean diaspora), these generations may still know *han,* both on an intellectual level and as a sentiment whose effects have shaped their lives in a myriad of ways. This phenomenon of knowing and feeling secondhand is one that Seo-Young Chu coins as "postmemory *han.*" By adapting Marianne Hirsch's concept of postmemory, Chu looks at the transmission of this specific form of Korean grief across generations. She suggests that the legacy of *han* for a postmemory generation is doubled because it involves the pain of seeing parents suffer and a profound sense of guilt for not suffering alongside them. This complicated affective positioning causes Chu to wonder, "How can a second-generation Korean American feel wounded by the Demilitarized Zone (DMZ)—as though the wound were still raw, as though the 38th parallel cut her own body in half?" (99). I think, though, that postmemory *han* illustrates the ways in which diasporic Koreans *have* had their bodies cut in half as they are trapped in a situation of knowing emotions they cannot feel, being haunted by histories they cannot access, and embodying both new and older forms of racialization. If, as Fredric Jameson has asserted, "history is what hurts" (102),[6] then Khang's projects demonstrate the complex ways in which history hurts and, curiously, perhaps even how the inability to feel that pain is a form of hurt. Watching footage of Khang performing *Wrong Places* and interrogating the divisions of countries, families, and individuals, I find myself yearning to feel the emotions he enacts and, in some sense, to feel the disruptions caused by imperialism in Asia, rather than to simply know them. But perhaps the absence of palpable emotions is precisely how these disruptions are felt given that diaspora involves dispersal not only in terms of geography and generation, but also the translation of affect and emotion. As Walter Benjamin suggests in his introduction to a translation of Baudelaire, the relationship between original and translation is neither about absolute fidelity nor seeking "likeness to the original" but rather one in which "the original undergoes a change" (*Illuminations* 73).

If affective grammars are specific to places and generations, then what possibilities exist for fostering intimacies between them and across the globe? Can a postcolonial public develop circuits that connect racialized subjects in terms of both knowledge and feeling? And can these binds ever be tighter than the ones that tie territories to imperial powers? Contemplating *Mom's Crutch* and *Wrong Places* makes me acutely aware of how I feel for, or perhaps more accurately, as part of, a North American center, and experience emotions akin to Canadian and American mourning much more easily than I feel for a Korean colony grappling with difficult histories that take the inscrutable form of *han*. Expanding upon Sianne Ngai's framing of "the difference between affect and emotion . . . as a modal difference of intensity or degree, rather than a formal difference of quality of kind," it seems clear that Khang's two projects provoke feelings that differ in terms of intensity as well as structure and style (27). In other words, through these works, I am forced to recognize the ways in which I, as a second-generation Korean Canadian, produce and reproduce the Asian/non-Asian (or Self and Other) binary through and within myself in complex, disorienting, and infuriating ways. The disconnectedness that Khang demonstrates as existing between postcolonial sites, made clear through the awkward experiences of secondhand feelings, also extends to an absence of intimacy within the postcolonial subject. These confusing and complicated affects are signs of a self-Orientalizing that still equates difference with the Other and Asia. As Naoki Sakai reminds us, the possibility of reconfiguring Asia as other than Other is riddled with difficulties given the extensive ways in which the West-Asia binary is sutured together: "The historical colonization of Asia by the West is not something accidental to the essence of Asia; it is essential to the possibility called Asia. Insofar as the *post* of postcoloniality is not confused with 'that which comes after' in chronological ordering, Asia was a *postcolonial* entity from the outset" (791). Thinking of an Asian subject then requires moving beyond the limits of a Western imagination that conceives of Asia in these ideological terms.

Considered together, *Mom's Crutch* and *Wrong Places* present the problem of feeling on the fringes of a North American public, of being shaped by those structures of feeling but disciplined as Asian through discourses of race. And at the same time, they also suggest that to be located within North American structures of feeling means to also be afflicted with amnesia about violent imperialist practices, at least on the level of affect. Khang's projects thus ask us to contemplate the affective consequences of inhabiting multiple positions as and in relation to Asia, always simultaneously if not consciously, and, moreover, of producing ourselves as Asian. To put this in another way, while we might be able to clearly comprehend on an intellectual level how international and national frames operate concurrently, we are not easily able to feel that knowledge and, additionally, we are compelled to forget that we do not feel these things. After reflecting on Khang's representations of Asian American relations and the complicated violences that underpin these imperialist circuits, I find myself wondering when it is that deliberate forgetting turns into actual not knowing. What *Mom's Crutch* and *Wrong Places* throw into relief is how imperialist structures of forgetting are structures of feeling that normalize a host of violences and encourage various forms of neglect. Perhaps, then, what is necessary in order to realize intimacies between postcolonial subjects is for a structure of remembering to shape global economies of caring. In such a scenario, we might find ourselves located within spaces of public feeling and also able to care about "minor" lives, regardless of where or when any of us are situated, without neglecting others.

Susan Choi's *The Foreign Student*

Like Khang's visual art, Susan Choi's *The Foreign Student* raises questions about how diasporic subjects negotiate multiple structures of feeling and memory. These various texts—*Mom's Crutch, Wrong Places,* and *The Foreign Student*—examine the curious legacy of the Korean War, one that remains almost completely illegible for many audiences despite the profound impacts it continues to have upon individual and collective psyches. Together, they ask how, even though details about this period have largely been suppressed or even erased from historical accounts,[7] a palpable affective residue continues to circulate within multiple social memories and, furthermore, what this might mean. *The Foreign Student* explores the complex construction of the Korean War, and more specifically, of it as an event produced through the intertwining of narratives that are told explicitly, memories that are rarely or perhaps never shared even as they are remembered constantly, and stories that are noticeably absent (and by this I mean as ones that must logically exist but are difficult, if not almost impossible, to find). Filtered through an omniscient narrator, the novel draws attention to the discrepancies between the accounts of the war that its protagonist, Chang Ahn, shares publicly with American audiences and those that he reflects upon in private. Chang hones his ability to select which version of a story to disseminate while working as a translator for Korean and American news agencies; he learns that audiences overseas desire particular kinds of stories about Korea—namely, ones that uphold existing beliefs about the vast cultural differences between Asia and the West, the necessity of American aid and intervention, and the spread of democracy as synonymous with the pursuit of social justice. That historical accuracy is of secondary importance to Chang and American readers becomes abundantly clear when, after a press conference,

Chang feeds a reporter from the *New York Times* a story about North Korean guerillas surrendering to the South Korean military police once they realized the error of their ways, a tale that both men realize is ludicrous (Choi 84). The exchange between Chang and the American reporter drives home Daniel Kim's point in his reading of Choi's novel that "what the narrator calls 'a potted history of the war'" can also be considered "as a selective translation of Korean events that serve a colonial purpose" (555).

Once Chang migrates to the American South in 1955, little changes in the sense that Chang remains a storyteller rather than a historian invested in accuracy. An international student at the University of the South in Sewanee, Tennessee, Chang holds a scholarship that covers his tuition and living expenses; in return, he is expected to give talks about Korea to various church groups across the region. The Korean history that he presents is crafted as 'an exciting, simple minded, morally unambiguous story" whose "plot was reduced and the number of details increased" (52). The considerable creative license that Chang exercises is evidenced by the fact that often the photos shown as part of his presentation do not accurately illustrate Chang's comments; for example, the image of the U.S. army that Chang shows to talk about the U.S. landing was taken five years earlier and had originally been captioned as "Liberation feels fine! US and their Soviet allies arrive to clean house in Korea" in reference to the Japanese defeat (52). These details make it clear that the goal of Chang's storytelling is not to revise existing histories of Korea by adding more accurate facts and details; in fact, the absence of a corrective impulse makes me wonder if Choi intends for Chang to promote these flawed histories and share the desire to believe, if not actual belief in, these simplified narratives of history and difference that write the Korean War as a minor, and consequently forgettable, episode of American heroism. By paring away the vexing details of wartime experiences that he is both incapable of and uninterested in sharing with his readers and listeners, Chang contributes a set of partially true narratives to this project. And as demonstrated by the optimistic photograph of liberation from Japanese occupation that Chang deliberately pairs with his overview of MacArthur's landing, Chang firmly commits himself to the work of promoting this particular narrative of the Korean War while remaining conscious of his dissimulations. This specific example of MacArthur's landing is intriguing since the novel informs us that Chang's actual experience of this event is anything but joyful. When U.S. troops landed at Inchon, Chang had been hiding for three months in a hole in his own home, trying to avoid being captured by the members of the Korean People's Army (KPA) that had taken over the house when it had captured the rest of the city. What Chang fails to tell his church audiences is that after months of lying cramped within the walls of his own home and in pools of his own urine and feces, MacArthur's liberation of Seoul literally freed him from the confines of his own domestic prison, but that this felt like "the beginning of a fresh agony as his body fought the alternation of light and dark and shrank in terror from the open space where nothing touched against him" because by then, "[h]e'd grown used to his hole" (103). Disseminating the celebratory narrative of Americans rescuing Seoul ironically saves Chang from explaining how, for him, the moment of freedom was almost unwelcome. And it is in this fashion that Chang becomes a conduit for Korean history without ever sharing his own personal story, liberating himself from the imperative to share emotionally taxing details about the journey he actually took in order to become the sole Korean student at the University of the South in Sewanee.

In disseminating these largely fabricated and thus simpler stories of Korea, Chang practices a kind of emotional avoidance (that is certainly not unique to either him or Korea in the 1950s) that permits him to metaphorically remain in his preliberation hole. This willed amnesia is further highlighted when Chang opts to introduce himself to his new acquaintances in Sewanee as Chuck, a renaming that had occurred earlier by Peterfield, his former boss at the United States Information Service in South Korea. When Katherine (a local woman that Chang develops a friendship with and romantic interest in) first meets him, she comments on the illogic of this renaming:

> "Somebody's changed your name from *Chang* to *Chuck*? Was the idea to make it easier to remember? Correct me if I'm wrong," she said to Mrs. Reston, "but you're not going to save any syllables going from 'Chang' to 'Chuck.' You're not even going to save any letters, unless you transliterate the name as the French would. And I don't see why you would want to do that." (9–10)

While this assessment of the shift from Chang to Chuck in terms of its pragmatic value is correct, I believe that Katherine misreads the intentions behind the transformation, which seem to be less concerned with the ease of remembering and more about the ease of forgetting. In Peterfield's case, this is most immediately about forgetting that he is in Korea as part of an impossible effort to report on an incomprehensible war; for Chang, the desire is to forget a history of himself before his encounter with America. It is perhaps worth noting that renaming Chang as Chuck also casts him as the diminutive version of Charles Addison, Katherine's lover, and in this way, reenacts the imperial relation between the United States and Korea on yet another level. Addison is also framed as a version of Chang's father as both men are professors, Addison at the University of the South and Dr. Ahn at Yonsei University, and both possess a deep love of the English language. And while his own father is a man that Chang "never knew whether he loved" or not, Dr. Ahn does manage to pass onto his son a passion for translation (81).

And although Chang avoids articulating these emotionally taxing experiences with those he encounters face to face, electing instead to practice a form of forgetting consistent with a more general amnesia about the Korean War, a certain kind of affective transmission occurs within the text in spite of his efforts. I do not believe that the significance of affective circulation in this context can be overstated given how this movement undoes illusions about individuals being self-contained in terms of their feelings, as well as the assumption that thought and affect are distinct capacities. This interplay is complex because the circulation of affect calls to consciousness an individual's own thoughts, but these "thoughts are not necessarily tied to the affects they appear to evoke. One may as well say that the affects evoke the thoughts" (Brennan 7). This transmission of competing affects, deliberate and unintended, occurs while Chang addresses his church audience. Here, as is conveyed by the earlier passage, Chang strives to convey a sense of positivity to his audience. However, when Katherine unexpectedly enters the room and stands 'looking lost" (Choi 53), Chang's thoughts and emotions escape his control:

> He couldn't remember where he'd left off. The awareness that he was blushing made him blush even more deeply. He wondered if anyone could see it. Often the darkness of his skin seemed to guard his emotions from notion, as if the fact of the color blotted out all that happened within it. He fingered the slide-changer nervously, and the carousel shot ahead, throwing a new picture onto the screen. For a terrifying eternity he stared at this without recognizing what is was. The rough grain of the image, fine rubble, a burial mound.... His gaze crisscrossed it wildly, searching for something that might help him locate himself. (53)

While this is certainly a moment that makes explicit Chang's desire for Katherine, his loss of control over his feelings—and more precisely the disappearance of the carefully orchestrated sense of glee that Chang projects when discussing MacArthur's landing—also occurs because he is receptive to Katherine's sense of displacement.

This scene with Chang and Katherine illustrates a social dynamic that is very different from another storytelling moment that occurs later in the novel when Chang visits Bill Crane's family for Thanksgiving. At the dinner table, Chang recounts a memory about his first experience with fried chicken en route from Juneau to Seattle and the awkwardness of not being able to figure out how to cut into what looked to him "like a bundle of elbows, wobbling with the movements of the plane" (60). Chang's story unquestionably speaks to his out-of-placedness on this flight full of Americans returning home, and this sense of dislocation is reflected in his retelling of this episode as Chang gets lost in his own story, accidently reliving more than he intends. Choi writes, "When he'd started to speak Chuck had only meant to say something, to make a friendly remark, but the longer the story grew the more it seemed to lash about on its own, in unintended directions. He went silent and there was an uncertain pause" (61). And yet, unlike his moment with Katherine, there is no apparent transmission of affect between Chang and the Cranes. Bill instead redirects the conversation toward his struggles with algebra, and even that is easily forgotten as the Cranes then "talked about other things, and the buzz between parents and son rose and covered him over" (61). This failure to transmit affect is perhaps as intriguing as the earlier success between Katherine and Chang for how it draws attention to audiences and the complex task of engaging them. The contrast between Chang's encounters with Katherine and the Cranes questions the nature of public formations; more precisely, it asks us to consider carefully what compels certain individuals to become part of these collectives while others feel no such call, remaining instead impervious to the very same stories and presences. How, in other words, are we to understand the various ways in which individuals are located as historical, social, and affective beings within empires?

While the moment of affective exchange that occurs during Chang's lecture is illuminating for the intimate connection between Chang and Katherine that it reveals, the novel further explores the relationality between these two characters from a number of other angles. Most obviously, the novel's structure suggests that the histories of South Korea and the American South might be read as parallel ones given the civil wars both feature, and that these narratives finally collide through Chang and Katherine's relationship. Their respective national histories mean that Chang and Katherine share an understanding of what it means to grow up in countries torn apart by political strife and overwhelming violence, and also of the fractured psyches produced under these kinds of circumstances. But Chang and Katherine mirror each other in at least one other significant respect; namely, that both grew up in privileged homes in which they no longer reside. For Chang's family, the end of Japanese colonial rule had disastrous consequences for, as part of the *yangban* class, they had benefited considerably from that social structure. Chang's father was deemed a traitor and punished by the new government, a sequence of events that precipitated a decline in his health. And even though the Ahn family is able to physically reclaim their house after the armistice is reached in 1953, the truth is that Chang's childhood home was destroyed long ago and his migration to the United States only formalizes the loss of this space.

While operating in less overt terms, Katherine's story also sutures together individual and national traumas; the affective legacy of Confederate loss is conveyed within the novel through Katherine's narrative, which pivots around sexuality and shame. She is initiated into an adult world of sexuality by Charles Addison, a lengthy affair that begins because she is deeply attracted to Addison, resentful toward her mother's feminine criticisms, and bored of Sewanee. The novel makes us aware of the complicated factors that fan Katherine's desire without taking away from the reprehensible fact that Addison, a grown man, seduced a fourteen-year-old Katherine. When Katherine's mother reads the correspondence between Addison and Katherine, the mother and daughter become estranged and the latter eventually takes up permanent residence in the family's summer home in Tennessee, away from her family, who continue to live in New Orleans. Like Chang, Katherine is a figure that lives in a present acutely aware of the past from which she emerged (and indeed, the very home that she lives in is literally an inheritance bequeathed by her father). Katherine is unable to break permanently with Addison for most of the novel, and there is a strong sense that part of her might have preferred to have never known him at all; this painful tie to an ongoing history of shame and ruptured familial relations is just one of the multiple similarities that link Chang and Katherine.

But even as the novel introduces the possibility of reading these characters as mirrors of each other and as likely allies, it undercuts such an interpretation by refusing to see American and Korean histories as distinct and separate. Chang's memories, which only he and the reader have access to, make it impossible to forget either the formative role that the United States played in the Korean situation or the callous way in which it did so. Here, it is useful to bear in mind Daniel Kim's suggestion that "[r]ather than reading its American narratives of race as somehow mirroring its Korean narrative of civil war, we might consider them both as fragments of a whole—a greater history of the Korean War that exceeds the sum of its parts" (D. Kim 561). For example, we witness Chang remembering his return to the U.S. Information Service office after North Korean forces had been driven out of Seoul and how Peterfield then made it clear that he would not try to protect Chang from being drafted by the South Korean army. Choi's description of Peterfield in this scene effectively summarizes the American attitude toward Korea as a whole:

> They opened the office again without discussing what Chuck thought of as Peterfield's abandonment of him. They never would. But seeing Peterfield that first day, undamaged and unrepentant, struck at him as powerfully as heartbreak. Sometimes his stomach would seem to drop away and there in the void was the realization that he had been discarded. Peterfield must have been affected as well, for their friendship was over. It seemed to have been corrupted by guilt, and the

resentment that a guilty man feels toward the source of his discomfort. Chuck recognized that Peterfield hated him, and why, but the recognition couldn't do him any good. (105)

Peterfield's deep animosity toward Chang emerges at this point in the novel when it becomes impossible to sustain a reading of American and Korean histories as echoing each other. Instead, Choi's text begins to push more forcefully for a recognition of how these histories are produced together and as part of a larger narrative of imperialism. Here, Peterfield's imperviousness to Chang's pain, or more specifically his resistance to the call of guilt, reminds us of the Teflon-like coating that shields the Cranes from Chang's memories of anxiety and displacement and the knowledge that Korean injury and American security are inextricably intertwined.

That such a tendency to frame the relations between the countries in parallel rather than interlaced terms is not simply limited to Peterfield and the Cranes, but also embedded within a dominant American imagination, becomes clear when, during Chang's lecture, he is

> called upon to deliver a clear explanation of the war. It defied explanation. Sometimes he simply skipped over causes, and began, "Korea is a shape just like Florida. Yes? The top half is a Communist state, and the bottom half are fighting for democracy!" He would groundlessly compare the parallel to the Mason-Dixon line, and see every head nod excitedly. "In June 1950, the Communist army comes over the parallel and invades the South. They come by surprise, and get almost all to the sea." (51)

The audience's enthusiastic reception for the idea that the Thirty-Eighth Parallel and the Mason-Dixon line might resemble each other indicates a strong willingness to explore these national histories in comparative terms, perhaps because such a framing absolves these audience members of the responsibility for American imperialism in Korea. These "groundless comparisons" that Chang draws are enticing because they offer the potential for cross-border alliances without demanding that a prior intimacy between these countries be acknowledged.

These examples of Chang's audience and Peterfield outline the strong and dangerous lures of reading the histories of Korea and America in parallel terms and make it apparent that to conceptualize Korean and U.S. histories as distinct entities that converge in the 1950s is to write American imperialism in a way that denies its much longer history. The problem of how to instead write U.S. imperialism in Asia as a project with an extensive and ongoing history is explored in *The Foreign Student*, on the one hand, by the narrative of Chang and Katherine's romance (one in which individuals seek to heal each other by taking solace in their shared vulnerabilities) and, on the other hand, through the stories that outline the larger social structures and political events of Korea and America. By shuttling between these narratives and their attempts to represent the violence of imperial encounters, *The Foreign Student* calls to our attention the multiple obstacles that hinder efforts to produce intimate publics. Even Chang and Katherine—who, as figures struggling with the histories of civil war, shame, and loneliness, bear certain striking similarities to each other and feel instinctively connected—find it difficult to negotiate their respective pasts and move toward more harmonious relations. This stems in part from the fact that Chang and Katherine are located within different racial formations designed to work against each other, and the tensions between these characters and racial formations remind us that to imagine future relations of alliance without interrogating the imperial structures that produce the terms of such encounters is dangerous. Indeed, throughout the course of Chang and Katherine's relationship, we are shown that social and political structures are designed to maintain the status quo and witness how they actively work to minimize disruptions. The novel teaches us that intimate publics cannot come into being without reckoning with the long history of U.S. imperialism throughout the globe given how "*The very identity of the actors depends upon the process of formation and maintenance of hegemony*" (Balibar, "Preface" 4; italics in original).

Diasporas, Asians, the "Partly Colored"

Choi's novel returns us to the problem of relationality in at least one other crucial way. As Leslie Bow notes in her literary study of Asians and the American South, narrative perspective in *The Foreign Student* matters: "Reversing the usual hierarchy of the West as a primary lens through which to read the developing world, Choi situates Asia as a vehicle for a commentary on domestic race relations, here, from the perspective of the interstitial Asian, the foreign student' (169). Channeling the novel through an omniscient narrator that takes as its primary focus Chang's and Katherine's stories not only makes the reader acutely aware of the competing desires at work in these narratives, but also foregrounds the paradigms through which such impulses are articulated. By employing an interstitial perspective, Choi's text simultaneously moves through race relations in the U.S. South and reflects upon the entangled nature of Korean and American histories, thereby unravelling the relations that suture together Asia and America. Choi's text, like Khang's art, generates questions about identification and social formations; but whereas I see the latter engaging with diasporic identification on the levels of politics and affect, the former writes about diasporic disidentification, or perhaps more accurately, about identification in much more singular terms. In *The Foreign Student,* Chang is framed not as part of a wave of migration to the American South, but rather as a lone individual who, after leaving behind his family and friends in Korea, never encounters another Korean figure again. Not only does Chang fail to cross paths with any other Koreans (or Asians at all, for that matter) in Tennessee, but this also remains true when he travels to Chicago and meets Asians in Little Tokyo and Chinatown that are Japanese, Chinese, and even occasionally Filipino, but never Korean. This association configures Chang as a foreign figure for the United States in particular terms—ones that sever him from a Korean collective and rewrite him as part of a more ambiguous or looser Asian immigrant population—that are noteworthy for the kinds of cultural identifications they embrace and those that they refuse. While the Asians that Chang finds in Chicago provide him with a community that he takes temporary refuge in, it is a collective that Chang becomes part of on the basis of shared racialized difference from non–Asian America, and not because they share a common past. The minimizing of these historical connections is underscored by the "grammatically arcane" Japanese (Choi 243) that Chang uses to communicate in Chicago, a language indelibly imprinted with the memories of Japanese colonialism for Koreans of this period, and for Chang in particular, with the failed promise of a prosperous future as what Homi Bhabha might call a mimic man. While race and language provide Chang entry into this community, they do not lead to an investigation of shared histories or the formation of deeper social bonds capable of easing the foreignness that Chang lives. The narrator notes it is uncertain whether Chang's new friends even realize his ethnicity, but that "[i]f these people knew he was Korean, they didn't seem to care" (244).

To explore the implications of Chang's subject formation, one that fails to recognize his specifically Korean dimensions in order to cast him as an Asian diasporic subject, I turn to Lily Cho's discussion of diasporic exceptionality in her essay on Chinese-Trinidadian Canadian filmmaker Richard Fung. Drawing on the work of Caribbean theorist Édouard Glissant to tease out the relations between the individual and collective, Cho asks how we might talk about the "specificity of Chineseness and, more specifically still, Chineseness in Trinidad through the lens of a filmmaker in Canada, without taking refuge in arguments for the unique experiences of Chinese diasporic subjects" ("Underwater Signposts" 191). Glissant opens up avenues for engaging with Fung (and by extension, the relations embedded in diaspora) when Glissant writes about how the experiences of slaves being sacrificed into the sea "became something shared and made us, the descendants, one people among others. People do not live on in exception. Relation is not made up of things that are foreign but of shared knowledge" (Glissant qtd. in Cho, "Underwater Signposts" 192). Here, Glissant suggests that the value of the stories of individual diasporans lies in their ability to make possible particular kinds of relationality. And while Cho fruitfully uses this idea to analyze the forms of knowledge and identifications produced by Fung's work, I suggest that this formulation is reversed in Choi's character of Chang. By writing Chang in terms that emphasize his singularity, the novel describes an alternate scenario in which diasporic relationality is refused, or perhaps more accurately, foreclosed. In the absence of other Koreans in his immediate vicinity and without a context of shared knowledge, Chang struggles to come into being as a subject. We must then ask about the possibilities for living for figures like Chang that can only ever exist as exceptions.

Choi's novel precludes Chang from identifying with a Korean collective by emphasizing his exceptionality within the United States, and this, oddly enough, becomes a way of folding Chang back into the Korean diaspora. Ironically, in his very singularity, Chang echoes President Rhee, the other foreign student that we encounter in the novel[8] (and one whose circumstances resemble Choi's fictional character as Rhee's doctoral tuition fees were waived by Princeton University and his room and board covered by the Princeton Theological Seminary). It is also important to note that Rhee is introduced to the reader of *The Foreign Student* as something of an unpleasant surprise for American forces and strategists:

> Only after installing Rhee as the Republic of Korea's president did the Americans realize he was unmanageable: bellicose, paranoid, and so undiscouragably [sic] determined to declare war on the Communist North that the United States deliberately underequipped his security forces. Rhee's government was repressive, incompetent, and stupendously unpopular. (64–65)

This relation between Rhee and Chang is crucial for how it historicizes the illegibility of Korea for the United States, and yet is one that is easily forgettable for those within the novel. While the American presence in Asia throughout the twentieth century produced very real displacing consequences for those in Asia, Chang's presence in Sewanee baffles the Americans he routinely encounters. As a legacy and repetition of Rhee, a figure framed by the novel as representing the ineptness of U.S. intervention, the illegibility of Chang's presence speaks volumes about how historical memories are buried even as their traces continue to circulate.

That the Korean diaspora is an unreadable phenomenon despite its historical force is a conundrum emphasized by the novel in other ways as well. Most obviously, by positioning Chang within the context of contemporary America, the text reminds us of the familiar problem of writing the Asian within a racial landscape conventionally understood in black and white terms. This challenge is highlighted frequently via the friendship between Chang and Katherine and the romantic possibilities of their relationship. While a mutual attraction between these characters exists, their future as a couple is difficult to envision given the unorthodox nature of this particular kind of interracial romance, the issue of Chang's emasculated identity as an Asian man, and the fact that Katherine has been having an affair with Charles Addison for the past fourteen years. Even though Chang and Katherine share certain characteristics and struggles—this is made evident with the descriptions of their common solitariness (10, 13)—it is hard to imagine how we might read them, as a Korean man and a white American woman, in collective terms despite the face that President Rhee and his wife Francesca offer up a historical model of interracial union. Rhee's second wife (and eventual first lady of the Republic of Korea) was an Austrian woman whom he married in the United States in 1934, setting a precedent that goes unrecognized by those in the Tennessee of the novel.

This challenge of comprehending interracial relations is described clearly in *The Foreign Student* when Katherine and Chang go for a drive and stop partway for a soda at a gas station. While waiting for the attendant to finish refueling Katherine's car, Katherine and Chang realize that they have attracted a considerable amount of attention from locals in the vicinity and Katherine thinks to herself that they might as well have been on a ship that had just docked "in a strange land" given the kind of scrutiny they receive (37). Afterward, Chang comments of the crowd, "They don't know what to make me" (37). As Daniel Kim suggests in his reading of this scene, the ship is a key trope for the novel because it "evokes the immigrant masses that enjoy a privileged place in American mythology, yet it also evokes a more shameful history of migration, of those who came to these shores by slave ship. Ultimately, this passage leaves unclear which analogy is more apt" (563). The oddness of the Asian within the U.S. racial landscape and, more pointedly, whether "the violently enforced taboo against miscegenation applies to Chang" (D. Kim 563) are also highlighted by the novel when Chang is invited to Bill Crane's home for Thanksgiving despite the fact that Bill's father is a senior member of the Klan.

The illegibility of Chang and Katherine as a couple here is directly tied to the ongoing erasure of a Korean diaspora within the United States. The metaphor of a ship bearing immigrants underscores the ongoing Korean displacement (and American culpability) at the same time that the curiosity elicited by potential interracial relationships addresses a willful forgetting of the American-orchestrated politics in Korea that produced Syngman and Francesca Rhee as South Korean president and first lady from 1948 to 1960, a period that precedes and succeeds the present moment of Choi's novel.

The persistent foreignness attached to Chang, as well as to Chang and Katherine as a couple, stands out within Choi's predominantly black and white racial landscape of the American South in the 1950s. By not including what Bow calls a "partly colored" population within the fictionalized terrain of the novel (with the exception of Chang's brief interlude in Chicago), Chang's alienness within the United States, and more specifically within the U.S. South, becomes impossible to ignore. While Chang remembers much movement occurring within Korea as people tried to escape the violent warfare (and that even the landscape itself changed profoundly as the country was divided into two nations), Chang himself is represented in singular terms and as if he is the sole individual migrating out of Korea and into the United States. Historically, of course, this portrayal is inaccurate because the 1950s saw a wave of Korean migration composed of international students, Korean children being adopted by Americans (in high concentrations to states such as California and Minnesota), and military brides; the exodus of the 1950s was significant even though it was much smaller than the later movement of Koreans into the United States that occurred post-1965. Setting Chang's experience in 1955 and framing him as the sole Asian in the region also obscures a longer history of Korean labor and settlement in America that emerges out of the needs of Hawaiian plantations in the nineteenth century. Thus, the novel seems deliberate in its decision to neither set its story within the context of more familiar Korean migration periods nor have Chang encounter other Korean, or even any Asian, figures within the South. These moves have the effect of rendering invisible the handful of Asians that might have been in the area at the same time as Chang and potentially provided him with a measure of community as it also writes the U.S. South as a distinct region from the North.

By writing Chang as a racial exception to his new American home, the novel begins to explore its inability to imagine the existence of Koreans strewn throughout the United States pre-1965, and moreover to imagine them as living intimately with other Americans, as symptomatic of how the North American social imagination operates. *The Foreign Student* interrogates the racial logic of the color lines by examining the bodies that lie in between them. As Bow argues in *Partly Colored,* reading segregation in the American South through the lens of Asians, American Indians, and mestizos draws the gaze toward "how color lines are drawn and what racial identity segregation demanded of those who seemed to stand outside—or rather, *between*—its structural logics" (5). Engaging with subjects racialized in terms other than black and white transforms cultural binaries into continuums and provides publics with a means of reworking current forms of relationality. And it is precisely because viewing race in more varied terms threatens to unsettle our understanding of the everyday that there is, as Bow notes, resistance to the interstitial and all of "the cultural anxieties that frame the space of the in-between" (5). By querying the work performed by black and white as structural logics, we can rethink the optics through which certain histories become visible and other relations obscured.

It is from this angle that I approach the illegibility of Chang and Katherine as a couple. By compelling us to focus on the difficulty of comprehending an interracial romance between a white woman and an Asian man, the novel stages the problem of illegibility as one that characterizes Asians in America more broadly. While this may or may not be true, such an approach implicitly encourages us to forget the very specific ways that the Korean diaspora is, by its very nature, always an illegible formation. Choi's novel therefore asks us to generate new ways of reading capable of recuperating the specific experiences of diasporas (such as the Korean diaspora) within a broader pan-Asian framework, strategies that can recognize the differences always present within racialized publics and diasporas, as these can also construct new forms of intimacy. And I want to be clear here that I do not imagine the intimate publics produced by *The Foreign Student* to be composed solely of those that already share an ethnic history or a racialized tie to Korea, but rather as a much larger potential formations that include all participants capable of understanding the impacts of the Korean War.

Grace Cho's analysis of the Korean War and the waves of migration it produced is pertinent here for how it suggests that the Korean diaspora—and perhaps this is true of all diasporas, not just the Korean one—is a formation that is fundamentally unknowable, even to itself. The silencing of Korean historical pain and violence must be read as a sign that, not only is "the diaspora... transgenerationally haunted by the unspoken traumas of war," but that it is, at its very core, "constituted by that haunting" as well (G. Cho 12). To be part of the Korean diaspora then is to be compelled to forget and, moreover, to know in affective terms that you have forgotten. And according to Cho, this problem of "enforced forgetting" is embodied most disturbingly by the *yanggongju*, a crucial figure in contemporary Korean and Korean diasporic history. Here, I turn to Cho's definition for how it translates the shifting meanings as well as the sexual politics of the term:

Yanggongju, literally meaning "Western princess," broadly refers to a Korean woman who has sexual relations with Americans; it is most often used pejoratively to refer to a woman who is a prostitute for the US military. It is a term that has been translated in various ways and whose meanings have shifted according to specific historical and political contexts. This word that is so full of meaning is at the same time an unspeakable and "phantomogenic" word for the Korean diaspora. The process of nurturing a ghost through shame and secrecy has made *yanggongju* both central and subjugated in the story that I want to tell. (3)

As a figure located at the intersection of sexuality, imperialism, and Westernization, the *yanggongju* occupies a complicated position in the historic and ongoing relations between Korea and the United States, one that is readily overlooked by the families and nations that are ashamed of her and the diasporas that are unaware of their connections to her (or sometimes even of her very existence). As a figure that renders visible the affective implications of this historical phenomenon, the *yanggongju* demands that we work through and against the Korean diaspora as a social formation based on "enforced forgetting" (G. Cho 12).

The framing of Chang and Katherine as an ideal but unlikely couple is another means by which the novel explores a social tendency to deny and forget traumatic Korean and American histories, this time by an American public. The illegibility of Chang's presence in Sewanee and his burgeoning romance with Katherine speak to the condition of "enforced forgetting" needed for Americans to disavow the lengthy history of imperialism that culminated with the installation of President Rhee and his first lady, Francesca. And yet, even as Chang and Katherine represent the problem of willful amnesia with respect to the Korean diaspora as produced by generations of shame, anger, and bitterness, in essence by *han,* the novel sidesteps any direct representation of the *yanggongju* even though she is such a central figure for the Korean diaspora. This is a curious move given the importance of the *yanggongju* as a figure of forgotten origins. As Cho argues, since

> half of those comprising the Korean diaspora in the United States are related by blood or marriage to a woman who married an American serviceman, the ghostly quality of this relationship is that one cannot know her past with any certainty. Others who arrived in the United States through a different trajectory may also be affectively connected to her through the larger unspoken traumas of the hidden history of the US-Korea relations. The patterns of connection across the Korean diaspora are the result of an uneasy configuration of traumatic effects; thus, the yanggongju articulates a monstrous family—a diaspora that is bound together through what cannot be known. (39–40)

And while this sense of unknown connection and shame are maintained in the public created by Chang and Katherine, what is to be made of the fact that the actual figure of the *yanggongju* is absent from the pages of the novel? This is an especially compelling question since, as Ji-Yeon Yuh claims, "military brides are the invisible backbone of the Korean American community in that for four decades following the Korean War the most common migration route for Korean immigrants was through sponsorship by one of the one hundred thousand Korean women who married American GIs" (Yuh qtd. in G. Cho 140). I read the exclusion of the *yanggongju* in the novel as a move that disassociates the sociological and affective dimensions of the Korean diaspora from each other. By framing Chang's story not within the structures of diaspora but instead in terms of individual migration, *The Foreign Student* emphasizes the Asian as a figure of perpetual newness, perhaps even of strangeness, and therefore always of foreignness.

It is, of course, displacement from Korea as it is transformed into two nations that turns Chang into a foreign student. That a desire to leave Korea rather than a desire to enter America propels his journey is crucial to keep in mind when thinking about Chang's circumstances toward the end of the novel, and moreover, the fact that he is left as a nonpermanent U.S. resident who does not appear to have any intention of returning to Korea. I now complicate my reading of Chang by pointing out that, as an international student, Chang fits into a tradition of migrant subjects—albeit in a way that is markedly different from unskilled migrant labor. Framing Chang as a migrant rather than a diasporic subject is an act with much significance because it locates him quite differently within various publics. Here, I find Jacqueline Lo's work on visual artist Fiona Tan provocative for thinking through what is at stake in the framing of subjects. Through a reading of the responses to Tan's art and her biography, Lo suggests that reading Tan and the figure of the Asian more generally in terms of migrancy is a displacement strategy that moves the Asian between multiple homes and denies the possibility that she might belong within a nation outside of Asia. Migrancy clearly performs very different kinds of work than diaspora; as a paradigm that demands that the long histories of dispersal and generational claims that racialized bodies assert on the nation be legitimated, diaspora resists framing Asians outside of Asia as a temporary phenomenon by demonstrating the very real ways in which they are rooted in these places. Lo's argument concludes by invoking the dangers of positioning migration as an earlier phase of diaspora, thereby the telos that underpins diaspora.

There is much conveyed through the aura of perpetual foreignness that is attached to Chang. If, as Bow writes, the foreigner is a figure of unbelonging, then we must recognize that it is always "a figure of only partial comprehensibility, one that must be self-consciously interpreted into the context of the local" but "is nonetheless essential to collective definition" (160–61). Chang is the paradigmatic figure of the foreigner in the novel, one that is always somewhat incomprehensible in terms of the collective possibilities that the novel suggests. Positioned beyond the imaginative limits of nation and diaspora, Chang asks us to think about a subjectivity that is always understood as estranged to some degree from those around him and to contemplate what would be required for figures like Chang to become legible. This novel then offers a rather different approach to Asia and its emotional and intellectual possibilities than does Khang's art. Whereas pieces and performances such as *Mom's Crutch* and *Wrong Places* raise questions about how to feel and imagine as part of a diaspora, a practice that claims affiliation beyond national borders, I understand Choi's novel as instead asking how to understand and feel as part of an empire with its structures of violence and domination. While, as *The Foreign Student* makes visible, the potential for the circulation of this affect always exists, it is a possibility that is often extraordinarily difficult to actualize. How to articulate—in both the senses of speaking and connecting—insights about the speaking and feeling practices of imperial diasporas is a trying task, especially since such a project involves unearthing what has been, or is still trying to be, forgotten.

CHAPTER 4

Global Loss

Metaphoric Substitution and the Logic of Human Rights

In an interview, Toronto-based poet Souvankham Thammavongsa states of *Small Arguments* (2003), her first book of poetry, that it "collects small lives and argues for their belonging. While doing so, it also serves as an argument for my own belonging. I was born in a refugee camp. I was not given a birth certificate. It is not enough that I am living. A piece of paper needs to prove this. *Small Arguments* offers this" ("*Small Arguments*").[1] In this description of her poetry, which suggests that to be born in a liminal place, a space between nations, means that one does not exist, Thammavongsa opens up for discussion the connection between legitimation and legibility. Without papers to officially speak to their existence, these lives are illegible in bureaucratic terms, transformed into what Giorgio Agamben calls bare life or *zoe,* and saved from complete erasure perhaps only by literary texts such as Thammavongsa's poetry. In drawing attention to the structures of power that exclude bare life in order to produce socially recognizable forms of life, as well as the larger polis to which they belong, *Small Arguments* and *Found* examine how print legitimates life, or perhaps more accurately, permits it to be recognized as human.

Homo Sacer, Agamben's study of sovereign power in the West, opens with the classical Greek distinction between *zoe* and *bios* as two different kinds of life, with the former referring to "the simple fact of living common to all living beings (animals, men, or gods)" and the latter to "the form or way of living proper to an individual or a group" (1). Agamben begins by tracing a line between Aristotle's definition of the perfect community (which takes for granted the opposition of *zoe* and *bios*) and Foucault's work on biopolitics, which examines the moment that "natural life begins to be included in the mechanisms and calculations of State power, and politics turns into *biopolitics*" (Agamben, *Homo Sacer* 3). In his reading of biopolitics, Agamben notes that this is unlike Foucault's other efforts to analyze how power operates through the State. In seeking to understand how these approaches to power—the totalizing structures and subjective individualization—cohere, Agamben responds to the question that Foucault's own work neglects. By connecting together the projects of Aristotle, Arendt, and Foucault, Agamben reaches the insight that "the two analyses [juridico-institutional and biopolitical] cannot be separated, and that the inclusion of bare life in the political realm constitutes the original—if concealed—nucleus of sovereign power. *It can even be said that the production of a biopolitical body is the original activity of sovereign power*" (*Homo Sacer* 6; italics in original). This realization asks important questions about the shape of Western politics—namely, why it "first constitutes itself through an exclusion (which is simultaneously an inclusion) of bare life. What is the relation between politics and life, if life presents itself as what is included by means of an exclusion?" (*Homo Sacer* 7).

Thammavongsa wrestles with similar kinds of philosophical problems, but turns to poetry to work through the tangled logics and regimes of representation that produce bare life on national and global scales. I place Thammavongsa's texts at the heart of this chapter because her poetry foregrounds the figures through which we imagine the human as it also opens up for consideration the narrative shape of human rights discourses so that we can consider how and why we are moved by certain lives and not others. Although the prototypical bare life of modernity via the Holocaust is typically the figure of the Jew and not the Asian refugee, I propose considering them together in order to position *zoe* and *bios* as part of a continuum rather than as categories produced through absolute division. As others writing about refugees and the war in Southeast Asia note, Agamben draws these figures together in his work because "the refugee brings into question the citizen, sovereignty, rights, people, and workers, everything associated with the nation-state and the struggle for inclusion and recognition within it. The refugee exists without rights and the protection of nation-states, in refugee camps and immigration detention centers that share a lineage with concentration and death camps" (V. Nguyen, "Refugee Memories" 930). In *Eichmann in Jerusalem,* Hannah Arendt reminds us that it was the stripping of national citizenship by the Nazis that transformed Jews into bare life and codified anti-Semitism as law. Thammavongsa's poems engage with a similar logic by examining the Southeast Asian refugee as another form of life situated outside the reaches of national citizenship and law; without collapsing the significant material and symbolic differences that distinguish the figures of the Jew and the Asian refugee, I suggest they share in common the condition of ephemerality because they exist outside of the legal and political parameters of national citizenship. In asserting the specificity of the Asian context while acknowledging similarities to the Jewish one, I reinforce the view of critics such as Cathy Schlund-Vials, who argues that although the Holocaust functions as a dominant referent for stories of trauma, we must also be conscious of the "very real differences between Jewish productions and Cambodian American life writing with regard to history, politics, and state-sanctioned justice" (118). One crucial difference that Schlund-Vials notes is that "[f]or those who recall the Holocaust, at stake is a 'never again' modality facilitated through a juridically acknowledged remembrance (e.g., *Yad Vashem*); for Cambodian American writers who recollect the Killing Fields era, the issue is an instantiating 'remember again' impulse intended to catalyze unrealized juridical processes" (118).

Small Arguments and *Found* resituate questions about bare life within the context of print publics in order to investigate how the logic of exception is exercised through the legitimating capabilities of print. Thammavongsa's work illuminates the human as a category produced through juridico-institutional and biopolitical power, and responds to an absence of legal and political documentation with poetry. In her poems, *zoe* appears in the shape of nonhuman life and the Asian refugee; as we are drawn further into the worlds sketched out by *Small Arguments* and *Found*, we see these forms of bare life differently as the rhetorical figures of the ant, earwig, and strawberry operate as eloquent and restrained arguments for recognizing a multitude of lives in the everyday. When read collectively, these lives generate provocative questions about the nature of public spaces and social intimacy and interrogate the logic of exception by which certain lives are diminished and reduced to bare, and even inhuman, life. How are we to understand the disturbing interchangeability of bugs, refugees, and rotting fruit that these poems sketch out? In what contexts and for what readers are these lives and objects rhetorical and conceptual substitutes for each other? These metaphorical substitutions draw attention to the particularities of the polis and ask whether seeing the limits of citizenry represented in either the form of insects or paperless people changes the particular figure through which *bios* is imagined.

In this chapter, I invoke Agamben's arguments about *homo sacer* as well as Lauren Berlant's and Michael Warner's theoretical explorations of publics to engage with Thammavongsa's poems and discourses of human rights. As these critics conceptualize excluded lives in distinct but nonetheless related ways, drawing on their analyses simultaneously sheds light on how the realm of the political operates in the West. This is particularly crucial for engaging with Thammavongsa's work as landmark Laotian Canadian writing that brings attention to war, genocide, and Southeast Asian refugees. As its "secret war," the United States' activities in Laos have not been part of the North American public imagination in the same way that Vietnam has been. Ma Vang describes how the United States undertook the war in Laos by secretly recruiting and training thirty thousand soldiers, mostly Hmong, and thousands of whom, along with their families and other civilians, perished in battle and from disease and starvation (688). Laos, Cambodia, and Vietnam were, however, all crucial stages in which the West undertook its crusade against communism. As a war not fought openly but largely through the training of Hmong soldiers after the United States had signed peace accords (such as the 1973 Peace Accords to end the fighting in Vietnam and cease U.S. direct military involvement), Laos illustrates how the logic of exception is used to maintain global order. In Agamben's work, bare life offers the conditions of possibility for politics even as these very possibilities are denied to it: "At once excluding bare life from and capturing it within the political order, the state of exception actually constituted, in its very separateness, the hidden foundation on which the entire political system rested" (*Homo Sacer* 9). While he grounds his discussion through important examples from twentieth- and twenty-first-century global politics such as the Nazi concentration camps in *Homo Sacer* and Guantanamo Bay in *State of Exception,* the exclusion of life is also a necessary precondition for the operations of law and state in an Asian North American context, and central to understanding the formation of minor publics in Canada.

Joseph Slaughter, whose work examines how mechanisms of inclusion and exclusion are implemented via human rights law and literature, extends Agamben's efforts to theorize human rights by investigating the relationship between the Universal Declaration of Human Rights (UDHR) and the literary form of the bildungsroman. Slaughter notes that these legal and literary forms share a vision of human development and that both privilege certain subjects at the expense of others, observations that further our understanding of how exclusionary principles of human rights are accepted as normative. Because the bildungsroman and human rights law intersect as extensions of the Enlightenment project, it is necessary that we be conscious of "the problems that such complicity creates, particularly with the *Bildungsroman*'s ambivalent capacity to disseminate and naturalize not only the norms of human rights but also the paradoxical practices, prejudices, and exclusions codified in the law" (Slaughter, *Human Rights* 5). Slaughter argues against the rhetorical appeal of human rights (which is generated in part through their framing as universal and self-evident principles) by encouraging us to investigate how literary and cultural forms reinforce the legibility and legislatibility of human rights norms (*Human Rights* 6).

To heed Slaughter's suggestion, we must rethink the idealized relations between individuals and society that human rights narratives promote in favor of conceptualizing other forms of sociality. This is crucial since the "enabling fiction" of the human personality as imagined within cultural and legal spheres produces a sense of collectivity that can only ever be achieved by obscuring the actual material and political inequalities that exist in the everyday (*Human Rights* 5). These enabling fictions mean that in practice, human rights are not bestowed upon all humans, but rather are the rights of citizens. As these cultural and legal fictions articulate the human, "the projection of a normative egalitarian imaginary not only sets the terms and limits of universality's cover; it becomes the discursive condition of possibility for nonhegemonic rearticulations of universality's compass" ("Enabling Fictions" 1408). That the political subject is produced through the exclusion of other forms of life and imagined in terms of rights and responsibilities is a particularly pertinent point when considering the figure of the excluded Asian within Canadian and American contexts. As demonstrated by multiple historical moments such as the Chinese Exclusion Acts, Canadian head-tax laws, the *Komagata Maru*, and Japanese Canadian and Japanese American internment, governments in Canada and the United States have denied Asians both entry to the country and the status of full citizenship, and reduced many to the invisible laboring bodies that enable a dominant public to exist. Henry Yu outlines this process with respect to the Chinese railroad workers in North America in "Global Migrants and the New Pacific Canada." Here, Yu notes that in the late nineteenth century, approximately 15,000 Chinese workers contributed their labor to building the Canadian Pacific Railway (CPR), which was essential for transporting goods from Canada to European markets as well as European migrants from the Atlantic coast to British Columbia. And even though these Chinese migrants had provided essential labor for building the CPR, their efforts only served to reinforce their exclusion from the national community:

> The irony is that the Chinese built the very means of transportation that allowed large numbers of migrants from the Atlantic coast to come to British Columbia and to begin displacing them and First Nations peoples. It is no coincidence that the 1885 Chinese head tax, designed to curb Chinese immigration to Canada, was passed at exactly the moment that the Chinese finished building the trans-

continental railroad that brought workers in large numbers from the east coast. ("Global Migrants" 1015)

But at the same time that the Asian as bare life acts as the other to the citizen, there are multiple levels of power and privilege within this racialized minority that need to be taken into account. The differences between Asian indentured workers, refugees, affluent merchants, and international students in Canada and the United States, for example, highlight the various ways in which the bare life and citizen spectrum operates for the Asian; this tension becomes even messier since, in the United States, citizenship was granted to American-born Asians while it was withheld in Canada.

In the case of Southeast Asians in North America, America's wars generated the conditions of displacement for Vietnamese, Cambodian, and Laotian refugees such as Thammavongsa's parents. The Canadian military was also involved in the wars in Southeast Asia in many different ways, first by supporting France's attempts to maintain control over Indochina and then by supporting U.S. aggression in Vietnam in defiance of the Geneva agreements. Canada provided information, ideological and material support to the United States, and soldiers as 20,000 to 30,000 Canadians enlisted in the U.S. military during the war in Vietnam (Engler 125–28). These historical inequalities substantiate Lisa Lowe's claim that the regulation of Asian racialized bodies is central to the logic of modern subjectivity ("Worldliness"). For this reason, I turn to alternate publics to conceptualize politics outside a dominant register and imagine other forms of political engagement and social intimacy.

Bare Life and Public Relations

While Agamben's lexicon of the sacred and the sovereign tethers exclusion to various forms and levels of biopolitical and juridico-institutional politics, somewhat different but nonetheless related possibilities for politics emerge when Thammavongsa's poems are read through the lens of publics, dominant as well as minor. Because discussions of publics and *homo sacer* share an interest in understanding how relations of power determine the value and legibility of lives, bringing together these theoretical approaches enables an examination of how principles of address and recognition operate in relation to state power and within minor publics. Thammavongsa's metaphorical substitution of bugs for Asian refugees addresses the mutual devaluation of both forms of life and gestures toward other modes of sociality capable of binding lives together in intimate ways.

According to Habermas, the public sphere is a space in which the greater common good is to be debated. While Habermas conceives of the bourgeois public as performing the necessary work of public critique and therefore as a key part of democracies, his understanding of the bourgeois public as coming together over shared concerns and rational debate already creates its space of the political by excluding "irrational" subjects. Remaining within this tradition of publics and sharing its commitment to collective spaces of discussion, theorists such as Warner, Berlant, and Nancy Fraser explore other potential uses and formations of publics. By focusing on less dominant publics, their work makes room for more nuanced critiques of power, politics, and strategies of legitimation useful for differentiating between *zoe* and *bios*.

In *The Female Complaint*, her book on feminine reading publics and nineteenth-century literature, Berlant analyzes political feeling and women's culture. Through chapters on celebrity deaths such as Princess Diana and John F. Kennedy and texts like *Uncle Tom's Cabin, Showboat,* and the work of Dorothy Parker, Berlant examines the aesthetic conventions that shape feminine publics and subjectivities. Particularly pertinent for my discussion of Thammavongsa's work is what Berlant calls "the critical intelligence of affect, emotion, and good intention" for its ability to provide

> an orientation toward agency that is focused on ongoing adaptation, adjustment, improvisation, and developing wiles for surviving, thriving, and transcending the world as it presents itself. It is not usually expressed in or addressed to the political register: as I indicated in the preface, generally intimate publics such as this one operate as aesthetic worlds that are juxtapolitical, flourishing in proximity to the political because the political is deemed an elsewhere managed by elites who are interested in reproducing the conditions of their objective superiority, not in the well-being of ordinary people or life-worlds. (*Female Complaint* 2–3)

That the public is a juxtapolitical space in Berlant's work is key because she sees it as operating not in or through the discourses of dominant politics, but rather near them. I do not read this necessarily as an abandonment of the space of politics, but rather as an attempt to expand the registers that compose that site and to provide new ways of returning to it. By making room for the "critical intelligence of affect" and using it as the grounds for an intimate public, Berlant imagines ways of connecting various forms of life and citizenry without necessarily translating them into the language of political representation.

Berlant's juxtapolitical world is markedly different from, yet not incompatible with, Warner's conception of the political (and this compatibility is perhaps most obviously suggested by their collaborative work on "Sex in Public"[2]). In

Publics and Counterpublics, Warner rethinks the forms of sociability that underpin political formations. Focusing primarily on queer publics, Warner notes the dissonance between the shape of queer political movements and queer sexualities and identities (18). He analyzes the inability of queer publics to promote their social movements without normalizing queer subjectivity, and thus pinpoints a problem with the language and audience of queer publics that can be transposed to other kinds of publics. What is necessary then, as becomes clear through his thinking about how principles and concepts of privacy and publicity operate with respect to sexuality, is an understanding that the "public sphere as an environment, then, is not just a place where one could rationally debate a set of gender or sexual relations that can in turn be equated with private life; the public sphere is a principal instance of the forms of embodiment and social relations that are themselves at issue" (54). The condition of feeling uneasy within the public sphere indicates a need for publics that welcome other habitus, "the conventions by which we experience, as though naturally, our own bodies and movement in the space of the world" (23). For Warner, the counterpublic is such a space; in "Public and Private" (a chapter in *Publics and Counterpublics*), he considers the tensions that exist between various forms of publics, and how one can think, feel, and be within various publics and counterpublics. The contributions of these counterpublics are multiple. Most obviously, counterpublics widen representative possibilities and consequently "can mediate the most private and intimate meanings of gender and sexuality. It can work to elaborate new worlds of culture and social relations in which gender and sexuality can be lived, including forms of intimate association, vocabularies of affect, styles of embodiment, erotic practices, and relations of care and pedagogy" (57). As sites that welcome new and complex ways of thinking and feeling subjectivity, counterpublics transform lonely and isolated individuals into a social world (57).

Influenced by Berlant's and Warner's investigations of intimate publics and counterpublics, my goal is to understand the formation of racialized publics made minor in their structural as well as affective relations to a dominant public. If we understand intimacy as a form of attachment, then the Asian refugee as a form of excluded life is necessary to the formation of Asian Canadian publics as intimate publics; the common experience of exclusion is frequently narrativized as part of a collective Asian Canadian experience. But as Mimi Nguyen and Yen Le Espiritu point out, for Southeast Asian refugees in North America, the structure of exclusion has operated inversely through narratives of rescue and redemption from state communism in Southeast Asia that produce the refugee as a marginalized condition in North America. It is, of course, precisely this equation of Asian and exclusion that renders impossible social intimacy between a dominant public and Asian Canadian publics. More recently, Berlant has explored the idea of "cruel optimism" as a form of relationality in which the desired object also functions as an obstacle (*Cruel Optimism* 1). Within the context of Asian Canadian publics, a historical investment in the political recognition of Asian Canadian subjects operates as an obstacle to their more comprehensive sociopolitical recognition. While the drive to obtain legal and political citizenship for racialized subjects is undeniably important, so too is the need to have these voices register affectively for a wider public. Within the framework of Canadian democracies, the perception that Asian Canadian concerns are, like those of other minority groups, special interest ones and not necessarily directly pertinent to the interests of a dominant public indicates a need to work through political and juxtapolitical avenues if a fuller sense of citizenship is to be accessible to Asian Canadians. If there is a cruel attachment operating in Asian Canadian publics, perhaps it is a belief that Asian Canadian subjects will start to matter affectively to a dominant public once they are granted equal protections under the law instead of the reverse scenario.

Reading together critical examinations of publics and human rights permits us to grasp how the inclusion and exclusion of bare life from politics has everything to do with how matters of address and attention operate. In performing this critical move—situating this conversation about bare life within the context of racialized publics, specifically those invoking the Asian refugee—I argue, via *Small Arguments* and *Found,* that the Asian refugee functions as a means of cohering a non-Asian public at the same time that it also works to generate intimate minor publics. By providing an exterior to the dominant public's interior, the Asian refugee produces the conditions of possibility needed for a dominant public to share a sense of intimacy. Concomitantly, as I argue later in this chapter, Thammavongsa's texts also engage racialized minor publics in intimate terms. Moving in a different direction from Agamben, Pheng Cheah explores how the human and human rights are conditioned by global capitalism; for Cheah, the inhuman is not simply an alienated human being, but rather "the inhuman or the non-human is something that precedes the human being and exceeds the human being. One has to look at how the human being emerges from these inhuman forces" (Hui). In refuting a normative understanding of the human that defines the inhuman as what is repressed or excluded (Hui), Cheah demands that we be conscious of how discourses of the human and human rights get invoked and argues for the need to notice how northern and southern states and NGOs mobilize human rights discourses (*Inhuman Conditions* 148). The paradox is that human rights are "violent gifts, the necessary nexuses within immanent global force relations that produce the identities of their claimants. Yet they are the only way for the disenfranchised to mobilize" (*Inhuman Conditions* 172). In light of these concerns, what can human rights discourses offer the Asian refugee that has always operated as a figure of the inhuman? How can the Asian refugee make use of these "violent gifts" if global audiences do not recognize her or his subjectivity?

As Naoki Sakai informs us, dismantling the colonial relations between Asia and the West requires that they be thoroughly historicized, particularly because, as he notes of these binary identities, "the putative unity of the West, the dominant and universalistic position, is sustained by the insistence on the equally putative unity of Asia, the subordinate and particularistic position" (801). In order to unravel the pernicious categories of Asia and the West, we must be conscious of how these terms are performed as well as our investments in them (Sakai 811). These binary oppositions continue to exist, despite their obvious falsity, because of "our prescribed investment for a certain distinction, for a justification for exclusion, and for own identity" (811). If Asia is a category that exists in relation to the West, and moreover works to unify it, then becoming aware of the various socioeconomic systems, colonial histories, and transforming nationalisms is a necessary step in decolonizing the relationship between Asia and the West. I see Thammavongsa's poems as undertaking precisely this work of interrogating Western perceptions of Asia and Asians and the kinds of publics they generate. By using the second person to directly address the reader, Thammavongsa calls attention to how relationality determines the legibility of representations. A pear, for instance, is described as reminding "you" of a guitar, a tangerine as a deferred orange because "It fits into you" (*Small Arguments* 19, line 3), and the word *na* as shifting meaning depending on whether "you keep / the last sound / you can / make / going" (*Found* 41, lines 39–43). These objects and sounds are denied intrinsic value and matter for how they resonate with the reader. By underscoring how audiences are addressed and attention held, these poems probe the category of nonhuman life as a means of withholding political subjectivity. Echoing international human rights struggles, Thammavongsa's poems about inanimate objects and minor forms of life striving for recognition illuminate much about how the language of rights, representation, and legitimation operates.

Public Materials

Thammavongsa's work addresses the legibility of minor lives by creating textual publics. As Berlant points out, textual publics bind strangers together via a shared text and the assumption that those who engage with these texts already share common perspectives, histories, and understandings of the world (*Female Complaint* viii). The circularity of the intimate public presumes that these texts express "that history while also shaping its conventions of belonging; and, expressing the sensational embodied experience of living as a certain kind of being in the world, it promises also to provide a better experience of social belonging" (*Female Complaint* viii). By highlighting the assumptions publics make as they emerge around particular texts, Berlant contributes to an understanding of the complex affective bonds that cohere collectives together. Thammavongsa's poems, however, approach textual publics from another angle as they examine the absence of a certain shared textual object—in this case, the birth certificate or passport—and question how this acts as a barrier to inclusion within national communities. Because she was born in a Thai camp, Thammavongsa was never given either a Thai or Lao passport. However, like other refugees from Southeast Asia, she would likely have been given other documentation, such as a refugee transit photo card, in order to be at the camp. Once she and her family arrived in Canada, they would have received immigration papers and then eventually a Canadian citizenship card and a passport. As a route to obtaining Canadian documentation familiar to many Southeast Asian refugees in Canada, *Small Arguments* and *Found* reframe Southeast Asian diasporas as print publics as they underline the importance of documentation to citizenship. The U.S. context reinforces this problem of documentation as many Southeast Asian refugees were never given citizenship, and this has resulted in the present-day deportation crisis of Cambodians, Vietnamese, and Laotians, many of whom grew up in the United States and do not speak fluently the languages of those countries. Thammavongsa's poems target the connection between print and being, not in order to eschew it completely, but rather to reformulate it; in doing so, the poems produce alternate forms of affective legitimacy that compete with citizenship and capital in order to regulate publics.

In lieu of official documentation, Thammavongsa's poems offer alternate modes of writing migrants into belonging and encourage us to consider how publics legitimate existences. Thammavongsa also examines this connection between written word and citizenship in entries published in *big boots,* a zine she cofounded and helped to edit. "there are no photographs of my mother," a poem published in the inaugural issue of *big boots,* describes her mother's experiences of migration, which ended with her eventually making her way to Canada. The poem states that while fleeing her homeland,

> her birth certificate
> on paper too weak to carry the weight of water

fell apart
nothing to prove the day of her birth
certain of one, she tells me:
it must have been on a day like the one we left to land
on white, cold ground
in a fire we leave with what we have on our backs
even then, that too must be left
("there are no photographs")

As the poem makes clear, it is the symbolic rather than physical act of displacement that makes the speaker's mother a refugee. The loss of official documents "made a familiar face, a stranger's" by transforming the mother from a citizen of Laos and a potential immigrant attractive to host countries given her finances, skills, and education into a homeless and destitute individual desperately seeking asylum in some part of the world ("there are no photographs"). As the editors of *Uprootings/Regroundings* note in the introduction to their volume, stasis and mobility are "privileges [that] are negotiated precisely in relationship to the inhabiting of spaces and to the 'passports' that are required not only to move between places, but also to stay 'at home' in them" (Ahmed et al. 7). The restrictions placed on the bodies of migrant laborers exploited by the machinery of various states find new expression in the mother of Thammavongsa's poem because the absence of even a less "desirable" passport means that her migration is continual and forced. While Canada finally permits the mother to settle within its borders, her description of the country as "white, cold ground" conveys her sense of feeling unwelcome and thus, in a very real sense, the experience of displacement fails to end. In this instance, written text in the form of documentation requirements for immigration is used to filter out as many migrant bodies from the country as is possible. "there are no photographs of my mother" critiques Canadian immigration policies and its multicultural ethos for being unable to either extend genuine hospitality to new migrants or engage with them as subjects.

This line of interrogation is pursued further in Thammavongsa's "photos and diary entries," a short essay published in a 2002 issue of *big boots*, which examines how written documents and laws prevent bodies from both traveling legally and making permanent homes. But this essay, like her poems, also explores the generative possibilities of noninstitutionalized forms of writing by returning to her parents' experiences as refugees. Here, written documents supplement visual images in order to convey stories that the parents are unable to share in everyday conversations In this respect, her parents' silences echo those of other Southeast Asian refugees:

Linguistically isolated, many first-generation refugee survivors kept to themselves, even within the confines of their own families. The struggle to mourn, memorialize, and heal thus competes with the struggle to survive against poverty and other symbolic forms of violence that are enacted daily upon vulnerable communities. For many, grieving comes as stolen moments. (Um 838)

Thammavongsa's curiosity about her parents' pasts and her own birthplace is partially satiated when she discovers a diary written by her parents in 1978, "one of the few things that was not lost or taken away," as it begins to document the daily lives of people rendered invisible by the juridical apparatuses of various nation-states (*big boots* 2). This diary is presumably the same one that she later engages with in order to write *Found,* her second book of poetry. While governmental papers such as "birth certificates, marriage certificates, childhood photos, were washed away as they crossed from laos to thailand," the parents continue to exist in written form (*big boots* 2). In the pages of the zine that follow, Thammavongsa shares some of these photographs and written entries with the reader, a couple of which are glossaries, perhaps used to help learn English, while the parents were hoping for entry into Canada. One list, written on the page of a daytime organizer dated February 19, contains words such as *barrack, lodging, belongings, insufficient,* and *freedom* (*big boots* 2). The collecting of English words pertinent to life in the refugee camp suggests that the writer of this diary was searching for a way to articulate his current state. And through the traces of camp life, we are compelled to ask how one speaks of lives that do not exist in legal terms and are rendered invisible in the eyes of a global public? What kind of vocabulary is adequate and appropriate to describe such experiences? While writing a diary obviously does not carry the same kind of symbolic or legal weight as official documents such as passports and birth certificates, it, like Thammavongsa's poems and essays, nonetheless demands a degree of legitimation simply by virtue of addressing a public. The diary, moreover, addresses potential readers in intimate terms by assuming they are interested in its confidences and are willing to participate in this textual public, thereby offering recognition to gendered and migrant speakers.

That print is not just a way of excluding but also a means of including subordinated peoples into the structure of publics is an idea examined further in "Materials." The first poem in *Small Arguments,* it carefully explores how the speaker's world shifts as she becomes literate. Raised in a space devoid of books and magazines, the only print materials available are discarded newspapers "laid out / on the floor / to dry / our winter boots / or wrap / things of glass" (*Small Arguments* 14, lines 5–10). Once the speaker learns to decipher lines of print, she experiences a radical epistemological shift, one mirrored by the two sections that constitute the poem's structure. The first five pairs of nonrhyming lines describe how newspaper is used to protect the household from daily wear and tear. However, by the time we reach the eleventh line (also the beginning of the second half of the poem), newspaper is no longer sacrificed to protect material objects. Boots are instead left dripping and glassware "broken / and uncovered" as the speaker realizes that written text provides access to different social realities (lines 15–16). The understanding that written text "would be my way in" is reflected formally as this final insight is the only line not part of a couplet, and therefore left open to future possibilities (line 19). "Materials" argues that print should be recognized for its ability to provide its readers with entry points into various publics, a sentiment that corresponds with Warner's insight that "a public enables a reflexivity in the circulation of texts among strangers who become, by virtue of their reflexively circulating discourse, a social entity" (11–12). Thinking of publics as sites of discussion that emerge around texts, requiring only that members be attentive to some degree, seems like a radical alternative to the restrictive terms of national citizenship and its cumbersome juridico-institutional apparatuses. Participation in textual discussions transforms the medium of print into a means of welcoming rather than excluding new members from public spaces, and encourages a rethinking of the terms of sociability that exist between strangers.

To be clear though, while "Materials" underscores matters of sociability with respect to textual publics and reading as a "way in" to these spaces, the poet never minimizes the painstaking labor this process demands or the degree of compassion it sacrifices. How the logic of exception is negotiated within textual publics is illustrated by a story that Thammavongsa recounts about being a child and learning to read at the same time that her father was learning to read English. They would read together books she brought home from school and collectively figure out the pronunciation for new words such as *knife*. Upon returning to the classroom, she remembers being told by her first-grade teacher that she was saying the word *knife* incorrectly and that the *k* was silent. Instead of deferring to her teacher, she says:

> I argued and argued to be right. I was sent to the principal's office to calm down. I see that it was never about the word "knife" but about the consequence of it. How pronouncing it incorrectly brought shame to me and said something about where I come from. I remember coming home and telling my dad the first letter was silent and him asking me why it was if it is there and especially if it was the first letter. That order, of it being first, meant something. Reading and writing,

for me, was not just to fill out a form or to read a book for pleasure—it was also about knowing where I come from and where I stood. (Barclay)

In this argument with her teacher, Thammavongsa defends her father's habitus and refuses to sacrifice his mode of moving through the world in order to uphold the disciplinary rules of English and, by extension, the colonizing impulses of the West with respect to Asian lives. At stake in this conflict are the intuitions she and her father have in common about how to survive with dignity the written world of English, ones that assume that all letters matter and that linguistic laws operate according to logical principles, to which Thammavongsa steadfastly clings. Learning English is clearly not simply a matter of acquiring vocabulary and mastering grammatical rules, but also an undertaking that forces the poet to struggle with the imperialist dimensions of English and her own affective relations to this cultural force. During this battle over pronunciation, the poet refuses to let English speak her or force her to disavow her ways of knowing the world. This experience is also examined in "how to pronounce *knife*," a poem published in *big boots*.

As *Small Arguments* and *Found* explore the affective and legal structures of citizenship through their content, they also draw attention to the circuits, corporeal and print, through which they move. Prior to being published as books of poetry by Pedlar Press, a small publisher (originally based in Toronto and now located in Newfoundland), several of these poems were self-published as chapbooks and, along with other essays and editorials by Thammavongsa, printed in *big boots*, a zine devoted to "women of colour reclaiming their voices and telling their own stories" (Untitled editorial, *big boots* 1). Thammavongsa's written work participates in multiple and somewhat differently configured publics, and consequently queries the nature of aesthetic and political representation from the angles of the decolonization of politics and public circulation. For example, the zines with their explicit antiracist feminist focus and project of reclaiming marginalized voices—aims made visible in the sharing of racialized women's stories and by maintaining control of the publication—address publics distinct from those that the very spare and highly metaphorical poetics of *Small Arguments* and *Found* engage. As a logical extension of their politics, the material form of *Small Arguments* and *Found*, and the circuits through which they move, offer sharp interventions within debates about Canadian neoliberalism and the juridico-institutionalization of immigration and multicultural policies. Moving through DIY publishing and small presses produces a measure of agency for the writer even as it potentially sacrifices degrees of visibility and power. And while "Materials" identifies participation in reading publics as a means of accessing larger public debates, the faith that it extols is somewhat naive, overly optimistic, and even somewhat at odds with other sections of *Small Arguments* as well as the interview cited earlier. Although these textual publics are democratic in theory because they are open to anyone willing to engage with them, numerous restrictions emerge in practice:

> A public seems to be self-organized by discourse but in fact requires preexisting forms and channels of circulation. It appears to be open to indefinite strangers but in fact selects participants by criteria of shared social space (though not necessarily territorial space), habitus, topical concerns, intergeneric references, and circulating intelligible forms (including idiolects or speech genres). (Warner 106)

This need to travel through already-established routes makes publics less permeable to migrants and also less amenable to reshaping. Those wanting to remake these publics must address how discussion is undertaken and, moreover, investigate the kinds of bodies, subjectivities, and modes of speaking that are symbolically and materially recognized as part of a public.

For this reason, Thammavongsa's work in *big boots* addresses what Warner calls a textual counterpublic rather than a public. Like his notion of publics, Warner's counterpublic understands the relations between readers as a form of discursive sociability between strangers; a key difference between publics and counterpublics, however, has to do with the kinds of subjects discussed. Members of counterpublics "are socially marked by their participation in this kind of discourse; ordinary people are presumed not to want to be mistaken for the kind of person who would participate in this kind of talk or be present in this kind of scene" (Warner 120). That the contributors to *big boots* perceive themselves as writing for just that kind of community is evident when they note that they, as visible minority women, some migrants, "come stranded with stories and images. but not alone" (*big boots* 2). Here, readers and writers are brought into sociability to form a counterpublic by the circulation of texts about women of color. As participants in a counterpublic explicitly interested in discourses of race, gender, and sexuality, they identify as social and cultural outsiders before they can take up this particular form of sociality; in this way, participation within publics and counterpublics are subject to comparable criteria. While these racialized readers and writers form the outskirts of dominant Canadian culture, they nonetheless assert their counterpublic as a site that belongs to a broader public. The editors underline their precarious positioning within Canada, simultaneously inside and outside the nation, when they comment on their use of written English: "that the zine is in english is proof that even here in this small space for which we have claimed for ourselves we are still very much without claim. who we really are, who we come from and where we come from falls into silence. and although silence is a language, it is a language no one listens to" (*big boots* 3). The zine, as a counterpublic forum, moves us outside of the dominant channels of discourse and terrain of literary high culture, and gestures toward how written language can be used to transform the terms of belonging in Canada.

While the work of *big boots,* with its clear opposition to a dominant public, fits squarely within the category of the counterpublic, I do not see *Small Arguments* and *Found* as necessarily addressing that same public even though some of her poems initially appeared in the zine. Instead, I view these poetic texts in terms of minor publics given how they emphasize the structural and affective relations that diminish them. Thammavongsa's poem "My Mother, A Portrait of," included as part of *Found,* echoes her earlier poem "there are no photographs of my mother," as both poems examine the sharp contrast between the mother's nonexistence in legal or state terms as she flees Laos and the weight that this places on her daughter. However, "My Mother, A Portrait of" resonates quite differently for the reader, in part because it is sandwiched in between a poem that critiques the standardized tools that measure and implicitly assess value and "Laos," a poem that remembers the burying of bodies killed in bombings and the use of the metal from the bombs "to lift / our homes / above / the ground" in order to survive (*Found* 33, lines 9–12). "Laos" speaks to the current plight of Laos as a country in which people are regularly killed by the accidental detonation of remaining bombs each year, but also as a place where people depend on the harvesting of scrap metal from the bombs in order to survive and these same bomb casings have been repurposed as stilts for houses. The documentary *Bomb Harvest* depicts this situation in a powerful fashion as it follows Lao children as they collect live bombs and bomb scraps to sell in order to feed their families. By identifying this tension, "Laos" speaks to the ongoing devaluation of Lao lives even as they struggle to survive. Speaking in a less overtly political but still critical voice, *Found* and *Small Arguments* highlight the production of the minor in order to make a compelling series of arguments for rethinking the terms of sociability within and between nations.

Thammavongsa's texts also remind us that counterpublics and minor publics are never outside the reach of dominant discourses; they are also subject to the very same discourses, forces, beliefs, and institutional logics that they intend to disrupt. Without being utopic spaces beyond the reach of the social norms and juridico-institutional powers that marginalize them, counterpublics and minor publics are sites that affirm the value of these lives by writing them into being. Literary work, while clearly incapable of rewriting the legal structures that regulate belonging within the nation, can push for a reformulation of the kinds of sociabilities produced within and alongside them. By underscoring the connections between written text and structures of citizenship, Thammavongsa's work directs our attention to the strategies and structures of representation that mediate between actual lives and political subjects. Lacking the legal documentation of birth certificate or passport to attest to the existence of the subject, the poems function as an alternate structure that yokes together paper and person. In doing so, the poems and essays highlight the process of substitution already at work in political forums with political and legal categories frequently standing in for subjects. Thammavongsa's texts suggest that often the process of representation has to do with how one is positioned within categories of citizenship rather than with the content of the story being told.

By reading these poems through the lens of publics, I focus on how this substitutive relation is also intimately bound to matters of address. Since the form of the public is self-reflexive and circular, addressing a public already presumes a sense of commonality between speaker and audience. In the case of the textual public, this cohesion is produced by the shared texts that bind individuals together. To perhaps belabor what is a simple point, the form of a public relies on the address to create social cohesion, and in this way differs in slight but significant ways from other collectives such as the community or the nation that are imagined along other lines. This turn to the form of the public (rather than to other collective imaginings such as the nation, community, or even market) acknowledges the tension between desire and belief with respect to participation as participants struggle between desiring validation from an audience and not necessarily believing that addresses will be heard. The belief that their addresses can be heard, however, is, I argue, an a priori condition of publics. The assumption of horizontal comradeship or collective solidarity therefore is not a given, but instead what is striven toward as a public is addressed. If, as Warner claims, "when people address publics, they engage in struggles—at varying levels of salience to consciousness, from calculated tactic to mute cognitive noise—over the conditions that bring them together as a public" (12), then Thammavongsa's poems compel us to rethink the critical terms through which publics differentiate between noise, speech, and sound.

The Human as Category, Discourses of Human Rights

The epigraph to *Small Arguments* by Bertrand Russell argues that philosophy has the ability to "show the strangeness and wonder lying just below the surface even in the commonest things in daily life" (Thammavongsa). The poems in

Small Arguments are like aphorisms given their ability to convey sharp insights through a few brief lines. Thammavongsa's verses deploy metaphors of nature to compel readers to see bodies that are typically overlooked within social and political Canadian spaces. For example, "The Weight of Salt," the second poem in Thammavongsa's collection, establishes an intimacy between human bodies and natural objects by suggesting that the mineral can best be measured according to the way it feels in a hand. This knowledge, however, comes at an emotional price. The phrase "an open hand / that knows the weight of how much" conveys an image of the hand as a vulnerable opening, thus alluding to the familiar adage about "salt in open wounds" (*Small Arguments* 15, lines 7–8). Subsequent poems move away from the painful wisdom that bodies accumulate about objects to focus on the lives of objects, or to phrase it slightly differently, objects as embodied. For example, in "Water," both water and light are given the human capabilities to wage deception and feel uncertainty and despair. By tracing the process through which water loses "itself / in what it didn't want, to become," water, a supposedly inanimate object, is described as having a rich inner life filled with desire and regret (*Small Arguments* 17, lines 20–21). The poem implicitly presents different forms of being as being capable of generating empathy in the reader, and makes the reader conscious of alternate ways of inhabiting the world.

The poems mark an epistemological shift in their refusal to privilege the category of the human in relation to other forms of life. Thammavongsa's poems advocate for a more comprehensive sense of belonging by recognizing human qualities in the natural world, progressing from supposedly inanimate objects to small creatures, a development that mirrors the transformation in the reader's consciousness as "minor" lives become increasingly significant. Strawberries, for instance, are depicted as continuously struggling against those incapable of distinguishing between particular strawberries or caring about how they differ from other types of fruit. The poem presents an image of the reader as gratuitously slicing open a strawberry to expose its insides, tearing "through skin" to confirm the berry's lack of bones, a violent act without purpose (*Small Arguments* 34, line 13). And despite the engagement with the blood and guts of this life, the poem predicts that the reader will remain unmoved by the strawberry's sacrifice and will instead continue to view this corpse much like the remains of a scientific experiment. The coconut is viewed in similar terms, presented as one that "does not know / tenderness" and as only ever feeling pain as the reader cracks it open, presumably to extract its soft flesh (*Small Arguments* 30, lines 1–2). In contrast, the final series of poems begins to recuperate beings such as grasshoppers, ants, and potato bugs, whose lives are typically regarded as having little, if any, value. The short life of the firefly is depicted as a heroic struggle to argue "against darkness and its taking" by making "tiny elegant speeches" even though they will never be heard (*Small Arguments* 41, lines 4, 11). The persistent firefly, like the grasshopper that continually "leaps / into heaven, / asking / for a place" and the ant that toils ceaselessly "to lift a world of crumb and bone," stands in for humans that rally against oppressive social, political, and legal structures (*Small Arguments* 42, lines 1–4; *Small Arguments* 43, line 12). Insects and slugs such as earwigs, worms, and cockroaches—creatures viewed as pests by humans—act as metaphors for the subaltern, a form of aesthetic representation that speaks loudly about how people are represented politically. That metaphor rather than simile structures these poems is key; the poems do not suggest that such individuals are treated *like* animals, but instead argue that in terms of dominant social, legal, and political institutions, they *are* subhuman.

And in making this move, the poems ask us to reflect upon what exactly occurs through this turn to metaphor. As a form of meaning making that operates via comparison, metaphor enables us to grasp dissimilarities as it highlights similarities between concepts and systems of meaning, and does so in a form more elegant and concentrated than the simile (Ricoeur 34). As Paul Ricoeur succinctly defines it, "As a figure, metaphor constitutes a displacement and an extension of the meaning of words; its explanation is grounded in a theory of substitution" (3). In the eight studies that constitute *The Rule of Metaphor*, Ricoeur analyzes metaphor on the levels of semantics, rhetoric, and hermeneutics in order to argue that the "metaphoric 'is' at once signifies both 'is not' and 'is like.' If this is really so, we are allowed to speak of metaphorical truth, but in an equally 'tensive' sense of the word 'truth'" (7). From his book, I take note of a couple of points particularly useful for thinking about metaphorical truth as it pertains to human rights discourses and Thammavongsa's poetry. Through his reading of Aristotle's *Rhetoric*, Ricoeur traces the role that metaphor plays in the fields of rhetoric and poetics. While the goal of rhetoric is to persuade and poetics is to act as a form of catharsis, both rely on metaphor's ability to transfer meaning in order to accomplish these ends (Ricoeur 12); moreover, this metaphoric transference also functions as a form of invention, one that "violates an order only to create another, that dismantles only to redescribe" (Ricoeur 23).

Metaphor, through its ability to make visible hidden resemblances, has the capacity to make us conscious of other forms of relationality. This is particularly relevant for *Small Arguments*, given how the poems investigate the systems of value and representation at work in the everyday by using insects as both rhetorical figures and conceptual metaphors. The poems work to humanize *zoe* by drawing attention to the social structures that make certain lives as inconsequential as those of insects. And yet, through their use of metaphoric substitution, the poems also underscore the limits of this form through which human recognition is bestowed. In the act of seeing and recognizing human and insect lives as interchangeable, an implicit question is raised about how demands for human recognition are made and heard; more precisely, the poems query whether the acts of humanizing—to be recognized *as* human—and human recognition—to be recognized *by* humans—might not also operate interchangeably at times. On the one hand, the turn to insects as metaphors for lives dehumanized by symbolic and material systems underscores the limitations of social orders and levies an implicit ethical demand on the poems' readers. On the other hand, if we read the metaphoric substitution on the level of the word rather than in terms of the statement or even within a broader historical horizon, then we are forced to confront the emptiness of these exchanges. By demonstrating that even a cockroach can substitute for the human, *Small Arguments* shows that the human is a category of indeterminable meaning, and moreover reminds us that recognizing lives as human does not actually transform them from *zoe* to *bios*. Instead, the substitution of cockroach for human makes visible how the human as a conceptual metaphor operates within the rhetoric of human rights.

The poems return us to the Aristotelian understanding of metaphor as central to the arts of poetry and rhetoric by asking whether the true work of this metaphorical substitution is to purge pity and fear from the public about *zoe* or if it is to persuade the public to think differently about how life is recognized. In either case, what becomes apparent is that the move to recognizing the humanity of *zoe* operates as a red herring because expanding the category of the human does not extend either human rights or citizenship rights. This point is corroborated by Slaughter when he reminds us that the "'human' cited in the title of the UDHR is not a human as such; it is a person as a member of a people or nation—a particular kind of human activated as a legal and moral unit" of social rights (*Human Rights* 58), and that the act of imagining one as human cannot compensate for the exclusionary legal and political structures that refuse to grant citizenship, a prerequisite to claiming human rights.

As George Lakoff and Mark Johnson observe in their discussion of what is highlighted and hidden by metaphor, "it is far more difficult to see that there is anything hidden by the metaphor or even to see that there is a metaphor here at all" (11). Thammavongsa's poems suggest a similar kind of entrenchment as occurring in human rights discourses with the human operating largely as an unrecognized metaphor for the citizen. Attempts to humanize subjects in order to access human rights misread how this discourse operates by forgetting that metaphoric substitution works differently on the levels of structure and rhetoric. As Agamben's distinction between *zoe* and *bios* and Slaughter's contrast between natural and human rights remind us, the attainment of rights requires that one belong to a polis rather than be recognized as a living being. In this sense, it is crucial that Thammavongsa's poems make use of a vocabulary of nature to represent how certain bodies are rendered invisible within national and global communities. To become naturalized, in this setting, is to become part of the background against which others act and live. This metaphoric use of nature is ironic given the meaning the term possesses in legal and political discourses of citizenship. To become naturalized, according to the language of state bureaucracies, is to be transformed into a legal citizen of a country and given all of the accompanying rights and responsibilities. In other words, it is naturalized citizenship rather than nature itself that allows an individual to exist, both on paper and because of that piece of paper.

By drawing attention to metaphor as it operates rhetorically and conceptually and shapes the impulse to humanize, *Small Arguments* questions the relations between the social and political, affect and rights, poetics and social narratives, and how these tensions distinguish between noise, speech, and publics. The poems suggest that to be either a cockroach or the reader recognizing the humanity of these subjects has everything to do with positioning and virtually nothing to do with actual feeling or ability. With this in mind, I return to Ricoeur's claim that metaphor has the ability to redescribe reality (6). Thammavongsa's poems contradict Ricoeur's insight, or at least sketch out something else, by offering moments when metaphor fails to open up ways of seeing differently. The inability to compel publics to forge other epistemological relations is conveyed through the form of the poems themselves as incomplete metaphors. While the poems in *Small Arguments* use a range of objects as their vehicles—raisins, strawberries, earwigs, snow—the tenor is never confirmed. We assume that what connects these poems is the struggle for various forms of life to be recognized and that this is itself a metaphor for the desire to be recognized as human, but this theme of the human is never confirmed. Instead, the poems invoke the form of human rights discourse in which publics are addressed through pleas for sympathy and human dignity, without wholeheartedly committing to this genre.

This appeal is clear in *Small Arguments*'s poems about the ground, trees, rain, and snow, most of which also offer fuller narratives than the other poems in the collection. "Poem for Trees," for instance, emphasizes the giving nature of the trees visible in the constant act of collecting rain to return to the sky. In a poignant fashion, the poem describes the branches as "hands / split and splayed, break and bend / from arguments / with gravity which were never won," an image that emphasizes the physical and spiritual costs of nurturing others that are exacted by the unrelenting nature of this labor (*Small Arguments* 37, lines 5–8). The goodness of trees is made indisputable with "each slender bone" steadfastly offering grace despite the number of times they have each been broken (37, line 9). Whereas the humanity of trees rests on their altruism and strong sense of ethics, in another poem, rain is made human through the deep loneliness and profound isolation it experiences as people continually avoid contact with it, choosing instead to employ umbrellas and hide in their homes. Rain is, like many of the other subjects in these poems, personified, but this time only partially so; we are encouraged to empathize with the rain for never having been held or kissed even as the poem acknowledges the impossibility of identifying its arms, hands, or mouth. "Poem for the Rain" is simultaneously speculative and insistent as it claims that "if there is a heart attached / to any of this, it is / as boundless as the rest" (*Small Arguments* 38, lines 14–16). In humanizing trees and rain and encouraging us to be moved by their neglect and exclusion, the poems underscore the difference between the recognition of humanity and the extension of human rights without setting aside the need for either act. Through this modified participation in the form of human rights, the poems engage cautiously with, rather than abandoning, this genre because its very investment in the monumental category of "human rights" mitigates the possibility for specific stories to be conveyed. Consequently, I read *Small Arguments* as taking a position similar to Pheng Cheah's when he argues, despite the contaminated nature of the normativity that is part of human rights, "Given that the transcendence of global capitalism is not in imaginary sight, we have no choice but to take the risk of conjuring with and against the inhuman force field of global capitalism as it induces changing forms of human dignity" (*Inhuman Conditions* 177). The metaphorical substitutions within the poems and their connections with broader discourses of the human and human rights speak to the difficulty of conveying particular narratives and transforming social relations and epistemologies, but do so without being able to propose an alternative to either this form or project. As Lisa Lowe notes in her analysis of metaphors and globalization, "Metaphoricity, then, names a tropological, but ultimately epistemological, dilemma of representing postmodern globalization; the rhetorical surplus expresses the still very 'modern' desire to master what will not be mastered, to rationalize as comprehensible the incomprehensible" ("Metaphors" 45). In a comparable fashion, Thammavongsa's poems explore "tiny" lives that exceed the metaphor of the human and remain incomprehensible.

This troubling problem of how the reader might know, and consequently engage with, the lives presented in *Small Arguments* and *Found* also poses a methodological question of how we are to read these poems (are they about recognizing the dehumanization of people? Or do they ridicule the desire to humanize everything?), and, by extension, how the genre of human rights narratives is read and produced. In making this point, I return to Agamben when he writes,

> To become conscious of this aporia is not to belittle the conquests and accomplishments of democracy. It is, rather, to try to understand once and for all why democracy, at the very moment in which it seemed to have finally triumphed over its adversaries and reached its greatest height, proved itself incapable of saving *zoe,* to whose happiness it had dedicated all its efforts, from unprecedented ruin. (*Homo Sacer* 10)

Like Cheah, Agamben directs our attention to the limitations of human rights principles without necessarily dismissing the need for human rights itself. To wonder about what makes something a human rights narrative and how we are to understand the terms of address it presupposes is also to ask a very simple question about how some utterances are recognized as calls for justice whereas others remain illegible and consequently in the domain of noise. Cheah reminds us of this problem when he notes that

> [v]iolations brought into the phenomenality of public light via the global mass media also tend to be of the most extreme or exceptional kind, such as genocide or massacre. When aligned with neoliberal arguments about the power of globalization to unify us into a common humanity, the moral universalism of human rights discourse can, paradoxically, be used to justify economic globalization as a form of postcolonial civilizing mission. (*Inhuman Conditions* 145)

Small Arguments and *Found* engage this genre by thinking through its conventions, essentially making use of this language of the human and the logic of human rights in order to question the subject imagined by them. And here, my framing of this exchange in terms of generic contracts is indebted to Fredric Jameson's formulation of genres as "essentially literary *institutions,* or social contracts between a writer and a specific public, whose function is to specify the proper use of a particular cultural artifact" (106). The poems sketch out the problem of relationality—between writer and text, text and reader, human and inhuman, human rights discourse and audience—and ask us to be conscious of the form these relations take as well as the long histories that shape them. Moreover, we are asked to reflect upon how we understand the series of substitutions that the poems make, and how they are able to move us between the domains and strategies of poetics and political rhetoric.

Inserting the figure of the Asian refugee into the form of human rights discourse again reinforces the importance of remembering that arguing for the recognition of common humanity is not the same as bestowing citizenship rights upon people. As Cheah writes, "Since rights come into existence only via political instruments that specify and protect them, dignity by itself is not the source of rights. Dignity is rather some contentless human attribute that is the basis of freedom in the world" (*Inhuman Conditions* 153). This point, coupled with Naoki Sakai's assertion that the category of the human cannot be expanded to include the Asian given that former is premised on the inhuman Asian (or perhaps more specifically on the barbaric that mediates between the human and the nonhuman), might be taken as marking the limits of human rights discourse for the Asian refugee. *Found* then shifts the conversation in significant and productive ways. The Asian refugee, as presented in *Found,* is clearly different from Thammavongsa's father, who originally kept the scrapbook. The former is a category that exists without a subject and attests to the effects of power and knowledge, whereas the latter is, of course, a living human being. It is key then that both *Small Arguments* and *Found* rely on metaphor in order to examine the connection between the human and strategies of voice and representation. By substituting the bug for the human, and the illegible history for the particular refugee narrative, the two books of poetry sketch out reasons that the project of substituting the Asian refugee for the human must be a failed one. Put simply, *Small Arguments* and *Found* remind us that because the Asian refugee is already a metaphor for the inhuman, to see the bug as human or illegible history as legible or the Asian as human would require a different set of relations no longer structured by the logic of exception. It would perhaps require that we be situated outside of the forces of history and global capital.

Here, I find it useful to turn to Paul de Man's essay on autobiography for how it critically engages with the complex problem of referentiality and reading practices. He argues that autobiography is not a genre, but instead is

> a figure of reading or of understanding that occurs, to some degree, in all texts. The autobiographical moment happens as an alignment between the two subjects involved in the process of reading in which they determine each other by mutual reflexive substitution. The structure implies differentiation as well as similarity, since both depend on a substitutive exchange that constitutes the subject. This specular structure is interiorized in a text in which the author declares himself the subject of his own understanding, but this merely makes explicit the wider claim to authorship that takes place whenever a text is stated to be *by* someone and assumed to be understandable to the extent that this is the case. ("Autobiography" 921–22)

By focusing on the substitutive relations that occur between autobiographical reading subjects, de Man explains a principle at work in all reading practices. The autobiography is of particular interest precisely because of its inability to reveal self-knowledge and tendency to instead reveal "in a striking way the impossibility of closure and of totalization (that is the impossibility of coming into being) of all textual systems made up of tropological substitutions" ("Autobiography" 922). Consequently, we must understand substitution as part of all texts and a fundamental, if necessarily flawed, way in which we generate meaning. This reading of autobiography and substitution guides our thinking about Thammavongsa's poetry and its refusal to permit us to complete the chain of substitutions that link her father, the figure of the Asian refugee, and the specter of *zoe* that desires to become *bios*. This series of metaphoric relations fails to stabilize itself, collapsing periodically with the knowledge that it is reliant upon the reader's identification with the textual subject, shuffling between the desire to make intelligible the figure of the father and understandings of ourselves. Thus, the impossibility of closure in *Found*'s textual system indicates an ongoing dismantling of the category of the Asian refugee even as it continues to rely on it to produce the human subject.

By refusing to offer testimony and instead foregrounding the possibility that it might be easier to humanize objects, insects, and fruit than Asian refugees, Thammavongsa's poetry queries what is at stake in conceptualizing something as human, and, more pointedly, what this work directs our attention away from. Consequently, the poems compel us to remember that the human in this formulation, just like the inhuman, operates as a metaphor for a series of other terms (such as the universal and the dominant). What interests me here is the opportunity to contemplate the metaphoric relations through which concepts such as the Asian refugee and the inhuman come to take on residual meanings, and in this way, refuse to remain closed off from other possibilities of meaning. As Paul de Man notes in his discussion of metaphor as a form of smuggling, "We have no way of defining, of policing, the boundaries that separate the name of one entity from the name of another; tropes are not just travelers, they tend to be smugglers and probably smugglers of stolen goods at that" ("Epistemology of Metaphor" 19). Whether these metaphors import meaning "with criminal intent or not" ("Epistemology of Metaphor" 19) is beyond the grasp of our knowing because we can only think about the meaning that is produced through the movement of language rather than the original intentions behind them. We might think of the work of metaphor as substituting meanings in a messier fashion and always leaving behind traces of meaning instead of operating in a more hygienic and surgical fashion. Laden with various histories and affects, it becomes more difficult to substitute the Asian refugee and the inhuman for each other because they fail to move with ease and, moreover, refuse to function as the antithesis of the human. If metaphors are smugglers, then we can imagine a scenario in which they begin to return stolen meaning, and relations between terms are adjusted.

Figures of Minor Histories

Found, Thammavongsa's second book of poetry, pushes further concerns about human rights discourse being fundamentally incapable of responding to the needs of *zoe*. Not a found poem in the way that the genre typically works (with pieces of text reproduced but meaning altered as the text is revised and reframed), *Found* is instead a collection of poems based on the diary that Thammavongsa's father kept while they fled Laos and as they lived in the refugee camp. She found the journal after her father had thrown it out in Canada. Thammavongsa's poems engage with the scrapbook without knowing exactly what it says; she did not have it translated and does not read Laotian. The diary cannot be seen as a historical object in the conventional sense (in which the object is accompanied by a reconstructed narrative or set of newly discovered facts), but instead is an artifact salvaged because the poet felt it did not belong in the garbage. She qualifies this by claiming it was too dirty for the garbage, and also that she was too deeply emotionally attached to it to let it be discarded (Thammavongsa, "Poet's Statement").

The scrapbook itself is certainly an affective document, but *Found* does not seek to explore the poet's feelings in response to these memories. Here, I agree with Carrie Dawson's reading of *Found,* which understands "these poems as a refusal of a confessional mode grounded in demonstrable truths and designed to affirm the innocence of its subject and the benevolence of its audience" (71). Instead, I understand the poems as moving us to think about the silences that surround these histories as well as the act of looking at what Dipesh Chakrabarty calls "minor histories," understanding them as particular kinds of figures. I invoke Chakrabarty's ideas about writing minor histories because of the valuable challenge they pose to the discipline of history. By considering the need for a form distinct from conventional good histories that seek to expand without necessarily critiquing the parameters of the genre, minor histories demonstrate the importance of interrogating how "the so-called universal ideas that European thinkers produced in the period from the Renaissance to the Enlightenment and that have since influenced projects of modernity and modernization all over the world, could never be completely universal and pure concepts" (Chakrabarty xiii). In the preface to the first edition of *Provincializing Europe,* Chakrabarty explains that in writing this project, he hoped to highlight the specific histories that shaped and imprinted universal concepts (xiii). Central to his argument is the insight that the universal operates as an unstable but necessary figure for modernity, and that it is always shaped by specific and unrecognized histories. Chakrabarty unravels universal concepts and locates Europe within a "particular accretion of histories that are not always transparent to us. To provincialize Europe was then to know how universalistic thought was always and already modified by particular histories, whether or not we could excavate such pasts fully" (xiii–xiv). This process of tracing how universal concepts are produced by specific histories is one that Thammavongsa's *Small Arguments* and *Found* also participate in; her poems ask for reading practices that employ a somewhat different angle by showing how minor histories are obscured by categories such as the universal and the human.

The challenge of showcasing minor histories is particularly poignant in *Found*; "*Found* was more difficult for readers because it was too particular. It was about a man no one knew and a life no one knew. I had a man's life and I had to prove why it was worth caring about him even though he never invented or created or took down or built a country. He was just my father" (Barclay). Instead of idealizing her father in order to persuade the reader of his intrinsic worth, the poet uses a series of small gestures to interrogate methods for valuing lives and objects. Laden with profound emotion and conveying sharp critiques of the surrounding social world that refuses to make them legible or to provide them with any measure of relief, the poems advocate in their own style for a recognition of quieter ways of speaking and different modes of engagement. To change the shape of publics and create new forms of intimacy, these poems suggest that publics might center on texts that they do not necessarily understand or even realize are addressing them. And here it may be useful to understand the poems as introducing a distinction between a public (one that "we" might be part of and is addressed by the text) and forms of kinship (that would generate the emotional power of the piece for those located within it and bonded by its connections, but would remain, by definition, closed to most people) to explain the particular ways in which it engages various readers and audiences. By asking us to reflect upon what we see and fail to see, the poems engage with the histories embedded within them and, furthermore, question how we are located in relation to and within these histories. While the poems reference the speaker being born in Nong Khai, a large Thai refugee camp historically significant for the Lao diaspora, and her connection to Laos, the particulars of the narrative or history are never spelled out. *Found* does not explain why or how the parents left Laos and ended up in a refugee camp, or share any details about the trajectory that eventually brought the family to Canada. Consequently, our not knowing the contents of the journal kept by the poet's father functions as a metaphor for how histories operate within *Found* and *Small Arguments*.

The reader of these poems, like the speaker, is unaware of the details of the family's history of migration. The reader might also be unfamiliar with the histories of Laos in the 1970s, particularly since the Lao are perhaps the most underrepresented of the Southeast Asian groups in North America in terms of literature and scholarship about them. Because the Hmong were allied with the CIA during the war, they have more representation within the U.S. public sphere than the Lao. This lack of information about Laos poses problems of comprehension, both in terms of the content of the books of poetry as well as the minor histories that stand in metaphoric relation to the figures of the Asian refugee and the inhuman. That our lack of knowledge about the specific histories that shape *Found* does not prevent the poems from being read through the lens of human rights discourse is troubling, and implies that the transformation and even obliteration of particular histories and stories into bare life is a requirement in order for narratives of the polis to function. I suggest though, that as appalling as that scenario is, that some kind of transformative work continues to occur in this act of substituting histories for minor histories. Along the lines of de Man's smuggling metaphors, we might hope that even without necessarily knowing the histories of the speaker's family or Laos more broadly, something—whether it be insight, affect, or curiosity—nonetheless is illicitly produced and conveyed to the reader. Perhaps then we might read Thammavongsa's poetry as operating along lines similar to Chakrabarty's minor histories that seek to write a different kind of project and demand a new form in order to write "plural ways of being in the world" (101), and even those "forms of democracy that we can not yet either understand or envisage completely" (107).

The political structures within which we are located produce the logic of exception, in part because they prevent us from engaging with stories and subjects, and this, moreover, prevents socially intimate publics from being formed. At stake in identifying this problem is how we are to respond to the politics of publics, and, more precisely, their reliance upon bare life to produce citizens and social intimacy. If, as John Erni argues, "the legal form of governmentality creates a sense of inclusion that is in fact in very close proximity to the sense of exclusion, and . . . this does not undo citizenship but in fact makes citizenship possible" (14), then what alternatives can we formulate that take this more contingent form of citizenship into account? *Small Arguments* and *Found* respond to this problem through the very smallness of their poems, a strategy that moves us away from grandiose categories such as the universal and the human. The poems are brief, spare, minimal, and remarkable not just for what they say, but also for reflecting upon how attention is paid to certain objects and speeches. Through the blank space surrounding the words on the page, the poems engage the eye and force the reader to become conscious of the act of looking. The poems are constructed through the relation between words and blank space, and consequently, what is written stands out in relief. One example in *Found* is that of the single diagonal line that is repeated over eight pages. Initially, we see the line crossing out the month of January in 1979, presumably marking the progression of time. As the height of the humanitarian crisis in Southeast Asia, when refugees started flooding the Thai camps, especially from Cambodia and Laos, 1979 is a particularly significant year. But the repetition of that line month after month slowly distances the slash from its purpose until we are left querying its meaning and our ability to respond to global crises. Is the slash finally an act of repeated negation, determined to continue crossing out even when there is nothing left to obliterate or even oppose? Or might we perhaps read commitment and futile hope into this act of marking, constant even when betrayed by the forward march of a calendar that does not correspond to the stagnant state of other affairs? What is this mark crossing into? And what do we cross into after focusing on it?

Relief is not simply a visual relation that makes the text stand out against its white space, but also one that occurs in affective terms. The poems eschew the mode of the confessional replete with large gestures and chest-beating in favor of subtle probings of the world. Thammavongsa's texts write a poetics of relation, to borrow Glissant's term, into the cusp of being:

> This is why we stay with poetry. And despite our consenting to all the indisputable technologies; despite seeing the political leap that must be managed, the horror of hunger and ignorance, torture and massacre to be conquered, the full load of knowledge to be tamed, the weight of every piece of machinery that we shall finally control, and the exhausting flashes as we pass from one era to another—from forest to city, from story to computer—at the bow there is still something we now share: this murmur, cloud or rain or peaceful smoke. We know ourselves as part and as crowd, in an unknown that does not terrify. We cry our cry of poetry. Our boats are open and we sail them for everyone. (9)

The shared relationality that is conveyed through poetry permits us to negotiate the violence of the everyday. Part of the work of poetry is to make demands on, and inquiries about, the very act of imagining. *Small Arguments* and *Found* strive to do this work by scrutinizing closely and listening carefully rather than amplifying speech and address. Thammavongsa's work suggests much about how the inclusion of bare life within the polis, on national and international scales, depends on the modes of perception deployed, and, as a consequence, argues for seeing and hearing lives rather than political apparatuses, and subjects rather than categories.

Conclusion
Ephemeral Publics and Roy Kiyooka's *StoneDGloves*

Kyo Maclear's first novel, *The Letter Opener,* explores the place that diasporic individuals occupy within the Canadian social imagination by focusing on the friendship between a recent Romanian refugee and a Japanese Canadian woman, both of whom work as mail-recovery employees, returning lost mail to their intended recipients. At the beginning of the novel, we are told that Andrei has disappeared without a word, leaving Naiko both grief-stricken and unsure about what to do with the bits of story that he has confided in her. The text's premise underscores a link between the task of remembering and the material objects that prompt memories, suggesting that this dialectical relationship produces value and possibility. And in this way, the novel cautions against the temptation to tightly hold onto physical souvenirs while neglecting the histories from which they emerge, an error that perpetuates the illusion that, as Sara Ahmed argues in *The Cultural Politics of Emotion,* affective value and emotions reside in objects (11). In their respective fashions, Ahmed and Maclear assert the need to undertake memory work rather than memorializing lost feelings and histories.

One strategy that *The Letter Opener* employs in its project of engaged remembering is to use a snippet from Roy Kiyooka's exhibition *StoneDGloves* (1970) as an epigraph: "the way they fell / the way they lay there // the dust sifting down, / hiding all the clues" (Maclear, *Letter Opener*). These lines are taken from the opening section of Kiyooka's piece, a combination of photographs and poetry that document multiple historical layers, the most immediate one being the forgotten labor of workers who constructed Expo '70. By focusing on the workers' gloves, Kiyooka draws attention to the aesthetic and political strategies of representation at work in public forms of memory and commemoration, and it is this line of inquiry that *The Letter Opener* extends to include the current moment. This return to Kiyooka, an interdisciplinary cultural producer, racialized modernist artist, and Japanese Canadian affected by internment but not himself interned, is provocative because Kiyooka is a figure that disrupts more familiar ways of telling cultural, artistic, national, and Asian Canadian histories. And yet, of course, it is precisely this very difficulty that he poses for conventional histories that is so generative for Asian Canadian publics as they interrogate their awkward and uneasy locations within Canadian, North American, and transnational discourses of sociability and citizenship. It is for this reason that *The Letter Opener* is one of several engagements with Kiyooka's work by contemporary Asian Canadian writers and critics such as Rita Wong, Roy Miki, and Christopher Lee. In her essay "Corrupted Lineage: Narrative in the Gaps of History," Larissa Lai suggests that Kiyooka is one of many writers (whom she lists alongside Roy Miki, Fred Wah, jamila ismail, and Marie Annharte Baker) whose work has been groundbreaking for a younger generation of writers, but largely ignored by the wider public. Lai interrogates this general neglect by asking us to "consider what this situation means for marginalized writers in terms of writing practice and, more widely as critical and creative subjects within a shifting social and political context, where certain inroads have been laid and certain power structures have transformed and adapted" (42). These multiple returns to Kiyooka's work suggest that it operates as a kind of Asian Canadian archive, one that offers its users valuable aesthetic, social, and political strategies. But if Kiyooka's work directs us to imagining unorthodox figures in relation to alternative histories in new ways, I want to underscore that it also reminds us that the minor publics called into being tend to be marked by impermanence. Kiyooka's ephemera, both as subject and style, pose important implications for the cultural politics of memory and institutionalization at work in minor publics that do not make the same claims to endurance as communities or nations. I end this book on Asian Canadian publics by looking at Kiyooka's work because his projects ask us to think about the temporality of intimate publics at the same time that they explore the aesthetics of racial representation. More specifically, *StoneDGloves* is an example of how race marks the limits of representation for dominant publics even as it remains a central logic for minor racialized publics; in negotiating this contradiction, Kiyooka's work produces a form of intimacy for racialized publics that is both ephemeral and generative.

In 1969, the Canadian government invited Kiyooka to construct a sculpture that would be part of the Canadian pavilion at Expo '70, which was to be held in Osaka, Japan. While working on this piece, Kiyooka became fixated upon the numerous workers' gloves that lay scattered about the Expo grounds, and snapped hundreds of photographs of them. A portion of these images were eventually transformed into an exhibition that he called *StoneDGloves: Alms for Soft Palms,* forty black-and-white photographs (some inscribed with poetry written in vinyl letters), that toured extensively in the early 1970s, making its way throughout Canada as well as to Japan and France. The actual photographs are large, ranging from two and a half to five feet in length, and Kiyooka suggested for at least one showing that they be hung from the ceiling as well as put on walls. This layout, which Scott Toguri McFarlane describes as "a cavernous, archaeological labyrinth," is one that I imagine would produce an intense, perhaps even overwhelming, aesthetic experience, flooding the viewer with images that literally touch her or him, thus preventing the possibility of distance (121). The sequence of *StoneDGloves* was later reworked, shortened, and is now available in print as part of his collected poems, *Pacific Windows.* The striking images in Kiyooka's early work give us a way of understanding the particular stakes in the notion of ephemerality for Asian Canadian publics. Kiyooka's ongoing use of ephemera, both as subject matter in the *StoneDGloves* collection and as a mode of production in his practice of self-producing limited-run poetry chapbooks and publishing correspondence during his lifetime, unseats easy distinctions between past and present, public and private, archive and text. It is also a means of apprehending the social and aesthetic mechanisms of forgetting and grasping how these processes locate Asian Canadian publics within larger national imaginaries.

At the end of *StoneDGloves,* Kiyooka includes a postscript: "the photos show how / the gloves fell / from the hands of work-men // flying home at 35000 ft / I imagined a cloud of whitegloves / falling into the Pacific /// the litter'd-site sings / thru in-sight. the poems link glove / to glove" (91). These words provide a powerful closing image that yokes the preceding portraits of workers' gloves to the countless lives destroyed by the WWII bombings, thereby making visible the disappearing bodies of both laborers and atomic victims. This link is reinforced in "Wheels," another sequence in *Pacific Windows* composed of photographs, poems, and fragments of text that appear to be letters, which documents Kiyooka's travels through Japan in 1969. Here, the speaker, after visiting the Hiroshima museum, is horrified, but also frustrated by the limits of representation and overwhelmed by personal memories from his childhood in Alberta. And so he writes:

Dear M: / no postcard / s. no images: though I took my / share of pictures of mute things inside the museum I won't / belabour their visual paucity, how they inevitably / leave out the stench of searing flesh and yes, all the offal desecration/ s ad / nauseam. John Hersey's "Hiroshima" / stands word-for-word behind these perambulatory thoughts . . . / I remember "JAPS SURRENDER!" / I remember all the flagrant incarceration / s / I remember playing dead Indian / I remember the RCMP finger-printing me: / I was 15 and lofting hay that cold winter day / what did I know about treason? / I learned to speak a good textbook English / I seldom spoke anything else. / I never saw the "yellow peril" in myself / Mackenzie King did). (170)

This section of "Wheels" links the spaces of Hiroshima and Alberta by transforming both Japanese and Japanese Canadian individuals into what Kiyooka calls "mute things" made silent by official social memory. While internment and atomic bombings represent two very different responses to the threat of "yellow peril," Kiyooka's reaction to the museum demonstrates an inability to separate these injuries as he is confronted by the violent traces of racism.

StoneDGloves effectively shows how ephemerality as a condition is attached to various publics in radically different ways. Photographing ephemera, the stoned gloves from the site of Expo '70, becomes a means of working through an unintentional forgetting of this Japanese trauma that was to some extent obscured by the pain of Kiyooka's own Japanese Canadian trauma and complicated by his geographical location. That the Japanese Canadian individual affected by internment becomes witness to the artifacts of Hiroshima is a provocative chain; these precarious existences locate and legitimate each other, however tentatively and provisionally, through their relations. *StoneDGloves* also reminds us of the cultural politics that determine ephemerality. At Hiroshima and Nagasaki, human bodies became ephemeral, disappearing almost without a trace after three-second bombings. This process of ephemeralizing Japanese lives extended to erasing those that died and those that survived for various lengths of time, bearing serious injury, as there was a U.S.-imposed ban against remembering. In Japan, the censorship of representations of the bombing meant that it was not until the documentary *Effects of the Atomic Bomb* was screened in 1952 that "most Japanese civilians . . . [had] their first opportunity to become visually and affectively immersed in the terrors of the atomic bomb experience" (Maclear, *Beclouded Visions* 41). In *Beclouded Visions*, her critical book on memory and the atomic bombs, Maclear firmly asserts that this censorship code was imposed from 1945 to 1952 because "the U.S. government did not want any evidence of the bombings to circulate" (41). Thus, the traces of these deliberately disremembered bodies that remain work against the grain of institutionalized memory and defy historical censorship.

What Can Ephemera Do?

In photographing the gloves and transforming them into a multilayered text composed of images and words, Kiyooka reckons with the complex position he occupies in relation to the host of memories he mediates. In "Wheels," he muses, "perhaps the photo / glyphs i took / of abandoned work gloves on the site of Expo 70 / will negotiate a tryst for my sense of / an un-embittered, well-being. what's the price / of clasping one another's hands ?" (171). Roy Miki, commenting on "Wheels," explains Kiyooka's unease about capturing the Hiroshima artifacts by noting, "[A]s he frames what has already been framed, he is suddenly caught in the aura of his own complicity in the aesthetic appropriation of images projecting intolerable suffering and trauma" ("Unravelling" 77). In deliberating the costs of "clasping one another's hands," a matter highlighted through the image of stoned gloves, and the problem of how to ethically engage with this suffering, Kiyooka and Miki emphasize the challenges of seriously engaging with ephemera as well as the need to be conscious of our motivations for wanting to preserve and capture it. Maclear asks a similar question in her critical work on visual art and witnessing, stating:

> Hiroshima and Nagasaki suggest that we must release ourselves of the ambition to see and know it *all*, while attending to the ethical consequences of our partial perceptions. But the space of witnessing is elongated or abbreviated in part by how we define our role as participants in the making of memory and meaning. How we frame questions about what we are seeing invariably shapes our answers: What kind of witnesses will we be? (*Beclouded Visions* 9)

Because memory work not only creates as it remembers but also needs to clear space within the consciousness in order to do so, the stakes of forming such a public are considerable.

The *StoneDGloves* sequence makes visible the histories and the ongoing circuits by which this particular configuration—a celebration of "Progress and Harmony for Mankind," the theme of Expo '70 in Japan—is arrived at. *StoneDGloves* contradicts the popular belief in the ability of objects to last indefinitely and independently, a view that can be used to excerpt objects from their histories and the networks that bestow them with meaning. Instead, the vulnerability of ephemera compels the viewer to remain vigilant and conscious of the constant risk of loss. And in the particular instance of Kiyooka's gloves, we are doubly cautioned about being wary because we are reminded of the all-too-recent forgetting of Japanese and Japanese Canadian traumas.

Ephemeralizing Institutionalized Memory

The transformative potential of Kiyooka's ephemera lies in the possibilities it poses for creating new forms of sociability. More specifically, ephemera demands attentiveness from its viewer by virtue of the fact that it cannot wait to be remembered. Thus, by its very nature, Kiyooka's ephemeral art addresses a public in intimate terms as it asks us to engage with the complexity of racialized histories and representations. Ephemera then, in its attentiveness to the present moment, gives Asian Canadian publics a strategy for engaging wider publics; by drawing attention to the fleeting aspects of objects, memories, and cultural production, Kiyooka's gloves make visible the transitory dimensions of even exclusionary institutional structures and produce hope for future social change. At the same time, Kiyooka's ephemera asks us to consider what has been and continues to be excluded from the social symbolic—namely, those dimensions of Asian publics that resist easy incorporation into the parameters of national memory—and it demands that we hold on to those bits. For while they mark the limits of dominant publics, these memories of racialization also produce a sense of intimacy within Asian Canadian publics. To return then full circle back to Maclear's *The Letter Opener*, that novel's invocation of Kiyooka's gloves becomes a remembering of remembering, a moment of serializing memory that remains conscious of the ongoing production. Kiyooka's ephemera acts as a model for Asian Canadian critical engagement, one that remains conscious of the need to disrupt history in order to remember the present. And it is in this way that Asian Canadian publics not only operate as a crucial site for understanding how race has and continues to operate locally, nationally, and globally, but also open up new ways of speaking, feeling, and thinking it.

Notes

Introduction: Multiculturalism, Minor Publics, and Social Intimacy

1. See, for instance, blog entries by Malaika Aleba, Rakhi Ruparelia, Todd Wong, and Phil Yu that contribute to this debate.

2. See, for example, scholarship by Seyla Benhabib, Nancy Fraser, Joan Landes, Mary Ryan, and Lynn Spigel on this subject.

3. The concept of minor empires is one that Christopher Lee and I develop through discussions of settler colonies and how the Asian is positioned within them. While countries such as Canada, Australia, and South Africa may not have been major imperial powers, they are nonetheless part of that imperial system and are still shaped by those desires. We explore minor empires and the Asian Pacific in our proposed special issue for the journal *Canadian Literature*.

4. See, for instance, Ali Kazimi's documentary film *Continuous Journey*, Radhika Viyas Mongia's "Race, Nationality, Mobility: A History of the Passport," Renisa Mawani's "Specters of Indigeneity in British-Indian Migration, 1914," and Hugh Johnston's *The Voyage of the "Komagata Maru."*

5. For further discussion of Linsanity (as it was dubbed by the media), see my 2014 article on this topic (Kim, "The Smell of Communities to Come," in the *Journal of Intercultural Studies* 35, no. 3).

Chapter 1. National Incompletion

1. See, for instance, work by Himani Bannerji, Smaro Kamboureli, and Minoo Moallem and Iain Boal.

2. My thanks to Ric Knowles for sharing insights about sitting knee to knee during his *Bioboxes* experience.

3. I should make it clear that I did not have the opportunity to see the performance. My only experiences with the Japanese *Biobox* have been with the script and discussions, through e-mail and in person, with Cindy Mochizuki, who generously shared her interview materials and thoughts with me. I am also grateful to Maiko Yamamoto of Theatre Replacement for graciously sharing promotional materials and images from the performance and to Natalie Brenton for carefully transcribing the interview.

4. While this is a general division that shapes conversations about history, memory, and injustice within academic and nonacademic spaces, many important contributions strive to disturb these divisions. A partial list of critical texts published in the past few years that seek to reconceptualize the relations between past and future as well as the kinds of historical legacies and responsibilities that shape the Canadian present include Ashok Mathur, Jonathan Dewar, and Mike DeGagné's *Cultivating Canada* (2011), Kirsten McAllister's *Terrain of Memory* (2010), Mona Oikawa's "Relations of Redress" (2012), and Paulette Regan's *Unsettling the Settler Within* (2011).

5. See Guy Beauregard's "After *Obasan*" for a detailed examination of this phenomenon.

6. David Gaertner's dissertation chapter on *The Rain Ascends*, Benjamin Lefebvre's journal article on *The Rain Ascends*, and Sheena Wilson's edited collection *Joy Kogawa: Essays on Her Works* are among the few scholarly investigations that look at Kogawa's work apart from *Obasan*.

7. See, for instance, Daniel Coleman's *White Civility*, Ruth Frankenberg's *White Women, Race Matters*, Sander Gilman's work on Jewish cultural studies (*Difference and Pathology*; *The Jew's Body*), and Toni Morrison's *Playing in the Dark*.

8. For a provocative look at this history through the visual culture of postwar Japan, see Linda Hoaglund's documentary film *ANPO* (2010).

Chapter 2. Transnational Triviality

1. For a more detailed comparison of Canadian and U.S. university admissions policies as they pertain to the "Too Asian?" debate, see David Weinfeld's "Asians and Affirmative Action on Campus."

2. More recent controversies fueled by social media include two led by Suey Park in 2014. Both the #CancelColbert (a response to a comment on *The Colbert Report*'s Twitter feed) and #HowIMetYourRacism (a response to a yellowface episode of the sitcom *How I Met Your Mother*) are examples of Twitter campaigns that elicited strong and immediate responses from Twitter followers and generated debates in other social media platforms.

3. Recent scholarship that explores Asian American and African American relations and the problem of citizenship includes Helen Jun's *Race for Citizenship*, Moon-Ho Jung's *Coolies and Cane*, Claire Kim's *Bitter Fruit*, James Lee's *Urban Triage*, Mae Ngai's *Impossible Subjects*, Viet Nguyen's *Race and Resistance*, and Min Song's *Strange Future*.

4. For a more detailed overview of the history of Canadian cultural industries, including book publishing, see Michael Dorland's *The Cultural Industries in Canada* and Roy MacSkimming's *The Perilous Trade*.

5. My examination of *Maclean's* as a publication venue for "Too Asian?" should also be read alongside Jeet Heer's introduction to *"Too Asian?"* for its brief biography of Ken Whyte, publisher and editor in chief of *Maclean's*, and underscoring of Whyte's consistently socially conservative politics. Heer's overview makes a strong case for seeing "Too Asian?" not "as an isolated mistake but as in keeping with the larger ideological imperative that has governed Whyte's career" ("Introduction" c).

6. Canadian responses include a YouTube video titled "'Asians in the Library': UCLA Girl Alexandra Wallace Gets Death Threats, Asian Godfather Responds" by Tetsuro Shigematsu, commentary in the *Vancouver Observer* about Shigematsu's video by Krissy Darch and Ray Hsu, and discussions in online forums about the University of British Columbia library in forum threads such as the one started by bebex3.

7. For a sample of this critical work in the Canadian context, see the introduction to Christine Kim, Sophie McCall, and Melina Baum Singer's *Cultural Grammars of Nation, Diaspora, and Indigeneity* as well as Roy Miki's *Redress* and Rinaldo Walcott's *Black Like Who?* Examples of American contributions include Lisa Lowe's *Immigrant Acts*, Judith Butler's *Precarious Life*, and Wendy Brown's *Regulating Aversion* and "Wounded Attachments."

8. The recent complaint by Dr. Jennifer Chan (against the University of British Columbia) and earlier cases such as Dr. Kin-Yip Chun (against the University of Toronto) are two high-profile examples that demonstrate what is at stake in the inability to easily name and understand race and racism.

Chapter 3. Diasporic Fragility and Brokenness

1. The newspaper article that David Khang is standing behind originally appeared on the front page of the *Globe and Mail* in 1995 and included a picture of Khang's aunt, Park Yong-Gil, visiting North Korea. Her husband, Moon Ik-Hwan, a minister turned political dissident activist, had been jailed for his Korean unification activism, which included a visit to North Korea. Moon passed away in 1994, the year before Park's visit (Khang, "Re: Abstract").

2. David Khang generously conducted a studio visit for graduate students in my English 843 course and Dr. Christopher Lee's English 545 course (offered at Simon Fraser University and the University of British Columbia, respectively) on November 7, 2010.

3. While the Korean War is frequently referred to as the Forgotten War in an American context (see, for instance, Clay Blair's *The Forgotten War,* Bruce Cumings's *Korea: The Unknown War,* and *Memory of Forgotten War,* a film by Deann Borshay Liem and Ramsay Liem), many understand it as having been forgotten by Canadians as well. John Melady writes in the preface to the second edition of *Korea: Canada's Forgotten War* that his initial impetus for writing his book in the 1980s came from a sense that "the

war in Korea, and the involvement of Canadians in it, was barely known about at the time" and, "[s]adly, not much has changed since then" (11).

4. For further discussion of racial identity and the language of woundedness, see Anne Anlin Cheng's *The Melancholy of Race* (2001), and David Eng and David Kazanjian's edited collection *Loss* (2003). Wendy Brown's "Wounded Attachments" (1993) and Judith Butler's *Precarious Life* (2004) also offer related and pertinent discussions of political identity and pain.

5. By emphasizing the Korean War as a historic moment that led to an outpouring of people who migrated to North America, among other places, my intention is neither to attribute a singular point of origin to the Korean diaspora nor is it to suggest that the work of imperialist displacement is over.

6. My thanks to Phanuel Antwi for astutely reminding me of Jameson's aphorism.

7. See, for instance, Grace Cho's *Haunting the Korean Diaspora* and Jodi Kim's *Ends of Empire*.

8. Syngman Rhee (president of South Korea from 1948 to 1960) received his BA from George Washington University, MA from Harvard University, and PhD from Princeton.

Chapter 4. Global Loss

1. The author's note in *Found* states that in 1978, her family lived in Nong Khai, a Lao refugee camp in Thailand.

2. Their essay was originally published in *Critical Inquiry* 24, no. 2 (Winter 1998) and then reprinted as a chapter of Warner's *Publics and Counterpublics*.

Works Cited

Acheson, Keith, and Christopher Maule. "No Bite, No Bark: The Mystery of Magazine Policy." *American Review of Canadian Studies* 31, no. 3 (Fall 2001): 467–81.

Agamben, Giorgio. *Homo Sacer: Sovereign Power and Bare Life*. Trans. Daniel Heller-Roazen. Stanford, CA: Stanford University Press, 1998.

———. *State of Exception*. Trans. Kevin Attell. Chicago: University of Chicago Press, 2005.

Ahmed, Sara. *The Cultural Politics of Emotion*. New York: Routledge, 2004.

———. "Multiculturalism and the Promise of Happiness." *New Formations* 63 (2007–8): 121–37.

Ahmed, Sara, Claudia Castaneda, Anne-Marie Fortier, and Mimi Sheller, eds. *Uprootings/Regroundings: Questions of Home and Migration*. Oxford: Berg, 2003.

Aleba, Malaika. "Mo' Money, Mo' Problems: Canada Whitewashes the New $100 Bill." *Autostraddle*. Excitant Group, 21 August 2012. Web. 21 June 2013.

Anderson, Benedict. *Imagined Communities: Reflections on the Origin and Spread of Nationalism*. Rev. and extended ed., 2nd ed. London: Verso, 1991.

Anderson, Kylie. "Re: UCLA Racist Rant." Online video clip. *YouTube*. YouTube, 13 March 2011. Web. October 2011.

ANPO. Dir. Linda Hoaglund. New Day Films, 2010.

Arendt, Hannah. *Eichmann in Jerusalem: A Report on the Banality of Evil*. New York: Viking Press, 1964.

Asakawa, Gil. "Aftermath of Alexandra Wallace 'Asians in the Library' Video: She Meant to Do It, and Two Great Responses." *Nikkei View: The Asian American Blog*. WordPress, 18 March 2011. Web. 2 August 2012.

Asian Pacific Coalition at UCLA. "In Response to 'Asians in the Library.'" Message to Asian American Studies Department and Center faculty, students, and staff. 16 March 2011. E-mail.

Austin, J. L. *How to Do Things with Words.* New York: Oxford University Press, 1965.

Balibar, Étienne. "Is There a 'Neo-Racism'?" In *Race, Nation, Class: Ambiguous Identities.* Étienne Balibar and Immanuel Wallerstein. Trans. Chris Turner, 17–28. London: Verso, 1991.

———. "Preface." In *Race, Nation, Class: Ambiguous Identities.* Étienne Balibar and Immanuel Wallerstein. Trans. Chris Turner, 1–13. London: Verso, 1991.

Banita, Georgiana. "Raymond Williams and Online Video: The Tragedy of Technology." In *About Raymond Williams,* edited by Monika Seidl, Roman Horak, and Lawrence Grossberg, 94–105. London: Routledge, 2010.

Bannerji, Himani. *The Dark Side of the Nation: Essays on Multiculturalism, Nationalism and Gender.* Toronto: Canadian Scholars' Press, 2000.

Barclay, Adèle. "Interview with Souvankham Thammavongsa." *The Journal* 136, no. 8 (19 September 2008). Web. 12 December 2012.

Beauregard, Guy. "After *Obasan*: Kogawa Criticism and Its Futures." *Studies in Canadian Literature* 26, no. 2 (2001): 5–22.

bebex3. "'Asians in the Library': UCLA Girl's Wild Racist Rant." *Mallvibes.* XenForo, 14 March 2011. Web. August 2012.

Beeby, Dean. "Are Canada's $100 Polymer Bills Really Maple-Scented?" *CTV News Vancouver.* Bell Media, 27 May 2013. Web. 19 June 2013.

———. "Canada $100 Bill Controversy: Mark Carney, Bank of Canada Governor, Issues Apology." *HuffPost Business.* TheHuffingtonPost.com, 20 August 2012. Web. 19 June 2013.

———. "Image of Asian-Looking Woman Removed from New $100 Bills after Complaints." *Thestar.com.* Toronto Star Newspapers, 17 August 2012. Web. 19 May 2013.

Benhabib, Seyla. "Models of Public Space: Hannah Arendt, the Liberal Tradition, and Jürgen Habermas." In *Habermas and the Public Sphere,* edited by Craig J. Calhoun, 73–98. Cambridge, MA: MIT Press, 1992.

Benjamin, Walter. "A Short History of Photography." Trans. Stanley Mitchell. *Screen* 13 (Spring 1972): 5–26.

———. *Illuminations.* Ed. and introduction by Hannah Arendt. Trans. Harry Zohn. New York: Harcourt, Brace and World, 1968.

Berlant, Lauren. *Cruel Optimism.* Durham, NC: Duke University Press, 2011.

———. *The Female Complaint: The Unfinished Business of Sentimentality in American Culture.* Durham, NC: Duke University Press, 2008.

———. "Intimacy: A Special Issue." In *Intimacy,* edited by Lauren Berlant, 1–8. Chicago: University of Chicago Press, 2000.

Berlant, Lauren, and Michael Warner. "Sex in Public." In *Publics and Counterpublics,* by Michael Warner, 187–208. New York: Zone Books, 2002.

Bhabha, Homi. *The Location of Culture.* London: Routledge, 1994.

Blair, Clay. *The Forgotten War: America in Korea, 1950–1953*. New York: Anchor Books, 1987.
Bomb Harvest. Dir. Kim Mordaunt. Lemur Films, 2007.
Bow, Leslie. *Partly Colored: Asian Americans and Racial Anomaly in the Segregated South*. New York: New York University Press, 2010.
Brennan, Teresa. *The Transmission of Affect*. Ithaca, NY: Cornell University Press, 2004.
Brown, Wendy. *Regulating Aversion: Tolerance in the Age of Identity and Empire*. Princeton, NJ: Princeton University Press, 2006.
———. "Wounded Attachments." *Political Theory* 21, no. 3 (August 1993): 390–410.
Brydon, Diana. "Dionne Brand's Global Intimacies: Practising Affective Citizenship." *University of Toronto Quarterly* 76, no. 3 (2007): 990–1006.
Butler, Judith. *Precarious Life: The Powers of Mourning and Violence*. London: Verso, 2004.
Canadian Coalition of Community Partners to Eliminate Anti-Asian Racism. "Open Letter—A Call to Eliminate Anti-Asian Racism." *AsianCanadianStudies.ca*. Pixeljets.com, 23 November 2010. Web. 11 December 2014.
Canadian Press. "Asian-Looking Woman Scientist Image Rejected for $100 Bills." *CBC News*. CBC.ca, 17 August 2012. Web. 19 May 2013.
Chakrabarty, Dipesh. *Provincializing Europe: Postcolonial Thought and Historical Difference*. Princeton, NJ: Princeton University Press, 2000.
Chan, Anthony. *Gold Mountain: The Chinese in the New World*. Vancouver: New Star Books, 1983.
Chang, Kornel. *Pacific Connections: The Making of the U.S.-Canadian Borderlands*. Berkeley: University of California Press, 2012.
Chariandy, David. "'The Fiction of Belonging': On Second-Generation Black Writing in Canada." *Callaloo* 30, no. 3 (Summer 2007): 818–29.
Cheah, Pheng. *Inhuman Conditions: On Cosmopolitanism and Human Rights*. Cambridge, MA: Harvard University Press, 2006.
———. "Crises of Money." In *The Creolization of Theory*, edited by François Lionnet and Shu-mei Shih, 83–111. Durham, NC: Duke University Press, 2011.
———. "Universal Areas: Asian Studies in a World in Motion." In *Traces 1: Specters of the West and the Politics of Translation, 2001*, edited by Naoki Sakai and Yukiko Hanawa, 37–70. Hong Kong: Hong Kong University Press, 2012.
Chen, Kuan-Hsing. "The Imperialist Eye: The Cultural Imaginary of a Subempire and a Nation-State." *positions: east asia cultures critique* 8, no. 1 (2000): 9–76.
Cheng, Anne Anlin. *The Melancholy of Race: Psychoanalysis, Assimilation, and Hidden Grief*. New York: Oxford University Press, 2001.
Chinese Canadian National Council, Toronto Chapter. "August 2012 Newsletter." Online posting. *Facebook*. Facebook, 29 August 2012. Web. July 2013.
Cho, Grace M. *Haunting the Korean Diaspora: Shame, Secrecy, and the Forgotten War*. Minneapolis: University of Minnesota Press, 2008.
Cho, Lily. "Diasporic Citizenship: Contradictions and Possibilities." In *Trans.Can.Lit*, edited by Smaro Kamboureli and Roy Miki, 93–109. Waterloo, ON: Wilfrid Laurier University Press, 2007.

———. "Underwater Signposts: Richard Fung's *Islands* and Enabling Nostalgia." In *Cultural Grammars of Nation, Diaspora, and Indigeneity in Canada*, edited by Christine Kim, Sophie McCall, and Melina Baum Singer, 191–205. Waterloo, ON: Wilfrid Laurier University Press, 2012.

Choi, Susan. *The Foreign Student*. 1998. New York: HarperCollins, 1999.

Chu, Seo-Young. "Science Fiction and Postmemory Han in Contemporary Korean American Literature." *MELUS* 33, no. 4 (2008): 97–121.

Chun, Wendy Hui Kyong. "Introduction: Race and/as Technology; or, How to Do Things to Race." *Camera Obscura* 24, no. 1 (2009): 6–35.

———. "Orienting Orientalism; or, How to Map Cyberspace." In *Asian America.Net: Ethnicity, Nationalism, and Cyberspace*, edited by Rachel C. Lee and Sau-ling Cynthia Wong, 3–36. New York: Routledge, 2003.

Clemchan17. "Asians in the Library—The Guy She Saw Speaks Up—UCLA Girl (Alexandra Wallace)." Online video clip. *YouTube*. YouTube, 18 March 2011. Web. 15 January 2015.

Coleman, Daniel. *White Civility: The Literary Project of English Canada*. Toronto: University of Toronto Press, 2006.

Compton, Wayde. *After Canaan: Essays on Race, Writing, and Region*. Vancouver: Arsenal Pulp Press, 2010.

Coyne, Andrew. "Canada's $100 Bill Flap a Teachable Moment." *National Post*. National Post, 23 August 2012. Web. 19 May 2014.

Cumings, Bruce. *Korea: The Unknown War*. New York: Pantheon Books, 1988.

Cvetkovich, Ann. *An Archive of Feelings*. Durham, NC: Duke University Press, 2003.

———. "Public Feelings." *South Atlantic Quarterly* 106, no. 3 (2007): 459–68.

Darch, Krissy, and Ray Hsu. "Tetsuro Shigematsu Responds to 'Asians in the Library' Video." *Vancouver Observer*. Observer Media Group, 18 March 2011. Web. 11 October 2011.

Dawson, Carrie. "On Thinking Like a State and Reading (about) Refugees." *Journal of Canadian Studies* 45, no. 2 (Spring 2011): 58–75.

D.D. "Asians in the Library: Part of a Series on Viral Videos." *Know Your Meme*. Cheezburger, Inc., n.d. Web. 11 July 2013.

Dean, Jodi. *Publicity's Secret: How Technoculture Capitalizes on Democracy*. Ithaca, NY: Cornell University Press, 2002.

de Man, Paul. "Autobiography as De-facement." *MLN* 94, no. 5 (December 1979): 919–30.

———. "The Epistemology of Metaphor." *Critical Inquiry* 5, no. 1 (Autumn 1978): 13–30.

Dorland, Michael, ed. *The Cultural Industries in Canada: Problems, Policies and Prospects*. Toronto: James Lorimer, 1996.

Dyer, Richard. "White." *Screen* 29, no. 4 (1988): 44–64.

"Editorial: The U.C.L.A. Video." *New York Times*. 17 March 2011. Web. 11 July 2013.

Ellis, John. "Mundane Witness." In *Media Witnessing: Testimony in the Age of Mass Communication*, edited by Paul Frosh and Amit Pinchevski, 73–89. Basingstoke, UK: Palgrave Macmillan, 2009.

Eng, David. *The Feeling of Kinship: Queer Liberalism and the Racialization of Intimacy*. Durham, NC: Duke University Press, 2010.

Eng, David, and David Kazanjian, eds. *Loss: The Politics of Mourning*. Berkeley: University of California Press, 2003.

Engler, Yves. *The Black Book of Canadian Foreign Policy*. Vancouver: Fernwood, RED Publishing in association with The Dominion, 2009.

Erni, John. "Citizenship Management: On the Politics of Being Included-out." *International Journal of Cultural Studies*. Prepublished 12 March 2015, 1–18. doi: 10.1177/1367877915573772.

Espiritu, Yen Le. *Body Counts: The Vietnam War and Militarized Refuge(es)*. Berkeley: University of California Press, 2014.

Findlay, Stephanie, and Nicholas Kohler. "Too Asian?" *Maclean's*. 10 November 2010. Web. 22 November 2010.

Frankenberg, Ruth. *White Women, Race Matters: The Social Construction of Whiteness*. Minneapolis: University of Minnesota Press, 1993.

Fraser, Nancy. "Rethinking the Public Sphere: A Contribution to the Critique of Actually Existing Democracy." In *The Phantom Public Sphere*, edited by Bruce Robbins, 1–32. Minneapolis: University of Minnesota Press, 1993.

Gaertner, David. "Beyond Truth: Materialist Approaches to Reconciliation Theories and Politics in Canada." PhD diss., Simon Fraser University, 2012.

Gilman, Sander. *Difference and Pathology: Stereotypes of Sexuality, Race, and Madness*. Ithaca, NY: Cornell University Press, 1985.

———. *The Jew's Body*. New York: Routledge, 1991.

Gilmour, R. J., Davina Bhandar, Jeet Heer, and Michael C. K. Ma, eds. *"Too Asian?": Racism, Privilege, and Post-Secondary Education*. Toronto: Between the Lines, 2012.

Gilroy, Paul. *The Black Atlantic: Modernity and Double Consciousness*. Cambridge, MA: Harvard University Press, 1993.

Glissant, Édouard. *Poetics of Relation*. 1990. Trans. Betsy Wing. Ann Arbor: University of Michigan Press, 1997.

Government of Canada. "Canadian Multiculturalism Act." *Department of Justice*. Canada.ca, n.d. Web. March 2012.

———. "Canada Periodical Fund." *Department of Canadian Heritage*. Canada.ca, 1 November 2013. Web. June 2014.

Gunadie, Andrew. "Canada's New Non-Asian $100 Bill." Online video clip. *YouTube*. YouTube, 19 August 2012. Web. 19 May 2014.

Habermas, Jürgen. *The Structural Transformation of the Public Sphere An Inquiry into a Category of Bourgeois Society*. Cambridge, MA/Cambridge, UK: MIT Press/Polity Press, 1989.

Hage, Ghassan. *Against Paranoid Nationalism: Searching for Hope in a Shrinking Society*. Annandale, NSW/London: Pluto Press/Merlin Press, 2003.

Hartley, John. "Uses of YouTube: Digital Literacy and the Growth of Knowledge." In *YouTube: Online Video and Participatory Culture*, edited by Jean Burgess and Joshua Green, 126–43. Cambridge, BC: Polity Press, 2009.

Heer, Jeet. "Introduction." In *"Too Asian?": Racism, Privilege, and Post-Secondary Education*, edited by R. J. Gilmour, Davina Bhandar, Jeet Heer, and Michael C. K. Ma, 1–13. Toronto: Between the Lines, 2012.

———. "Too Brazen." *The Walrus Blog*. The Walrus Foundation, 24 November 2010. Web. 15 June 2011.

———. "*Maclean's* Article on Asians Familiar to Anti-Semites of Old." *National Post*. 15 November 2010. Web. November 22, 2010.

Henning, Michelle. "New Lamps for Old: Photography, Obsolescence, and Social Change." In *Residual Media*, edited by Charles R. Acland, 48–65. Minneapolis: University of Minnesota Press, 2007.

Herzfeld, Michael. "The Cultural Politics of Gesture: Reflections on the Embodiment of Ethnographic Practice." *Ethnography* 10, no. 2 (2009): 131–52.

Hirsch, Marianne. "The Generation of Postmemory." *Poetics Today* 29, no. 1 (Spring 2008): 103–28.

House of Commons Debates. 28th Parliament, 3rd Session: Vol. 8. October 8, 1971. 8545–8585. Web. 15 October 2013.

Hui, Yuk. "Interview with Pheng Cheah on Cosmopolitanism, Nationalism and Human Rights." *Theory Culture and Society*. Sage Publications, 17 March 2011. Web. 1 June 2014.

Huyssen, Andreas. *Present Pasts: Urban Palimpsests and the Politics of Memory*. Stanford, CA: Stanford University Press, 2003.

Jameson, Fredric. *The Political Unconscious: Narrative as a Socially Symbolic Act*. Ithaca, NY: Cornell University Press, 1981.

Jenkins, Henry. "What Happened before YouTube." In *YouTube: Online Video and Participatory Culture*, edited by Jean Burgess and Joshua Green, 109–25. Cambridge, MA: Polity Books, 2009.

Johnston, Hugh. *The Voyage of the "Komagata Maru": The Sikh Challenge to Canada's Colour Bar*. 2nd ed. Vancouver: University of British Columbia Press, 1989.

Jun, Helen Heran. *Race for Citizenship: Black Orientalism and Asian Uplift from Pre-Emancipation to Neoliberal America*. New York: New York University Press, 2011.

Jung, Moon-Ho. *Coolies and Cane: Race, Labor, and Sugar in the Age of Emancipation*. Baltimore: Johns Hopkins University Press, 2006.

Kamboureli, Smaro. *Scandalous Bodies: Diasporic Literature in English Canada*. 2000. Waterloo, ON: Wilfrid Laurier University Press, 2009.

Kay, Barbara. "A Tale of Two Quotas." *National Post*. 24 November 2010. Web. 24 November 2010.

Kaye, Nick. "Displaced Events: Photographic Memory and Performance Art." In *Locating Memory: Photographic Acts*, edited by Annette Kuhn and Kirsten Emiko McAllister, 173–97. New York: Berghahn Books, 2006.

Kazimi, Ali, dir. *Continuous Journey*. Peripheral Visions Film and Video, 2004.

Keeling, Kara. "I=You." In *Strange Affinities: The Gender and Sexual Politics of Comparative Racialization*, edited by Grace Kyungwon Hong and Roderick Ferguson, 53–75. Durham, NC: Duke University Press, 2011.

Khang, David. *Mom's Crutch*. 2004. Photographic installation. Orange County, CA.
——. "Re: Abstract." Message to the author. 21 September 2012. E-mail.
——. "Re: Images." Message to the author. 16 December 2010. E-mail.
——. *A Wrong Place: Greening the DMZ*. Performance art. *Centre for Innovation in Culture and the Arts in Canada*. 2007a. Web. November 2010.
——. *A Wrong Place (Greening the DMZ)*. Performance art. *David Khang*. 2007b. Web. November 2010.
Kim, Christine. "The Smell of Communities to Come: Jeremy Lin and Post-Racial Desire." *Journal of Intercultural Studies* 35, no. 3 (2014): 310–27.
Kim, Christine, Sophie McCall, and Melina Baum Singer, eds. *Cultural Grammars of Nation, Diaspora, and Indigeneity in Canada*. Waterloo, ON: Wilfrid Laurier University Press, 2012.
Kim, Claire. *Bitter Fruit: The Politics of Black-Korean Conflict in New York City*. New Haven, CT: Yale University Press, 2000.
Kim, Daniel. "'Bled In, Letter by Letter': Translation, Postmemory, and the Subject of Korean War: History in Susan Choi's *The Foreign Student*." *American Literary History* 21, no. 3 (2009): 550–83.
Kim, Elaine. "Home Is Where the *Han* Is: A Korean American Perspective on the Los Angeles Upheavals." In *Reading Rodney King/Reading Urban Uprising*, edited by Robert Gooding-Williams, 215–35. New York: Routledge, 1993.
Kim, Jodi. *Ends of Empire: Asian American Critique and the Cold War*. Minneapolis: University of Minnesota Press, 2010.
Kiyooka, Roy. *Pacific Windows: Collected Poems of Roy K. Kiyooka*. Ed. Roy Miki. Burnaby. Talonbooks, 1997.
Kogawa, Joy. *Emily Kato*. Toronto: Penguin Books Canada, 2005.
——. *Itsuka*. Toronto: Penguin Books Canada, 1993 (original 1992).
——. *Obasan*. Toronto: Penguin Books Canada, 2003 (original 1981).
——. *The Rain Ascends*. Toronto: Vintage Canada, 1996 (original 1995).
——. *The Rain Ascends*. Rev. ed. Toronto: Penguin Books Canada, 2003.
Lai, Larissa. "Corrupted Lineage: Narrative in the Gaps of History." *West Coast Line* 33 (2001): 40–53.
Lake, Marilyn, and Henry Reynolds. *Drawing the Global Colour Line: White Men's Countries and the International Challenge of Racial Equality*. Cambridge: Cambridge University Press, 2008.
Lakoff, George, and Mark Johnson. *Metaphors We Live By*. Chicago: University of Chicago Press, 1980.
Landes, Joan. *Women and the Public Sphere in the Age of the French Revolution*. Ithaca, NY: Cornell University Press, 1988.
Landsberg, Alison. *Prosthetic Memory: The Transformation of American Remembrance in the Age of Mass Culture*. New York: Columbia University Press, 2004.
Lee, Christopher. "Asian Canadian Performance and the Politics of Misrecognition." In *Asian Canadian Theatre*, edited by Nina Lee Aquino and Ric Knowles, 102–14. Toronto: Playwrights Canada Press, 2011.

———. "The Lateness of Asian Canadian Studies." *Amerasia* 33, no. 2 (2007): 1–17.
Lee, James. *Urban Triage: Race and the Fictions of Multiculturalism.* Minneapolis: University of Minnesota Press, 2004.
Lee, Yoon Sun. *Modern Minority: Asian American Literature and Everyday Life.* New York: Oxford University Press, 2013.
Lefebvre, Benjamin. "In Search of Someday: Trauma and Repetition in Joy Kogawa's Fiction." *Journal of Canadian Studies* 44, no. 3 (2010): 154–73.
Levin, Laura, Marlis Schweitzer, Kim Solga, Jenn Stephenson, and Belarie Zatzman. "Performing outside the Box." *Canadian Theatre Review* 137 (Winter 2009): 61–67.
Liem, Deann Borshay, and Ramsay Liem, dir. *Memory of Forgotten War.* Mu Films and Channing and Popai Liem Education Foundation, 2013.
Litvak, Isaiah, and Christopher J. Maule. "Bill C-58 and the Regulation of Periodicals in Canada." *International Journal* 36, no. 1 (1980–81): 70–90.
Lo, Jacqueline. "Moving Images, Stilling Time: The Art of Fiona Tan." *Third Text* 28, no. 1 (2014): 56–66.
Lowe, Lisa. *Immigrant Acts: On Asian American Cultural Politics.* Durham, NC: Duke University Press, 1996.
———. "The International within the National: American Studies and Asian American Critique." *Cultural Critique* 40 (1998): 29–47.
———. "Metaphors of Globalization." In *Interdisciplinarity and Social Justice: Revisioning Academic Accountability,* edited by Joe Parker, Ranu Samantrai, and Mary Romero, 37–62. Albany: State University of New York Press, 2010.
———. "The Worldliness of Intimacy." In *Edward Said: The Legacy of a Public Intellectual,* edited by Ned Curthoys and Debjani Ganguly, 121–51. Carlton, Victoria, BC: Melbourne University Press, 2007.
Lye, Colleen. *America's Asia: Racial Form and American Literature.* Princeton, NJ: Princeton, University Press, 2005.
Mackey, Eva. *The House of Difference: Cultural Politics and National Identity in Canada.* Toronto: University of Toronto Press, 2002.
Maclear, Kyo. *Beclouded Visions: Hiroshima-Nagasaki and the Art of Witness.* Albany: State University of New York Press, 1999.
———. *The Letter Opener.* Toronto: HarperCollins, 2007.
MacSkimming, Roy. *The Perilous Trade: Book Publishing in Canada, 1946–2006.* Toronto: McClelland and Stewart, 2007.
Martin, Sandra, and Sonia Sarfati. "Magazines." *The Canadian Encyclopedia.* Historica Foundation, 3 December 2012. Web.
Mathur, Ashok, Jonathan Dewar, and Mike DeGagné, eds. *Cultivating Canada: Reconciliation through the Lens of Cultural Diversity.* Ottawa: Aboriginal Healing Foundation, 2011.
Marx, Karl. *Capital.* Vol. 1. Trans. Samuel Moore and Edward Aveling. Moscow: Progress Publishers, 1887.
Mawani, Renisa. "Specters of Indigeneity in British-Indian Migration, 1914." *Law and Society Review* 46, no. 2 (2012): 369–403.

McAllister, Kirsten Emiko. *Terrain of Memory: A Japanese Canadian Memorial Project*. Vancouver: University of British Columbia Press, 2010.
McFarlane, Scott Toguri. "Un-Ravelling *StoneDGloves* and the Haunt of the Hibakusha." In *All Amazed: For Roy Kiyooka*, edited by John O'Brien, Naomi Sawada, and Scott Watson, 117–47. Vancouver: Arsenal Pulp Press, 2002.
McGonegal, Julie. "The Future of Racial Memory: Forgiveness, Reconciliation, and Redress in Joy Kogawa's *Obasan* and *Itsuka*." *Studies in Canadian Literature* 30, no. 2 (2005): 55–78.
Melady, John. *Korea: Canada's Forgotten War*. 2nd ed. Toronto: Dundurn Group, 2011.
"Merit: The Best and Only Way to Decide Who Gets Into University." *Maclean's*. 25 November 2010. Web. 26 November 2010.
Miki, Roy. *Broken Entries: Race, Subjectivity, Writing*. Toronto: Mercury Press, 1998.
——. *In Flux: Transnational Shifts in Asian Canadian Writing*. Edmonton: NeWest Press, 2011.
——. *Redress: Inside the Japanese Canadian Call for Justice*. Vancouver: Raincoast Books, 2005.
——. "Unravelling Roy Kiyooka: A Re-Assessment amidst Shifting Boundaries." In *All Amazed: For Roy Kiyooka*, edited by John O'Brien, Naomi Sawada, and Scott Watson, 69–83. Vancouver: Arsenal Pulp Press, 2002.
Moallem, Minoo, and Iain A. Boal. "Multicultural Nationalism and the Poetics of Inauguration." In *Between Woman and Nation*, edited by Caren Kaplan, Norma Alarcón, and Minoo Moallem, 243–63. Durham, NC: Duke University Press, 1999.
Mochizuki, Cindy. "Discussion of Arts of Conscience." *Arts of Conscience: From Hiroshima to Vancouver* symposium. Vancouver, BC. 15 October 2011. Panel discussion.
——. "Japanese Biobox." Unpublished script, 2007.
Mongia, Radhika Viyas. "Race, Nationality, Mobility: A History of the Passport." *Public Culture* 11, no. 3 (1999): 527–56.
Morozov, Evgeny. *The Net Delusion: The Dark Side of Internet Freedom*. New York: Public Affairs, 2011.
Morrison, Toni. *Playing in the Dark: Whiteness and the Literary Imagination*. Cambridge, MA: Harvard University Press, 1992.
Nakamura, Lisa. *Digitizing Race: Visual Cultures of the Internet*. Minneapolis: University of Minnesota Press, 2008.
Newton, Elizabeth. "The Great Maple Syrup Controversy." Eliznewton. N.p., 2 July 2012. Web. 25 November 2014.
Ngai, Mae. *Impossible Subjects: Illegal Aliens and the Making of Modern America*. Princeton, NJ: Princeton University Press, 2004.
Ngai, Sianne. *Ugly Feelings*. Cambridge, MA: Harvard University Press, 2005.
Nguyen, Mimi. "Tales of an Asiatic Geek Girl: *Slant* from Paper to Pixels." In *Technicolor: Race, Technology, and Everyday Life*, edited by Alondra Nelson and Thuy Linh N. Tu with Alicia Headlam Hines, 177–90. New York: New York University Press, 2001.

———. *The Gift of Freedom: War, Debt, and Other Refugee Passages.* Durham, NC: Duke University Press, 2012.

Nguyen, Viet. *Race and Resistance: Literature and Politics in Asian America.* Oxford: Oxford University Press, 2002.

———. "Refugee Memories and Asian American Critique." *positions: east asia cultures critique* 20, no. 3 (2012): 911–42.

Oikawa, Mona. "Relations of Redress." In *Tracing the Lines: Reflections on Contemporary Poetics and Cultural Politics in Honour of Roy Miki,* edited by Maia Joseph, Christine Kim, Larissa Lai, and Christopher Lee, 60–65. Vancouver: Talonbooks, 2012.

Park, Jane. *Yellow Future: Oriental Style in Hollywood Cinema.* Minneapolis: University of Minnesota Press, 2010.

Price, John. "'Orienting' the Empire: Mackenzie King and the Aftermath of the 1907 Race Riots." *BC Studies* 156/157 (2007): 53–81.

Regan, Paulette. *Unsettling the Settler Within.* Vancouver: University of British Columbia Press, 2011.

Reitz, Jeffrey, and Rupa Banerjee. "Racial Inequality, Social Cohesion and Policy Issues in Canada." In *Belonging? Diversity, Recognition and Shared Citizenship in Canada,* edited by Keith Banting, Thomas Courchene, and F. Leslie Seidle, 1–57. Montreal: Institute for Research on Public Policy, 2007.

Ricoeur, Paul. *The Rule of Metaphor.* 1975. Trans. Robert Czerny with Kathleen McLaughlin and John Costello, SJ. Toronto: University of Toronto Press, 1977.

Rivas, Jorge. "Alexandra Wallace's Anti-Asian Rant Draws . . . Misogyny and Death Threats." *Colorlines.* 18 March 2011. Web. 20 January 2015.

Ross, Sandy. "Canada's $100 Bill: Money, Representation and Multiculturalism." *Everyday Economies.* 29 October 2012. Web. 19 May 2014.

Ruparelia, Rakhi. "Professor Rakhi Ruparelia on the 100$ Bill." *Blogging for Equality.* Creative Commons, 23 August 2012. Web. 24 June 2013.

Ryan, Mary. "Gender and Public Access: Women's Politics in Nineteenth-Century America." In *Habermas and the Public Sphere,* edited by Craig Calhoun, 259–88. Cambridge, MA: MIT Press, 1992.

Said, Edward. *Orientalism.* 1978. New York: Vintage Books, 1994. 25th anniversary edition.

Sakai, Naoki. "'You Asians': On the Historical Role of the West and Asia Binary." *South Atlantic Quarterly* 99, no. 4 (Fall 2000): 789–817.

Schlund-Vials, Cathy. *War, Genocide, Justice: Cambodian American Memory Work.* Minneapolis: University of Minnesota Press, 2012.

Sherrett, Monique. "The Smell of Money—Canada's New $100 Bill Smells Like Maple." *So Misguided.* ExpressionEngine, 28 January 2012. Web. 25 November 2014.

Shigematsu, Tetsuro. "'Asians in the Library': UCLA Girl Alexandra Wallace Gets Death Threats, Asian Godfather Responds." Online video clip. *YouTube.* YouTube, 17 March 2011. Web. 5 August 2012.

Sia, Beau. "Asians in the Library of the World: A Persona Poem in the Voice of Alexandra Wallace." Online video clip. *YouTube*. YouTube, 16 March 2011. Web. 15 January 2015.
Silva, Denise Ferreira da. "Towards a Critique of the Socio-Logos of Justice: The Analytics of Raciality and the Production of Universality." *Social Identities* 7, no. 3 (2001): 421–54.
———. *Toward a Global Idea of Race*. Minneapolis: University of Minnesota Press, 2007.
Simmel, Georg. *The Philosophy of Money*. Ed. David Frisby. Trans. Tom Bottomore and David Frisby. London: Routledge, 1978.
Slaughter, Joseph. "Enabling Fictions and Novel Subjects: The 'Bildungsroman' and International Human Rights Law." *PMLA* 121, no. 5 (2006): 1405–23.
———. *Human Rights, Inc.. The World Novel, Narrative Form, and International Law*. New York: Fordham University Press, 2007.
"*Small Arguments* by Souvankham Thammavongsa." *Poetry Spoken Here: Canada's Poetry Webstore*. Poets.ca, n.d. Web. 3 March 2006.
"Sniff Test: Does the New $100 Bill Smell Like Maple Syrup?" CTVNews.ca. online newsvideo. *Globe and Mail*. 28 May 2013. Web. 25 November 2014.
So, Christine. *Economic Citizens: A Narrative of Asian American Visibility*. Philadelphia: Temple University Press, 2007.
Solga, Kim. "Artifacting an Intercultural Nation: Theatre Replacement's BIOBOXES." *TDR: The Drama Review* 54, no. 1 (Spring 2010): 161–66.
———. "Meet Me at the Border: Theatre Replacement's *Bioboxes*." In *Theatres of Affect*, edited by Erin Hurley, 171–91. Toronto: Playwrights Canada Press, 2014.
Song, Min Hyoung. *Strange Future: Pessimism and the 1992 Los Angeles Riots*. Durham, NC: Duke University Press, 2005.
Spigel, Lynn. *Welcome to the Dreamhouse*. Durham, NC: Duke University Press, 2001.
Stoler, Ann Laura. *Carnal Knowledge and Imperial Power: Race and the Intimate in Colonial Rule*. Berkeley: University of California Press, 2002.
Taylor, Charles. "The Politics of Recognition." In *Multiculturalism. Examining the Politics of Recognition*, edited by Amy Gutmann, 25–73. Princeton, NJ: Princeton University Press, 1994.
Thammavongsa, Souvankham. *big boots* 2, no. 1 (n.d.): n.p.
———. *big boots* 3 (n.d.): n.p.
———. *Found*. Toronto: Pedlar Press, 2007.
———. "how to pronounce *knife*." *big boots* 1 (n.d.): n.p.
———. "photos and diary entries." *big boots* 2, no. 1 (2002): n.p.
———. "Poet's Statement." *Found: The Poetry of Souvankham Thammavongsa. A Film by Paramita Nath*. n.d. Web. 5 December 2012.
———. *Small Arguments*. Toronto: Pedlar Press, 2003.
———. "there are no photographs of my mother." *big boots* 1 (n.d.): n.p.
———. Untitled editorial *big boots* 1 (n.d.): n.p.

"'Too Asian?' Critics Ignoring Reality." *The Ubyssey.* 18 November 2010. Web. 19 January 2015.

"'Too Asian?' Talkback." *Facebook.* Facebook, 29 June 2013. Web. 25 November 2014.

Ty, Eleanor. *The Politics of the Visible in Asian North American Narratives.* Toronto: University of Toronto Press, 2004.

———. *Unfastened: Globality and Asian North American Narratives.* Minneapolis: University of Minnesota Press, 2010.

Ty, Eleanor, and Donald Goellnicht, ed. *Asian North American Identities: Beyond the Hyphen.* Bloomington: Indiana University Press, 2004.

UCLA. "UCLA Chancellor Appalled by Student Video." Online video clip. *YouTube.* YouTube, 14 March 2011. Web. August 2012.

Um, Khatharya. "Exiled Memory: History, Identity, and Remembering in Southeast Asia and Southeast Asian Diaspora." *positions: east asia cultures critique* 20, no. 3 (2012): 831–50.

Vang, Ma. "The Refugee Soldier: A Critique of Recognition and Citizenship in the Hmong Veterans' Naturalization Act of 1997." *positions: east asia cultures critique* 20, no. 3 (2012): 685–712.

Walcott, Rinaldo. *Black Like Who? Writing Black Canada.* 1997. Toronto: Insomniac Press, 2003. 2nd rev. ed.

Wallace, Alexandra. "Asians in the Library." Online video clip. *YouTube.* YouTube, 13 March 2011. Web. 15 March 2011.

Warner, Michael. *Publics and Counterpublics.* New York: Zone Books, 2002.

Wegner, Phillip E. *Life between Two Deaths, 1989–2001: U.S. Culture in the Long Nineties.* Durham, NC: Duke University Press, 2009.

Weinfeld, David. "Asians and Affirmative Action on Campus." In *"Too Asian?": Racism, Privilege, and Post-Secondary Education,* edited by R. J. Gilmour, Davina Bhandar, Jeet Heer, and Michael C. K. Ma, 28–37. Toronto: Between the Lines, 2012.

Wente, Margaret. "Where Cherished Values Collide." *Globe and Mail.* 23 November 2010. Web. June 15, 2011.

Wiegman, Robyn. "Whiteness Studies and the Paradox of Particularity." *boundary 2* 26, no. 3 (Autumn 1999): 115–50.

Williams, Raymond. "Structures of Feeling." In *Marxism and Literature.* 1977. Repr., Oxford: Oxford University Press, 1988, 128–35.

Wilson, Sheena, ed. *Joy Kogawa: Essays on Her Works.* Toronto: Guernica Editions, 2011.

Winks, Robin W. *The Blacks in Canada: A History.* 1971. 2nd ed. Montreal and Kingston: McGill–Queen's University Press, 1997.

Wong, Cori. "Think for a Change (9): RE: Asians in the UCLA Library." Online video clip. *YouTube.* YouTube, 15 March 2011. Web. August 2012.

Wong, Jimmy. "Ching Chong! Asians in the Library Song." Online video clip. *YouTube.* YouTube, 15 March 2011. Web. 15 January 2015.

Wong, Todd. "Canada Likes Females on the New $100 Bill to Be 'White-Washed' and Racially-Neutral?" *Gung Haggis Fat Choy.* WordPress, 7 September 2012. Web. 24 June 2013.

Yu, Henry. "Global Migrants and the New Pacific Canada." *International Journal* 64, no. 4 (Autumn 2009): 1011–26.
———. "The Parable of the Textbook." In *"Too Asian?": Racism, Privilege, and Post-Secondary Education,* edited by R. J. Gilmour, Davina Bhandar, Jeet Heer, and Michael C. K. Ma, 17–27. Toronto: Between the Lines, 2012.
Yu, Phil. "'Asian-Looking' Woman Removed from Canada's New $100 Bill." *Angry Asian Man.* Blog, 17 August 2012. Web. 24 June 2013.
———. "Bank of Canada Apologizes for $100 Bill Race Redesign." *Angry Asian Man.* Blog, 21 August 2012. Web. 24 June 2013.

Index

Note: Page numbers in **bold** refer to figures.

Agamben, Giorgio, 16, 124–25, 127, 129, 145, 147
Ahmed, Sara, 43, 96, 135, 154
the American South, 29, 55, 80, 109, 110, 112–16, 119–20
Anderson, Benedict, 85–36, 87
Arendt, Hannah, 125
Aristotle, 51, 124–25, 143, 144
Asia, construct of, 67–68. *See also* Orientalism
Asianness, feeling of, 53, 57–60
"Asians in the Library" (Wallace), 7, 17, 25, 28, 57–63, 66, 67, 76–84, 163n6
Asian students. *See* "Asians in the Library"; "Too Asian?"

Balibar, Étienne, 79, 115
Banerjee, Rupa, 11–12
banknote controversy. *See* currency controversy
Beclouded Visions (Maclear), 157, 158
Benjamin, Walter, 97, 106
Berlant, Lauren: and intimate publics, 40, 41, 42, 43–44, 55, 130, 132, 133–34; and social intimacy, 5–6, 12

Bhabha, Homi, 86–87, 116
big boots (Thammavongsa), 29, 134–36, 138–40
Bioboxes (Mochizuki/Theatre Replacement), 17–18, 27, 31, 33–37, **36**, 39, 41–45, 162nn2–3
bios, 124, 125, 126, 130, 144, 145, 149
Bow, Leslie, 115, 119–20, 122–23
Broken Entries (Miki), 49–50, 51–52

Cambodia, 126, 127; refugees from, 129, 134, 153
Canadian Charter of Rights and Freedoms, 9, 32
Canadian Multiculturalism Act, 3, 9, 32
Chakrabarty, Dipesh, 150–51, 152
Chang, Kornel, 62
Chariandy, David, 10
Cheah, Pheng, 14, 67, 132, 146, 147, 148
Chen, Kuan-Hsing, 66
Cheng, Anne Anlin, 55, 82
Chinese Canadian National Council, 2
Chinese Exclusion Acts, 128
Cho, Grace, 103–4, 120–22
Cho, Lily, 15–16, 116–17
Choi, Susan, *The Foreign Student*, 25, 28–29, 92, 93, 108–23

Index

Chow, Olivia, 71, 74
Chu, Seo-Young, 106
Chun, Wendy, 81, 82, 88, 89
citizenship: national, 9–18, 20–22, 26, 30, 45–47, 75, 125–26, 134–35, 137; social (*see* "Asians in the Library"; "Too Asian?")
Cold War, 11, 54, 104
Coleman, Daniel, 72
colonialism, 9, 12, 20–23, 25, 33, 133; and Korea, 97–103, 106–12, 116; and Orientalism, 19–20, 66–68; and postcolonial intimacy, 29, 87–88, 97–108, 147. *See also* imperialism
Compton, Wayde, 69–70
counterpublic, definition of, 5–6, 44, 47–48, 130–31, 139
currency controversy, 1–5, 12–15
Cvetkovich, Ann, 56, 100

Dean, Jodi, 87, 88
diaspora, 16–17, 24–25, 29, 91–92, 164n5. *See also* Choi, Susan; Khang, David; Thammavongsa, Souvankham
digital media. *See* "Asians in the Library"; "Too Asian?"
Dyer, Richard, 80

Ellis, John, 60, 90
Emily Kato (Kogawa), 45, 48
Eng, David, 55–56
Erni, John, 13, 152
Ethnic Diversity Study (Statistics Canada), 10

Findlay, Stephanie: "Too Asian?" (*Maclean's* magazine), 28, 57–59, 61, 64–67, 71, 74, 163n5
The Foreign Student (Choi), 25, 28–29, 92, 93, 108–23
Found (Thammavongsa), 29–30, 124, 126, 132–36, 138, 140, 146–53, 164n1
Fraser, Nancy, 75, 79, 84, 130
Fung, Richard, 116–17

Gilroy, Paul, 89
Glissant, Édouard, 116–17, 153
Goellnicht, Donald, 16

Habermas, Jürgen, 5, 12, 68, 79, 84, 88, 130
Hage, Ghassan, 75–76
han, 105–7, 121
head tax, 22, 40, 128
Heer, Jeet, 62–63, 75–76, 81, 83, 163n5
Herzfeld, Michael, 6–7
Hiroshima, 35, 37, 54, 156–58
the Holocaust, 125–26
human rights, 70–71, 125, 127–28, 141–49; and refugees, 29–30, 131–33, 147–49

immigration, 71, 98, 125, 134; experience of, 11–12, 33–34, 63, 80, 105–16, 118, 122; policies, 20–23, 33, 62, 128–29, 135, 138. *See also* head tax; *Komagata Maru*; passports; refugees
imperialism, 12; American, 20, 55, 62, 104; British, 21, 22–23, 62; Japanese, 22, 55; and minor empires, 17, 19–20, 22, 161n3. *See also* colonialism; Orientalism
In Flux (Miki), 8, 16, 20
Itsuka (Kogawa), 45, 48, 49, 53

Jameson, Fredric, 106, 147
Japanese Canadians, internment of, 25, 35, 54, 55, 128, 155, 157; in Joy Kogawa's work, 40, 45–46, 48, 49, 50, 51–52, 53

Kamboureli, Smaro, 10–11, 37–38
Kay, Barbara, 63, 75–76, 81
Keeling, Kara, 91–92
Khang, David, 163nn1–2; *Mom's Crutch*, 17, 28–29, **94–95**, 96–100, 107–8, 123; *Wrong Places*, 28–29, 97–103, 106–8, 123
Kim, Daniel, 109, 113, 118
Kim, Elaine, 105–6
Kim, Jodi, 19, 104–5
Kiyooka, Roy: *StoneDGloves*, 30, 154–59
Kogawa, Joy: *Emily Kato*, 45, 48; *Itsuka*, 45, 48, 49, 53; *Obasan*, 40, 46, 48, 49, 51–53; *The Rain Ascends*, 7, 27, 31, 45–47, 48–53, 56
Kohler, Nicholas: "Too Asian?" (*Maclean's* magazine), 28, 57–59, 61, 64–67, 71, 74, 163n5
Komagata Maru, 21–22, 71, 128
Korean War, 29, 92, 99, 103–5, 108–23, 163–64n3, 164n5

Landsberg, Alison, 93, 97
Laos, 127, 135; refugees from, 136, 140, 150, 151–52, 153
Lee, Christopher, 38–39, 54, 155, 161n3
The Letter Opener (Maclear), 154–55, 159
Levin, Laura, 35, 36
literary works. *See* Choi, Susan; Kogawa, Joy; Maclear, Kyo; Miki, Roy; Thammavongsa, Souvankham
Lo, Jacqueline, 122
Lowe, Lisa, 19, 98–99, 102–3, 104, 129, 146

Maclean's magazine: "Too Asian?" (Findlay and Kohler), 7, 18, 28, 57–90, 163n5
Maclear, Kyo: *Beclouded Visions*, 157, 158; *The Letter Opener*, 154–55, 159
Man, Paul de, 148–49, 152
masculinity, Asian men and, 25, 118
McAllister, Kirsten, 46
McFarlane, Scott Toguri, 156
Miki, Roy, 155, 158; *Broker Entries*, 49–50, 51–52; *In Flux*, 8, 16, 20
Mochizuki, Cindy: *Bioboxes*, 17–18, 31, 32, 33–37, **36**, 39, 41–45, 162nn2–3
Mom's Crutch (Khang), 17, 28–29, **94–95**, 96–100, 107–8, 123
Mongia, Radhika Viyas, 20–21, 22
Morozov, Evgeny, 85–86
multiculturalism, policy of, 3–12, 23
Multiculturalism Act. *See* Canadian Multiculturalism Act

Nagasaki, 45, 51, 54, 157–58
the nation-state, 3, 11–13, 15, 25, 67, 125–26; and racialization, 16–17, 45–46, 49. *See also* citizenship
Ngai, Sianne, 50–51, 52, 107
Nguyen, Mimi, 81, 88, 131
Nguyen, Viet, 125
9/11 (September 11), 29, 54, 85, 92, 96, 99–100

Obasan (Kogawa), 40, 46, 48, 49, 51–53
Orientalism, 18, 19–20, 23–24, 28, 61, 67–71, 77, 81–84, 86, 107

passports, 12, 20–22, 134–35

performance art. *See Bioboxes*; Khang, David
photographs. *See Bioboxes*; Khang, David; Kiyooka, Roy
poetry, 144, 153. *See also* Kiyooka, Roy; Miki, Roy; Thammavongsa, Souvankham
Price, John, 22–23
print media. *See* "Asians in the Library"; "Too Asian?"
publics, definition of, 4–5. *See also* counterpublics

The Rain Ascends (Kogawa), 7, 27, 31, 45–47, 48–53, 56
refugees, 16, 26, 29–30, 124, 125–27, 129; from Cambodia, 129, 134, 153; and human rights discourses, 29–30, 131–33, 147–49; from Laos, 134–36, 140, 150, 151–52, 153, 164n1; from Vietnam, 129, 134. *See also* diaspora
Reitz, Jeffrey, 11–12
Rhee, Francesca, 119, 121
Rhee, Syngman, President, 117–19, 121, 164n8
Ricoeur, Paul, 143, 145
Royal Commission on Bilingualism and Biculturalism, 9–10

Said, Edward, 19–20, 23–24, 68. *See also* Orientalism
Sakai, Naoki, 67–68, 107, 133, 148
Schlund-Vials, Cathy, 126
sexuality, 5, 15, 112–15, 120–21, 131, 139; colonial, 12, 103; and the Internet, 82, 86, 88; and Orientalism, 82, 86; queer, 44, 131
Silva, Denise Ferreira da, 65–66, 78–79
Slaughter, Joseph, 127–28, 144, 145
Small Arguments (Thammavongsa), 29–30, 124, 126, 132–34, 136–39, 140–48, 151–53
So, Christine, 14–15
social intimacy, definition of, 5–6, 12
social media, 7, 18, 59, 162n2 (chap. 2). *See also* "Asians in the Library"; "Too Asian?"
Solga, Kim, 36, 39–40, 41, 43

Stoler, Ann Laura, 12
StoneDGloves (Kiyooka), 30, 154–59

Taylor, Charles, 37–39, 41
Thammavongsa, Souvankham, 7–8; *big boots*, 29, 134–36, 138–40; *Found*, 29–30, 124, 126, 132–36, 138, 140, 146–53, 164n1; *Small Arguments*, 29–30, 124, 126, 132–34, 136–39, 140–48, 151–53; "there are no photographs of my mother," 134–35, 140
theater. See *Bioboxes*
Theatre Replacement. See *Bioboxes*
"there are no photographs of my mother" (Thammavongsa), 134–35, 140
"Too Asian?" (*Maclean's* magazine), 7, 18, 28, 57–90, 163n5
trauma, 26, 35, 40, 53–54, 162n4. *See also* Hiroshima; the Holocaust; Japanese Canadians, internment of; Nagasaki
Trudeau, Pierre, 9–10
Ty, Eleanor, 16

Um, Khatharya, 136
universities, 163n8. *See also* "Asians in the Library"; "Too Asian?"
U.S. South. *See* American South

Vang, Ma, 127

Vietnam, 127, 129, 134
visual art, 17, 102, 122, 158. *See also* Khang, David; Kiyooka, Roy; Mochizuki, Cindy

Wallace, Alexandra: "Asians in the Library," 7, 17, 25, 28, 57–63, 66, 67, 76–84, 163n6
Warner, Michael, 137; and counterpublics, 5–6, 44, 47–48, 130–31, 139, 141
Wegner, Phillip, 53–54
whiteness, 2, 4, 20–23, 41, 61–64, 86–87; denaturalizing, 27, 31–32, 45–47, 50, 55–56, 77; and privilege, 7, 53, 58, 67, 71, 75, 78, 80, 81
Wiegman, Robyn, 80–81
Williams, Raymond, 100–101
Wong, Cori, 83–84
Wong, Jimmy, 58, 76
Wrong Places (Khang), 28–29, 97–103, 106–8, 123

yanggongju, 120–22
Yellow Peril, language of, 28, 64, 65, 71, 157. *See also* Orientalism
Yu, Henry, 64, 128–29
Yuh, Ji-Yeon, 122

zines, 29, 134–36, 138–40
zoe, 124–25, 126, 130, 143–44, 145, 147, 149, 150

CHRISTINE K M is an associate professor of English at Simon Fraser University.

THE ASIAN AMERICAN EXPERIENCE

The Hood River Issei: An Oral History of Japanese Settlers
   in Oregon's Hood River Valley   *Linda Tamura*
Americanization, Acculturation, and Ethnic Identity:
   The Nisei Generation in Hawaii   *Eileen H. Tamura*
Sui Sin Far/Edith Maude Eaton: A Literary Biography   *Annette White-Parks*
Mrs. Spring Fragrance and Other Writings   *Sui Sin Far;
   edited by Amy Ling and Annette White-Parks*
The Golden Mountain: The Autobiography of a Korean Immigrant, 1895–1960
   Easurk Emsen Charr; edited and with an introduction by Wayne Patterson
Race and Politics: Asian Americans, Latinos, and Whites
   in a Los Angeles Suburb   *Leland T. Saito*
Achieving the Impossible Dream: How Japanese Americans Obtained
   Redress   *Mitchell T. Maki, Harry H. L. Kitano, and S. Megan Berthold*
If They Don't Bring Their Women Here: Chinese Female Immigration
   before Exclusion   *George Anthony Peffer*
Growing Up Nisei: Race, Generation, and Culture among Japanese Americans
   of California, 1924–49   *David K. Yoo*
Chinese American Literature since the 1850s   *Xiao-huang Yin*
Pacific Pioneers: Japanese Journeys to America
   and Hawaii, 1850–80   *John E. Van Sant*
Holding Up More Than Half the Sky: Chinese Women Garment Workers
   in New York City, 1948–92   *Xiaolan Bao*
Onoto Watanna: The Story of Winnifred Eaton   *Diana Birchall*
Edith and Winnifred Eaton: Chinatown Missions
   and Japanese Romances   *Dominika Ferens*
Being Chinese, Becoming Chinese American   *Shehong Chen*
"A Half Caste" and Other Writings   *Onoto Watanna;
   edited by Linda Trinh Moser and Elizabeth Rooney*
Chinese Immigrants, African Americans, and Racial Anxiety
   in the United States, 1848–82   *Najia Aarim-Heriot*
Not Just Victims: Conversations with Cambodian Community Leaders
   in the United States   *Edited and with an introduction by Sucheng Chan;
   interviews conducted by Audrey U. Kim*
The Japanese in Latin America   *Daniel M. Masterson with Sayaka Funada-Classen*
Survivors: Cambodian Refugees in the United States   *Sucheng Chan*
From Concentration Camp to Campus: Japanese American Students
   and World War II   *Allan W. Austin*
Japanese American Midwives: Culture, Community,
   and Health Politics   *Susan L. Smith*
In Defense of Asian American Studies: The Politics of Teaching
   and Program Building   *Sucheng Chan*

Lost and Found: Reclaiming the Japanese American Incarceration *Karen L. Ishizuka*
Religion and Spirituality in Korean America *Edited by David K. Yoo and Ruth H. Chung*
Moving Images: Photography and the Japanese American Incarceration *Jasmine Alinder*
Camp Harmony: Seattle's Japanese Americans and the Puyallup Assembly Center *Louis Fiset*
Chinese American Transnational Politics *Him Mark Lai, edited and with an introduction by Madeline Y. Hsu*
Issei Buddhism in the Americas *Edited by Duncan Ryûken Williams and Tomoe Moriya*
Hmong America: Reconstructing Community in Diaspora *Chia Youyee Vang*
In Pursuit of Gold: Chinese American Miners and Merchants in the American West *Sue Fawn Chung*
Pacific Citizens: Larry and Guyo Tajiri and Japanese American Journalism in the World War II Era *Edited by Greg Robinson*
Indian Accents: Brown Voice and Racial Performance in American Television and Film *Shilpa S. Davé*
Yellow Power, Yellow Soul: The Radical Art of Fred Ho *Edited by Roger N. Buckley and Tamara Roberts*
Fighting from a Distance: How Filipino Exiles Helped Topple a Dictator *Jose V. Fuentecilla*
In Defense of Justice: Joseph Kurihara and the Japanese American Struggle for Equality *Eileen H. Tamura*
Asian Americans in Dixie: Race and Migration in the South *Edited by Jigna Desai and Khyati Y. Joshi*
Undercover Asian: Multiracial Asian Americans in Visual Culture *Leilani Nishime*
Islanders in the Empire: Filipino and Puerto Rican Laborers in Hawai'i *JoAnna Poblete*
Virtual Homelands: Indian Immigrants and Online Cultures in the United States *Madhavi Mallapragada*
Building Filipino Hawai'i *Roderick N. Labrador*
Legitimizing Empire: Filipino American and U.S. Puerto Rican Cultural Critique *Faye Caronan*
Chinese in the Woods: Logging and Lumbering in the American West *Sue Fawn Chung*
The Minor Intimacies of Race: Asian Publics in North America *Christine Kim*

The University of Illinois Press
is a founding member of the
Association of American University Presses.

University of Illinois Press
1325 South Oak Street
Champaign, IL 61820-6903
www.press.uillinois.edu